CAMBRID
HISTORY

SAMUEL CLARKE
*A Demonstration of the Being and
Attributes of God*

CAMBRIDGE TEXTS IN THE
HISTORY OF PHILOSOPHY

Series editors

KARL AMERIKS
Professor of Philosophy at the University of Notre Dame

DESMOND M. CLARKE
Professor of Philosophy at University College Cork

The main objective of Cambridge Texts in the History of Philosophy is to expand the range, variety and quality of texts in the history of philosophy which are available in English. The series includes texts by familiar names (such as Descartes and Kant) and also by less well-known authors. Wherever possible, texts are published in complete and unabridged form, and translations are specially commissioned for the series. Each volume contains a critical introduction together with a guide to further reading and any necessary glossaries and textual apparatus. The volumes are designed for student use at undergraduate and postgraduate level and will be of interest not only to students of philosophy, but also to a wider audience of readers in the history of science, the history of theology and the history of ideas.

For a list of titles published in the series, please see end of book.

SAMUEL CLARKE

A Demonstration of the Being and Attributes of God

And Other Writings

EDITED BY

EZIO VAILATI
Southern Illinois University, Edwardsville

CAMBRIDGE
UNIVERSITY PRESS

PUBLISHED BY THE PRESS SYNDICATE OF THE UNIVERSITY OF CAMBRIDGE
The Pitt Building, Trumpington Street, Cambridge CB2 1RP, United Kingdom

CAMBRIDGE UNIVERSITY PRESS
The Edinburgh Building, Cambridge CB2 2RU, United Kingdom
40 West 20th Street, New York, NY 10011–4211, USA
10 Stamford Road, Oakleigh, Melbourne 3166 Australia

© Cambridge University Press 1998

First published 1998

Typeset in Ehrhardt

A catalogue record for this book is available from the British Library

Library of Congress cataloguing in publication data
Clarke, Samuel, 1675–1729.
[Selections. 1998]
A Demonstration of the Being and Attributes of God and Other Writings /
Samuel Clarke; edited by Ezio Vailati.
p. cm. – (Cambridge Texts in the History of Philosophy)
Includes bibliographical references and index.
ISBN 0 521 59008 6 (hardback). – ISBN 0 521 59995 4 (paperback)
1. God–Proof–Early works to 1800. 2. God–Attributes–Early works to 1800.
3. Natural theology–Early works to 1800. 4. Revelations–Early works to 1800.
I. Vailati, Ezio. II. Title. III. Series.
BB100.C542 1998
212'.1–dc21 97–22309 CIP

ISBN 0 521 59008 6 hardback
ISBN 0 521 59995 4 paperback

Transferred to digital printing 2002

Contents

To the memory of Wilbur Knorr

Acknowledgments

In carrying out this project, I have incurred many debts which I gladly acknowledge. John Perry first drew my attention to Clarke's work. Julie Ward and Edwin Lawrence have helped with the notes, especially the Greek; of course, any remaining errors are entirely mine. Desmond Clarke, one of the two general editors of Cambridge Texts in the History of Philosophy, has been both critical and encouraging. Special thanks go to the National Endowment for the Humanities for a one-year grant in 1996 during which I did most of the work. Finally, I wish to thank the staff of Cambridge University Press for their professional help.

Abbreviations

Cl   Clarke's letter to Leibniz, in *The Leibniz–Clarke Correspondence. With extracts from Newton's "Principia" and "Opticks,"* ed. H. G. Alexander (Manchester University Press, 1956), followed by letter number and section.

E   Spinoza, B. *Ethica more Geometrico Demonstrata* in *Spinoza: Opera,* ed. C. Gebhardt (Heidelberg, C. Winters, 1925), vol. 2.

Lz   Leibniz's letter to Clarke, in *The Leibniz–Clarke Correspondence. With extracts from Newton's "Principia" and "Opticks,"* ed. H. G. Alexander (Manchester University Press, 1956), followed by letter number and section.

NP   Newton, I. *Isaac Newton's Philosophiae Naturalis Principia Mathematica. The third edition (1726) with variant Readings,* eds. A. Koyré and I. B. Cohen (Cambridge, MA, Harvard University Press, 1972), followed by book, section, proposition, and page.

W   Clarke, S. *The Works* (London, 1738; reprint New York, Garland Publishing Co., 1978), followed by volume and page.

Introduction

The sixteenth and seventeenth centuries saw the reoccurrence in western thought of methods and procedures in the study of the natural world which had been largely forgotten or not systematically used since Archimedes. The reawakening of western science was so fast and momentous as to be truly revolutionary. Especially in physics, the new science centered on the mathematization of nature, a process which accelerated as more and more powerful mathematical tools, from analytic geometry to calculus, were developed.

The relation of modern science to traditional religion soon proved problematic. Some natural philosophers, e.g., Galileo Galilei (1564–1642), thought that the new science was incompatible with a literal reading of the Scriptures; others, for example, Benedictus de Spinoza (1632–77) and Thomas Hobbes (1588–79), believed that it was in conflict with many of the traditional tenets of natural religion, and consequently were considered, perhaps somewhat unjustly, atheists by their contemporaries. However, many of the natural philosophers involved in the scientific revolution thought that religion or, at a minimum, natural religion, and the new science could be made compatible once the philosophical ramifications of modern science were properly understood.

The first great systematic attempt to harmonize religion and modern science was carried out by René Descartes (1596–1650), who produced a metaphysical system in which a perfect God exists, the soul is immaterial and immortal, and matter, being nothing but tridimensionally extended substance, is the proper subject of mathematization. However, Descartes' system soon ran into difficulties. Its scientific part, especially the fundamental laws of impact, proved unsatisfactory and, more importantly, many philosophers of different persuasion, for example, Henry More (1614–87), Clarke himself, Gottfried Wilhelm Leibniz (1646–1716), and Isaac Newton (1642–1727), came to believe that, whatever Descartes' intentions had been, Cartesianism, far from securing natural religion, could be, and had been, used to subvert it.

In 1687, Newton published *Philosophiae Naturalis Principia Mathematica*, the book that represented the culmination of the scientific revolution. Edmond Halley (1656–1742) had written a long review of the work for the *Philosophical Transactions* shortly before its publication, and upon the book's appearance news of Newton's achievement spread quickly, both in Great Britain and on the Continent, not only among mathematically sophisticated scientists like David Gregory (1661–1708), Christiaan Huygens (1629–95), Johann Bernoulli (1667–1748), Guillaume de L'Hôpital (1661–1704) and Leibniz, but also among philosophers who, like John Locke (1632–1704), or Pierre Bayle (1647–1706), found much of the mathematics insurmountable. Newton, a very religious man with an abiding interest in theology and scriptural exegesis, viewed favorably the attempt to put his physical discoveries in the service of religion. The Boyle Lectures provided an ideal vehicle for that attempt.

The Lectures had been instituted through the will of Robert Boyle (1627–91), the great English physicist, who had left a modest sum, later increased by others, establishing a series of sermons for "proving the Christian Religion against notorious Infidels, viz., Atheists, Theists, Pagans, Jews, and Mahometans." The first lecturer had been Richard Bentley (1662–1742), the famous classical scholar. He had asked Newton's advice in the composition of his 1692 lecture, and Newton had obligingly replied, pointing out that he had composed *Principia* "with an eye upon such Principles as might work with considering men for the beliefe of a Deity & nothing can rejoyce me more than to find it usefull for that purpose."[1] Several of the lectures were given by members of the Newtonian circle, for example, Clarke, William Whiston (1667–1752), and William Derham (1657–1735), and the Boyle Lectures to a good extent became a vehicle for the dissemination of Newtonianism. In 1704, Samuel Clarke delivered that year's lecture under the title *A Demonstration of the Being*

---

[1] For Boyle's will, see R. Boyle, *The Works of the Honourable Robert Boyle*, ed. T. Birch (London, 1772; reprint Hildesheim, G. Olms, 1966), vol. 1, p. 105; for Newton's reply to Bentley, see H. W. Turnbull, J. F. Scott, A. R. Hall, and L. Tilling (eds.), *The Correspondence of Isaac Newton* (Cambridge University Press, 1959–77), vol. 3, p. 233. Unless otherwise noted, reference page numbers in the introduction refer to this volume.

and Attributes of God; it proved very successful, so that he was asked to deliver the following year's lecture, which he did with the title *A Discourse Concerning the Unchangeable Obligations of Natural Religion, and the Truth and Certainty of the Christian Revelation*.

Samuel Clarke was born at Norwich on 11 October 1675. He took his B.A. degree at Cambridge in 1695 by defending Newton's views, which then were still far from uncontroversial at Cambridge. His tutor apparently convinced him to provide a new Latin translation, with notes, of Rohault's *Treatise of Physics*. The translation, first published in 1697, was very successful; it went through four editions and was often used at Cambridge as a textbook. Jacques Rohault (1620–72) was a Cartesian scientist, and Clarke's notes, which became longer and more abundant as the translation went through its editions, in effect criticized Cartesian physics in favor of Newton's. In that same year, Clarke befriended Whiston, who just five years later was to be Newton's hand-picked successor to the Lucasian Chair; it was, presumably, this relation which introduced him into the Newtonian circle, of which he soon became a leading figure. His relation with Newton is somewhat unclear, in part because none of their correspondence (if there was any, since they were neighbors for many years) survives; however, in contrast to many members of the Newtonian circle, it seems that he never fell out of favor with Newton. The 1704–5 Boyle Lectures gave him great notoriety, and his connection with Newton became, as it were, official in 1706, when he translated, to Newton's satisfaction, the *Opticks* into Latin. In the same year, Clarke attacked Henry Dodwell (1641–1711), who had claimed that the soul is naturally mortal and receives immortality by the supernatural efficacy of baptism. Clarke's criticism drew a reply by Anthony Collins (1676–1729), a materialist follower of Locke's, and the ensuing exchange on whether matter can think brought Clarke even greater notoriety. His reputation had become so great that in 1710 George Berkeley (1685–1753) sent him the first edition of the *Principles* (Clarke declined to comment on them), and in 1713 Joseph Butler (1692–1752) consulted him on some difficulties in *A Demonstration*. In the meantime, he had been introduced to Queen Anne (1665–1714), who made him one of her chaplains in 1706, and three years later he was elevated to the rectory of St. James's, Westminster.

In 1712, apparently against the advice of some of Queen Anne's ministers, Clarke published *The Scripture Doctrine of the Trinity*, which was, not altogether unfairly, accused of Arianism, the theological view that Christ is divine but created. The ensuing controversy culminated two years later in his promise to the Upper House of Convocation not to preach and not to write on the topic any longer. This act of submission did not please outspoken Arians like Whiston, who in 1710 had been expelled from Cambridge because of his heterodox views; nor did it silence the (correct) rumors that he, like many of the Newtonian circle, including Newton himself, was still an Arian. How much these suspicions of heterodoxy damaged his ecclesiastical career is unclear. However, Voltaire (1694–1778) reports that Bishop Gibson effectively prevented Clarke's elevation to the See of Canterbury by pointing out that Clarke was indeed the most learned and honest man in the kingdom, but had one defect: he was not a Christian.

After the Hanoverian accession, Clarke developed a close relationship with Caroline of Anspach (1683–1737), the Princess of Wales and future queen. Caroline was an intelligent woman with philosophical interests who, in earlier years, had been a pupil of Leibniz. It was through her mediation that Clarke engaged Leibniz in the most famous philosophical correspondence of the eighteenth century (1715–16). The exchange dealt with many of the issues which had occupied Clarke in his Boyle Lectures, such as divine immensity and eternity, the relation of God to the world, the soul and its relation to the body, free will, space and time, and the nature of miracles. It also discussed more strictly scientific topics, such as the nature of matter, the existence of atoms and the void, the size of the universe, and the nature of motive force, which were then often given both a philosophical and a scientific treatment.

In 1717, Clarke published the correspondence with Leibniz together with an attack on a work by Collins denying the existence of free will. This was his last significant philosophical work. However, his remaining years were not spent idly. He continued to defend his theological views; in 1728 he wrote a short essay for the *Philosophical Transactions* trying to show, against the Leibnizians, that the proper measure of force is not mv^2 but mv; in 1729, by royal command, he edited and translated into Latin the first twelve books of the *Iliad*, showing the same skill in classical languages he had manifested in his edition of the works of Caesar seventeen years earlier. He died in 1729 after a very short illness, survived by his wife Katherine and five of his seven children.

Clarke was a polite and courtly man who, however, was vivacious with his friends and seems to have been fond of playing cards. Voltaire, who met him, was impressed by his piety and admired his logical skills so much that he called him "a veritable thinking machine." His philosophical interests were in theology and metaphysics; epistemology seems to have held little attraction for him. His philosophical vocabulary and some of his metaphysical ideas were influenced by Descartes, whom he followed in holding that the world contains two types of substance, mind and matter, the combination of which constitutes humans. However, he sided with Nicolas Malebranche (1638–1715) and Locke in denying that introspection lets us reach the substance of the soul. Indeed, like Locke and Newton he held that we just do not know the substance of things (p. 30). Furthermore, Clarke's overall judgment of Descartes was quite critical. He told Butler that Descartes' views that matter is infinite and eternal, that the behavior of all bodies can be explained mechanically, and that final causes ought to be expunged from physics had been deleterious to religion (p. 111).

One could, of course, debate Clarke's exegetical accuracy. For example, although Descartes had told More that the thesis that the world is finite is contradictory, he had also claimed that the world is indefinite rather than infinite. But this objection would miss the real thrust of Clarke's point. For he thought that natural religion was under attack by naturalism (the view that nature constitutes a self-sufficient system of which we are but a part), which had been revived by Hobbes and, especially, Spinoza. He also shared the view expressed by other philosophers, for example, More in England, and Blaise Pascal (1623–62), Bayle, and Leibniz on the Continent, that Descartes' system could be, and had been, used to further irreligion. In particular, he believed that Descartes' main fault was the identification of matter with extension, and therefore space, which entailed bestowing on matter the eternity and infinity of space. Cartesianism, then, opened the way for naturalism and the demise of natural religion, whose defense through philosophy and science he made his philosophical mission.

Clarke's attack against naturalism revolved around five connected points. First, God is a necessarily existent omnipotent, omniscient, eternal, omnipresent, and supremely benevolent person. Second, nature and its laws are radically contingent. God, endowed with a libertarian will, chose to create the world and operate in it by a reasonable but uncaused fiat (pp. 46–7, 73–4). Third, although space and time are infinite, matter is spatio-temporally finite, and being endowed only with *vis inertiae* it has no power of self-motion (p. 149). Fourth, God is substantially present in nature (or, better, nature is literally in God, since space and time are divine attributes) and constantly exercises his power by applying attractive and repulsive forces to bodies (pp. 158–9). With the exception of the law of inertia, which describes the essentially passive nature of matter, strictly speaking the laws of nature (e.g., Newton's inverse law) do not describe the behavior of matter, which is just dead mass constantly pushed around, but modalities of operation of the divine power: as in the case of occasionalism, they prescribe the actions of the divine will rather than describe those of bodies (p. 149). Fifth, although the soul is extended and interacts with the body, it is necessarily immaterial because matter, being constituted of merely juxtaposed parts, cannot possibly think even by divine intervention; moreover, the soul has been endowed by God with a libertarian will (pp. 63–6, 153–8). The first four points guaranteed that nature is not a self-sufficient system, so much so that without direct and constant divine physical intervention planets would fly away from their orbits, atoms break into their components and the machinery of the world literally grind to a halt; the fifth guaranteed that the soul is not a part of nature. In the following, we shall see these points emerge from a consideration of Clarke's views on God, free will, matter and the laws of nature, space and time, and the soul. Finally, we shall briefly consider the fortunes of *A Demonstration*.

God

The proof of the necessary existence and attributes of God occupies most of *A Demonstration*, and it is beyond the scope of this introduction to discuss it in detail. If we are to believe Whiston's testimony, Clarke preferred the argument from design to the cosmological argument.[2] Indeed, he held that the former argument is more easily understood, and therefore more apt for unphilosophical minds than the latter, and at times he claimed that the reasons behind his use of the cosmological argument were essentially occasional and strategic: *a priori* atheistical arguments required *a priori* answers (p. 119). However, he also noted that the argument from design, in contrast to the cosmological argument, cannot prove the immensity and infinity of God, and therefore we may assume that Clarke's use of the argument *a priori*, as he called it, was not merely occasioned by his adversaries' modes of argumentation (p. 119). The main lines of the argument are as follows. Since something exists now, something has existed from eternity, otherwise nothing would exist now because from nothing nothing comes.

---

[2] W. Whiston, *Historical Memoirs of the Life of Dr. Samuel Clarke* (London, 1730), p. 11.

What has existed from eternity can only be either an independent being, i.e., one having in itself the reason of its existence, or an infinite series of dependent beings. However, such a series cannot be the being which has existed from eternity because, by hypothesis, it can have no external cause, and no internal cause, i.e., no dependent being in it, can cause the whole series. Hence, an independent being exists (pp. 8–12). As a side argument, Clarke also argued that since space and time cannot be thought of as non-existent and they are obviously not self-subsistent, the substance on which they depend, God, must exist necessarily as well (pp. 13, 108). Clarke identified self-existence with necessary-existence, and embarked on obscure considerations about the necessity of the self-existing being in which, at times, this necessity seems to be some sort of entity antecedent in nature to God as the reason for God's existence (pp. 12–13, 113, 118–19). This was an unfortunate move which generated a good deal of controversy that continued after Clarke's death. Finally, teleological considerations show that the independent being, God, is necessarily endowed with intelligence and wisdom (pp. 38, 79). In addition, God is endowed, though not with metaphysical necessity, with all the moral perfections (p. 83).

Clarke said little about the divine nature, perhaps because he held that the manner of divine existence infinitely transcends that of creatures, and that consequently we cannot have an adequate notion of the divine being and attributes. However, he rejected not only Spinoza's view that a word can refer both to human and divine properties only equivocally, but also Aquinas' position that it can do so only analogically. Instead, he adopted the Latitudinarian view that human and divine attributes, especially the moral ones, have the same nature, although God's are infinite (pp. 8, 144–5).

Clarke's most characteristic and controversial views about God concerned divine eternity and immensity. According to traditional Christian theology, God is eternal and immense (omnipresent). The claim that God is eternal can be taken to mean two different things. In one sense it means that God is a timeless being whose duration is not successive, with no before or after: past, present, and future are all timelessly present to God. In another sense, it means that God is sempiternal, i.e., a being existing throughout time but whose duration is successive and for whom there is a before and an after.[3]

---

[3] For the first view, see S. Boethius, *De Consolatione Philosophiae*, v; St. Anselm, *Monologion*, chs. 20–3; St. Thomas Aquinas, *Summa Theologiae*, Ia Iae, Q. 10. For an account of the second view, R. Sorabji, *Time, Creation and the Continuum* (Ithaca, Cornell University Press, 1983), ch. 16.

Similarly, divine immensity or omnipresence can be understood in different ways. God can be taken to be present everywhere by operation but not by situation; i.e., God is present by being in a place not as a human would be, but by acting there. God fills a room by causing it and its contents in a way remotely analogous to that in which I can fill a glass by pouring water in it. By contrast, one could claim that divine operational presence requires situational presence, and hold that the divine substance is, in some sense to be specified, coextended with what it fills. However, divine extension can itself be taken in two ways. It can be understood in terms of local extension; God, then, would be extended like, say, a stone or perhaps space are, with the proviso that God, unlike a stone, could penetrate all other extended things. Or, it can be understood in non-local terms, in accordance with what More dubbed "holenmerism"; the divine substance, then, would be whole in the whole of space and whole in each and every place, in a way analogous to the presence in space of an instant of time.[4]

Clarke rejected the view of God as substantially removed from space and time. Divine eternity involves both necessary existence and a "Duration of inexhaustible and never failing permanency," which, however, could not be identified with the traditional notion of the eternal present (*nunc stans*) according to which God exists in an unchanging permanent present without any successive duration (pp. 32–3). Like Newton, Clarke considered such a view unintelligible at best and contradictory at worst (pp. 32–3, 138).[5] The attribution of successive duration to God might suggest that God, like us, is in time but, unlike us, does not change. However, this was not Clarke's view. For one thing, he made clear in his exchanges with Butler that God is not in space and time (p. 105). Moreover, he attributed distinct and successive thoughts to God, otherwise God could not "vary his will, nor diversify his works, nor act successively, nor govern the world, nor indeed have any power to will or do anything at all" (pp. 159–60). Hence, God is

---

[4] For operational presence, see e.g., St. Thomas Aquinas' *Summa Theologiae*, Ia Iae, Q. 8, a. 2. For ancient and medieval examples of holenmerism, see St. Augustine, *Liber de Praesentia Dei* (Letter 187) secs. 11, 25; St. Anselm, *Monologion*, ch. 22; for modern examples, see N. Malebranche, *Dialogues on Metaphysics*. trans. W. Doney (New York, Abaris Books, 1980), dialogue VIII, section iv; R. Cudworth, *The True Intellectual System of the Universe* (London, 1678; reprint New York, Garland Publishing Co., 1978), pp. 781–3.

[5] For Newton, see McGuire's "Existence, Actuality and Necessity: Newton on Space and Time," *Annals of Science*, 35 (1978), 463–508, especially 495, and A. Koyré and I. B. Cohen, "Newton & the Leibniz-Clarke Correspondence," *Archives Internationales d'Histoire des Sciences*, 15 (1962), 63–126, especially 97.

immutable with respect to his will and his general and particular decrees only in the sense that he does not change his mind (pp. 138–9).

Clarke's criticism of the Scholastic view of divine immensity or omnipresence was analogous to that of eternity: the claim that "the immensity of God is a point, as his eternity ... is an instant" was, he held, unintelligible (p. 35). However, while, for Clarke, God's temporal presence is analogous to ours by involving temporal succession, his views about God's spatial presence were somewhat less clear because he did not explicitly state whether he adopted holenmerism or not. Nevertheless, there are good reasons for holding he did not. Clarke vigorously denied Leibniz' charge that extension is incompatible with divine simplicity because it introduces parts in God without making any reference to holenmerism, and this intimates that he thought of divine omnipresence in terms of local extension and dimensionality. Nor did he attempt any defense of holenmerism from More's famous critique, and in addition there is some indirect contemporary evidence that Clarke took God to be literally dimensional.[6]

For Clarke, divine eternity and immensity are to be identified with space and time. This identification, however, was fraught with difficulties, in part because Clarke's position was not clear. Usually, he held that space and time are just divine properties (p. 31; *Cl* v, 36–48, note). However, he also told Leibniz that, in addition, they are necessary effects of God's existence and necessary requirements for divine eternity and ubiquity, without supplying any argument to show that these different accounts are equivalent or even compatible (*Cl* IV, 10). At other times, as in the letter to Daniel Waterland (1683–1740) and in the *Avertissement* to Pierre Des Maizeaux (1666–1745), in the latter of which Newton had more than a hand, he held that they are not, strictly speaking, properties (p. 122–3).[7]

Moreover, as Leibniz and an anonymous correspondent (almost certainly Waterland) readily noted, the identification of divine immensity with

[6] Collins mentions More, Turner, and Clarke among the supporters of the dimensional extension of God: A. Collins, *A Discourse of Free Thinking* (London, 1713), pp. 47–8. Similar issues arise with respect to Newton; see E. Grant, *Much Ado about Nothing. Theories of Space and Vacuum from the Middle Ages to the Scientific Revolution* (Cambridge University Press, 1981), pp. 244–6, 416, note 420; R. S. Westfall, *Never at Rest. A Biography of Isaac Newton* (Cambridge University Press, 1980), p. 647.

[7] P. Des Maizeaux, *Recueil de diverses pièces ... par Mrs. Leibniz, Clarke, Newton, & autre autheurs celèbres* (Amsterdam, 1720), tome 1, p. v. Koyré and Cohen have shown that the *Avertissement* was written by Newton by publishing the several drafts by his own hand. However, as they themselves point out, there is no reason to doubt that Clarke contributed to it. See their "Newton & the Leibniz-Clarke Correspondence," *Archives Internationales d'Histoire des Sciences*, 15 (1962), 63–126, especially 95.

space endangers the simplicity of the divine being because space has parts, albeit not separable ones. The objection, though formidable, was not new; Bayle had chided the Newtonians for identifying space with divine immensity in order to solve the ontological problem created by the positing of an infinite space and had compared this solution to Malebranche's placement of "intelligible extension" in God, a solution which, he claimed, Antoine Arnauld (1612–94) had shown to lead to the destruction of divine simplicity.[8]

Clarke's solution was to claim parity between spatial and temporal extendedness: since the former is compatible with the simplicity of what "stretches" temporally, the latter is compatible with the simplicity of what stretches spatially (pp. 115–16). But the parity between space and time, were it to be granted, rather than showing that spatial extendedness is not detrimental to a thing's simplicity because temporal extendedness is not, could be taken to show that the latter is detrimental to a thing's simplicity because the former is. Moreover, the objection could be reinforced by noting that time, as space, is subject to the category of quantity, traditionally taken to be incompatible with the divine essence.

The same critic also argued that extension is incompatible with divine "spirituality," as Clarke put it, namely with the claim that God thinks. This, too, aimed at showing that Clarke's God is not a unity. For, according to Clarke, only an essentially simple substance can think, and consequently matter, being a compound, cannot possibly be the subject of consciousness (pp. 153–8). While unfortunately we do not have the letter of Clarke's critic, presumably the objection was that if the divine consciousness were extended, then it would be possible to consider a spatial part of it as being itself conscious. But this possibility shows that an extended consciousness is not a unity because if a spatial part of consciousness were a consciousness, then the whole consciousness would be a multitude of consciousnesses. And this would not only be incompatible with divine simplicity, but with Clarke's point that consciousness is a unity in the sense of not being composed by several consciousnesses (p. 157).

As before, Clarke's reply invoked the symmetry between space and time. He started by pointing out, as Newton had done in the General Scholium to book III of *Principia*, that an instant of time is the same everywhere. But, Clarke thought, the spatial extension of one instant of time does not affect

---

[8] P. Bayle, *Dictionnaire historique et critique* (Paris, Editions sociales, 1974), s.v. Leucippus, remark G.

its unity and does not justify the claim that it stretches for, say, one mile. The evidence for this conclusion, Clarke seemed to hold, is given by the fact that one does not think, or talk, about time in terms of miles. Similarly, he concluded, from the fact that the divine consciousness is extended, one should not infer that it is proper to talk about it in terms of its spatial parts (p. 116). However, Clarke's point seems hardly compelling: if one assumes that an instant of time is infinitely extended, one is implicitly assuming that it is extended for at least one mile.

Free will

Clarke attached great importance to the issue of free will (p. 63). Like many philosophers, he held that the highest form of freedom involves willing as one should, namely, having one's will in step with one's right values. He also believed that freedom of the will, or liberty, involves a libertarian power of self-determination and that it is a necessary condition both for that higher form of freedom and for religion. Hobbes's and Spinoza's views that everything happens deterministically or necessarily, he thought, destroy it. However, Spinoza, Hobbes, and their followers could be defeated by noticing that the very causal version of the principle of sufficient reason, customarily used to show that no self-determining will is possible because each of its determinations is the effect of previous causes, in reality entails that God has a self-determining free will. The reason is that the causal version of the principle of sufficient reason in the cosmological argument shows that the necessary being on which the contingent world depends must have in itself "a principle of acting ... which is the idea of liberty" (pp. 53–4).

Clarke's argument is disconcerting. At most, the cosmological argument shows that the first cause cannot be acted upon by any other cause and consequently must be an original causal principle. Spinoza knew this, and pointed out that God is self-existent and self-determined, i.e., a free cause in his sense, and that its essence is power. But whether the divine power operates in accordance with metaphysically necessary laws themselves arising from the divine nature or not, is left open by the causal version of the principle of sufficient reason. Clarke thought he had an answer to this sort of objection by showing that the notion of a necessary agent is contradictory because agency involves the libertarian capacity of suspending action (pp. 46, 74–5, 132–5). Therefore, since God must be an agent, he cannot operate necessarily, and, since being an agent and being free are the same thing, God is free as well (p. 75). Of course, the identification of agency with the capacity to choose provided further evidence against the view that Spinoza's god is an agent, as Clarke did not fail to point out (W II, 586). But Clarke failed to justify his libertarian view of agency, and finally could not explain why the first cause ought to be an agent in his sense rather than just a Spinozistic cause which produces all that can be produced without choosing. Ultimately, the causal version of the principle of sufficient reason cannot yield the conclusion Clarke wanted.

However, Clarke had other arguments against the view that divine operations are necessary. If God operated necessarily, things could not be different from how they are. But the number of planets, their orbits, indeed, the law of gravitation itself, could have been different, as any reasonable person (but not Spinoza) could plainly see. Further, the obvious fact, despite Spinoza and Descartes, that final causes are at play in the world, indicates that divine activity follows, not necessary, but architectonic, patterns (p. 51).

Clarke did not content himself with attacking necessitarianism and determinism with arguments drawn from general metaphysical considerations; he also criticized the specific theories of volition which determinists and necessitarians had put forth, in particular the view that volition is caused by, or even identical with, the last evaluative judgment. He did not identify whom he had in mind, but certainly the targets were Spinoza and Hobbes. Spinoza had argued that every act of volition is an act of affirmation and vice versa. Presumably, what he had in mind is that every volition is identical with a value judgment: to will to do X is to judge that X is the best thing to do. Hobbes had not identified the volition with the evaluative judgment, but had told John Bramhall (1594–1666) that the latter was the final and decisive cause of the former, since the last judgment of the understanding "may be said to produce the effect *necessarily*, in such manner as the last feather may be said to break a horse's back, when there were so many laid on before as there wanted but that one to do it."[9]

Clarke was ready to grant that the understanding is fully determined to assent to a proposition which is perceived to be true in the same way in

[9] B. Spinoza, *Ethics*, part II, proposition 49, corollary; T. Hobbes, *Of Liberty and Necessity* in *English Works*, ed. W. Molesworth (London, 1839; reprint Aalen, Scientia Verlag, 1966), vol. 4, pp. 247, 268. For Hobbes's definition of volition, see *Leviathan*, ed. C. B. Macpherson (New York, Penguin Books, 1968), part I, ch. 6. For Hobbes's point to Bramhall, see T. Hobbes, *English Works*, vol. 5, p. 73.

which an open eye is fully determined to see objects. In this sense, the assent is necessary (p. 125). However, the necessity of the last evaluative judgment is totally immaterial to the issue of freedom. His opponents, Clarke thought, were guilty of basic philosophical errors. If they maintained that the content of the evaluation, the evaluative proposition, is identical with the volition or causes it, then they were confusing reasons with causes or, as he put it, "moral motives with physical efficients" (pp. 54, 73). The understanding presents the agent with a value judgment, e.g., "doing X is better than doing Y," which the agent has the power to follow or not. The reason, Clarke explained to Collins, is that the motive, e.g., the proposition "doing X is better than doing Y," cannot cause anything because it is an abstract entity. Holding the contrary is taking an abstract entity for a substance (pp. 134, 136).

On the other hand, if Clarke's opponents maintained that, not the evaluative proposition, but one's perceiving, judging, or otherwise believing it, is identical with, or a partial cause of, volition, then they were falling foul of a basic causal principle. Against Descartes, Clarke insisted that judging, i.e., assenting to what appears true and dissenting from what appears false, is not an action but a passion. But what is passive cannot cause anything which is active (p. 134). So, there is no causal link between evaluation and volition or, as Clarke put it, "approbation and action" (p. 126). Nor is there any causal link between previous non-volitional mental states and any volition. What causes the volition is the principle of action itself, which Clarke identified with the agent, that is, the spiritual substance.

Having shown that God is necessarily endowed with liberty, Clarke tried to show that we are as well. His argument was based both on metaphysics and experience. It is clear that liberty is a communicable power because it does not entail such incommunicable qualities as total causal independence and self-existence (p. 61). We do not know how the power of action can be transmitted, but considerations drawn from experience assure us that it has been, since our actions seem to us to be free, exactly as they would do on the supposition that we are really free agents (p. 62). Of course, this does not amount to a strict demonstration; but denying that we have free will is on a par with denying the existence of the external world, a coherent but unreasonable option. The burden of proof is not on the supporter of liberty, but on its denier.

In addition to providing evidence for the libertarian position, Clarke also endeavored to answer arguments against it. Against the claim that divine foreknowledge is incompatible with free will, Clarke objected that since knowledge does not affect the thing known, our free choices are unaffected by divine omniscience (pp. 140–3). He also addressed the Hobbesian argument that, since thought is a mode of matter and matter has no self-moving power, there cannot be any freedom of the will. Against this, he advanced two objections (p. 64). One is a complex argument, which we discuss later, for the claim that thought cannot possibly inhere either naturally or supernaturally in matter. The other consists in the claim that Hobbes and his followers were guilty of sliding from meaning by "matter" "extended solid substance" (which of course would not have free will even if it were to think *per impossibile*) to meaning "substantial *substratum* or subject of inherence" (to which any previous conclusion regarding free will based on solidity and extension need not apply) (p. 71).

Another objection Clarke considered is that a free agent cannot choose whether to have a will or not; "but (the two contradictories of acting or not acting being always necessarily before him) he must of necessity, and essentially to his being a free agent, perpetually will one of these two things, either to act or to forbear acting" (p. 74). This fact, Clarke continued, induced even "some considerate persons" to entertain "great doubts concerning the possibility of liberty." Clarke did not identify the philosophers he had in mind, but probably one of his targets was Locke, who, at *Essay* II, 21, 23–4, seemed to move from the claim that an action can take place or not only if the agent wills it or not and the claim that necessarily an action must take place or not, to the conclusion that the will of the agent is determined. Clarke pointed out that the argument was guilty of confusing *de dicto* and *de re* necessity. It might be true that if I think about doing A, then it is necessary that either I will to do A or will not to do A. However, from this it does not follow that if I think about doing A, then necessarily I will to do A. Nor does it follow that if I think about doing A, then necessarily I will not to do A (pp. 74–5).

Matter and the laws of nature

Clarke's views on matter are best seen in connection with his ideas about miracles. Like Joseph Glanville (1636–80), Thomas Sprat (1635–1713), Boyle, and Locke, he belonged to that group of English intellectuals associated with the Royal Society who thought that miracles could be used as evidence for the claim that Christianity is the true religion. According to

Clarke, a miracle is a "work effected in a manner unusual ... by the inter-position either of God himself, or of some intelligent agent superior to man, for the proof or evidence of some particular doctrine, or in attest-ation to the authority of some particular person" (*W* II, 701).

However, Clarke claimed, "Modern Deists," noticing that nature is regular and constant and that certain causes produce certain effects accord-ing to fixed laws, have come to the conclusion that "there are in matter certain laws or powers the result of which is ... the course of nature; which they think is impossible to be changed or altered, and consequently that there can be no such things as miracles" (p. 150). Prima facie, it is difficult to see why Clarke worried about this allegedly deist view. Certainly, even in a physical world ruled by metaphysically necessary laws, events can have unusual causes, e.g., by being brought about by invisible agents. Presumably then, when Clarke claimed that miracles are "effected in manner unusual, or different from the common and regular method of providence," he meant that the causes of a miracle are not subsumable under the laws of nature; consequently, if the natural laws are unbreakable and all pervasive, as the deists and Spinoza claim, then miracles are impossible.

The deistic view, Clarke argued, is completely wrong because "all things done in the world, are done either immediately by God himself, or by created intelligent beings: matter being evidently not at all capable of any laws or powers whatsoever" except for the negative power of inertia. Consequently, the so-called "effects of the natural powers of matter, and laws of motion; of gravitation, attraction, or the like" properly speaking are but the "effects of God's acting upon matter continually and every moment, either immediately by himself, or mediately by some created intelligent beings." The course of nature is "nothing else but the will of God producing certain effects in a continued, regular, constant and uniform manner which ... being in every moment perfectly arbitrary, is as easy to be altered at any time, as to be preserved" (p. 149). So, the possibility of miracles, and ultimately the strongest evidence for the divine commission of Christ, for Clarke depends upon a form of theological voluntarism and the denial of the activity of matter.

Clarke's theological voluntarism was moderate if compared with the extreme views of Descartes. For him, moral laws are independent of the divine will, and even the absolute power of God (*potentia dei absoluta*) is limited to what is logically possible. Nor is the divine will inscrutable, if that entails that divine attributes and powers are absolutely different from the human ones, since, as we saw above, they have the same nature and differ only in degree. Moreover, the "arbitrariness" of God's will is not to be construed as irrationality; rather, the divine will infallibly follows his necessarily correct judgment, and consequently God always acts on the basis of rules of "uniformity and proportion." However, true to his libertarian position, Clarke held that the will, in God as in us, is not causally determined by the understanding, and therefore the rules governing the ordinary power of God (*potentia dei ordinata*), a subset of which are the laws of nature, are freely self-imposed, and not the result of the necessarily correct divine understanding: they are a manifestation of God's moral, and therefore free, attributes, not of God's metaphysical, and therefore necessary, ones.

Clarke steadfastly maintained that matter has neither an essential nor an accidental power of self-motion. The first claim was very common among early modern philosophers, and held not only *a fortiori* by an occasionalist like Malebranche, but also by thinkers of different persuasions like Descartes, Locke, and Boyle. In fact, even Pierre Gassendi (1592–1655), who had upheld the notion of an active matter by claiming that atoms have an internal corporeal principle of action, had fallen short of claiming that they possess it essentially.[10]

Clarke's second claim, however, was more controversial. For, although most early modern mechanists programmatically tried to substitute a nature made of inert particles for the living nature of Renaissance philosophy, the attempt soon ran into great difficulties. Strict mechanism proved inadequate to explain phenomena like exothermic reactions (where does the explosive motion of gunpowder come from?) or the spring of the air (why does a deflated closed balloon expand in a vacuum tube?). In order to explain such phenomena, mechanism was altered by philosopher-scientists like Boyle, Walter Charleton (1619–1707), William Petty (1623–87), and Newton to include particles variously endowed with powers of motion, attraction, and repulsion.

Clarke's position on the issue was radical: the various non-mechanical powers of particles are the result of direct divine or spiritual activity. He could not bring himself to accept active matter because he thought of it as a prelude to atheism, for, as we noticed above, Clarke believed that deny-

---

[10] R. Boyle, *Works*, vol. 5, p. 46; J. Locke, *An Essay concerning Human Understanding*, ed. P. H. Nidditch (Oxford University Press, 1979), IV, 10,10; R. Descartes, *Principia Philosophiae*, II, 36, in *Oeuvres de Descartes*, eds. C. Adam and P. Tannery (Paris, 1897–1913; reprint Paris, J. Vrin, 1964–76), vol. IXB, p. 61; P. Gassendi, *Opera Omnia in sex tomos* (Lugduni, 1658; reprint Stuttgart-Bad Canstatt, F. Fromann, 1964), vol. 1, pp. 336–7.

ing God's continuous direct intervention in nature in effect amounts to eliminating him, as John Toland (1670–1722) had done by endowing matter with essential "autokynesis" (pp. 19, 120–30). Clarke's views, however, had their own problems. A God who is actually extended and constantly operates physically on matter looked suspiciously like the soul of the world, as Leibniz charged using Newton's identification (in the *Opticks*) of space as the *sensorium* of God. Similarly, the placement of gravitational forces within the purview of ordinary divine activity which Clarke openly accepted, in contrast with Newton's officially agnostic position, drew from Leibniz the accusation of obscurantism.

Space and time

According to Clarke, the ideas of space and time are the two "first and most obvious simple Ideas, that every man has in his mind" (p. 114). Like many of the philosophers who investigated the nature of space and time, he tended to produce arguments with regard to space, leaving the reader to infer that parallel arguments could be drawn with respect to time. While matter can be thought of as non-existing, space exists necessarily because "to suppose any part of space removed, is to suppose it removed from and out of itself: and to suppose the whole to be taken away, is supposing it to be taken away from itself, that is, to be taken away while it still remains: which is a contradiction in terms" (p. 13).[11]

Although space is not sensible, Clarke rejected its identification with nothingness because nothing has no properties, while space has some, e.g., quantity and dimensions (pp. 13, 114–15, 152). One might add other properties which he accepted, such as homogeneity, immutability, continuity, and probably impenetrability. Space, then, is an entity in which things are, and not the mere absence of matter, as at least some of the ancient atomists seem to have thought. Space is also not an aggregate of its parts, but presumably an essential whole preceding all it parts, a view motivated at least in part by theological considerations (*Cl* IV, 11–12).

Like Newton, Clarke adopted the view that space is necessarily infinite because "to set bounds to space, is to suppose it bounded by something

---

[11] Clarke's views were similar to Newton's. See *NP* I, definition 8, scholium, pp. 46–8; in addition, see Newton's early *De Gravitatione* for the claim that space cannot be thought as non-existent, in *Unpublished Scientific Papers of Isaac Newton*, eds. and trans. A. R. Hall and M. B. Hall (Cambridge University Press, 1962), p. 104.

which itself takes up space" or else that "this bounded by nothing, and then the idea of that nothing will still be space," and both suppositions are contradictory (p. 115). What Clarke had in mind here is rather unclear. He seemed to think that what has a boundary must be bounded by something else. If so, the argument was not well taken because a sphere, for example, has a boundary which stems from its own nature, not by the presence of something external bounding it: one need not think of space by analogy with a gas kept in place by the walls of a vessel. Perhaps, however, he had in mind Archyta's powerfully intuitive argument, which Locke had recently repeated, that one could, in principle, stretch one's hand out of any edge allegedly bounding space, and therefore that space is infinite. If so, the argument counters the objection that one cannot, in principle, stretch anything into nothing by stating, albeit without argument, that the alleged nothing bounding space in reality is more space.[12]

Since absolute space has an essential and invariable structure which is independent of the bodies in it and which is not altered by their presence, any possible world must conform to it, as creatures must be in space and God cannot alter essences because his power is limited to the metaphysically possible. The same is true of time, which "flows equably" independently of anything in it. Creatures occupy an absolute position in space and time which we may or may not be able to establish because we have no direct access to absolute space and time. Such a position is privileged in the sense that the true spatio-temporal relations among creatures are completely parasitic upon the spatio-temporal relations of the spatio-temporal locations they occupy.

The introduction of absolute space, allegedly demanded by Newtonian physics, offered Clarke an immediate philosophical advantage in the fight against Spinoza, for it showed that the Cartesian identification of extension with matter, which had made possible Spinoza's excesses, was wrong, a consequence which was not lost on Bayle and insisted upon by Colin Maclaurin (1698–1746).[13] Of course, the existence of absolute space introduced the new difficulty of its relation to God, but, as we saw, Clarke thought he had solved it by claiming that space and time are attributes of God or the result of divine existence.

---

[12] J. Locke, *An Essay*, ii, 13, 21. See also I. Newton, *De Gravitatione* in *Unpublished Scientific Papers*, pp. 101–2.

[13] See P. Bayle, *Dictionnaire*, s.v. Leucippus, remark G; C. Maclaurin, *An Account of Sir Isaac Newton's Philosophical Discoveries* (London, 1748), p. 77.

The soul

In 1706, Henry Dodwell published a book in which he defended conditional immortality: our souls are naturally mortal and upon the death of the body can be kept in existence only by divine supernatural intervention. Clarke wrote an open letter to Dodwell complaining that he had opened wide the floodgates to libertinism by providing an excuse for the wicked not to fear eternal punishment. He then argued that the soul, being immaterial, is naturally immortal and gave his own version of the traditional argument for the immateriality of the soul from the alleged unity of consciousness, insisting that not even God could endow matter with consciousness.

Clarke's argument was very ambitious, as one can see by comparison with Locke's argument from consciousness to immateriality. Locke agreed that matter on its own cannot possibly produce thought either in itself or in anything else. He concluded, from the fact that we think, that our maker must be immaterial. However, Locke was ready to admit that God could superadd thought to matter and, consequently, that we could not exclude with metaphysical certainty that our minds are material.[14] By contrast, Clarke's argument attempted to prove, not merely that matter cannot possibly produce thought, but also that it is metaphysically impossible for matter to be the subject of inherence of thought. Not only is it impossible for matter to think on its own, but not even God could make it think (p. 72).

Clarke's argument failed to convince Anthony Collins, who made no bones about his materialist leanings and whose intervention in defense of Dodwell started a protracted controversy. Clarke told Collins that if thinking in humans were a mode of matter, then "it [would] be but too natural a consequence, to conceive that it may be only the same thing in all other rational beings likewise; and even in God himself. And what a notion of God this would give us, is not difficult to imagine" (*W* III, 851). For then, Clarke continued, every thinking being, including God, would be governed by "absolute necessity, such as the motion of a clock or a watch is determined by." The result would be the destruction of every possibility of self-determination and the undermining of the very foundations of religion.

In the course of the exchange with Collins, it became clear that Clarke's argument for the immateriality of the soul revolved around three basic claims, namely:

[14] J. Locke, *An Essay*, IV, 10, 16; IV, 3, 6.

1. Necessarily consciousness is an individual power.
2. An individual power cannot result from, or inhere in, a divisible substance; or, alternatively, an individual power can only be produced by, or inhere in, an individual being.
3. Matter is not, and cannot possibly be, an individual being.

The conclusion is that consciousness cannot possibly be the product of, or inhere in, matter.

The first premise, Clarke explained, must be understood as expressing the obvious truth that consciousness is "truly one undivided consciousness, and not a multitude of distinct consciousnesses added together" (*W* III, 784). Collins accepted Clarke's first premise, and was also ready to accept the third premise, not with respect to matter *per se*, but with respect to systems of matter such as the brain. However, he disagreed with Clarke's claim that an individual power such as consciousness can inhere only in an individual subject, namely a being which, as Clarke put it, is "essentially one," i.e., such that any division in it destroys its essence (pp. 152–3). Consequently, he disagreed with Clarke's contention that only an individual substance like an immaterial soul can be the subject of consciousness. Clarke's attempts to meet Collins' objections are too complex to be considered here; the interested reader should look at their full exchange.

For Clarke, although the soul is necessarily immaterial, it can causally affect the body because material qualities such as figure and mobility are "negative qualities, deficiencies or imperfections" which can be effected by consciousness, which is a positive quality (p. 41). One can appreciate the theological, moral, and broadly philosophical motivations for such a position. He clearly wanted to leave the door open for arguing that God, the maker of matter, is immaterial, and the claim that a thinking immaterial substance can produce material modifications is an essential component of his argument. Moreover, for Clarke the capacity of the soul to affect the body causally is a consequence of our being endowed with liberty (*Cl* IV, 32, 33; V, 92, 93–5). In addition, Clarke was convinced that we experience the causal power by which we move our body (p. 62). However, his position on whether the body causally affects the soul was less than clear. At times, he leaned towards the view that is does, and at others that it does not (pp. 116, 41).

Collins not only rejected Clarke's argument from the unitary nature of consciousness to the immateriality of its subject, but also wondered how an immaterial substance like the soul can be indivisible if one assumes, as Clarke had obliquely intimated, that it is extended. To Collins's apparent surprise, instead of rejecting the view that the soul is extended, Clarke replied that whether the soul is extended was immaterial to the issue at hand (p. 151). Moreover, "as the parts of space or expansion itself can demonstrably be proved to be absolutely indiscerpible, so it ought not to be reckoned an insuperable difficulty to imagine that all immaterial thinking substances (upon supposition that expansion is not excluded out of their idea) may be so likewise" (*W* III, 763). The point is that, for Clarke, space is extended and yet indivisible because of the interdependence of its parts (p. 152). All one has to do is to think of the soul as a substance whose parts depend on each other, like those of space (p. 152).

One can sympathize with Clarke's guarded reply. On the one hand, he understood the problems involved in the claim that the soul is extended and is also the individual, essentially indivisible, immaterial subject of consciousness and, consequently, tried to separate the issue of immateriality from that of extension. On the other hand, Clarke did indeed maintain that the soul is extended. He held that while God is not in space, everything else is (p. 105). As he eventually told Leibniz, not only is the soul in space, but it is in a particular place, the *sensorium*, which a part of the brain occupies (*Cl* IV, 37). Clarke inferred the presence of the soul in the *sensorium* through an argument which employed two independent premises: first, that something can act only where it is substantially, and, secondly, that the soul interacts with the body. The conclusion is that the soul is substantially present where (at least) a part of the body is (*Cl* III, 11–12).

Saying that the soul must be substantially present where a part of the brain is does not fully determine how the soul is present. It certainly rules out mere Cartesian operational presence, but it fails to determine whether the soul's presence is to be understood in terms of holenmerism or in terms of mere extension. However, there is cumulative evidence that for Clarke the soul is merely coextended with a part of the brain. Clarke used an analogy with space, which he took to be both extended and indivisible, to explain how the soul could be extended and indivisible; but certainly holenmerism does not apply to space. He did not address More's critique of holenmerism, as one would expect him to do had he adopted it. He did not address Leibniz' accusation that the extension of the soul destroys its unity by appealing to holenmerism; rather, he defended the claim that, as he put it, the soul "fills the sensorium" (*Cl* v, 98). In sum, Clarke's views on freedom, with their ties to morality and religion, together with his views on causality, pushed him towards the thesis that the soul is extended.

The fortunes of *A Demonstration*

Given Clarke's position in the Newtonian circle, the influence of *A Demonstration* was strongest in England during the first half of the eighteenth century. Since its publication, it was subjected to intense criticism, e.g., by Butler and Waterland, to which Clarke himself occasionally replied. It is also reasonable to assume that, in section 117 of the *Principles*, Berkeley had Clarke in mind when he attacked the "divines" who make space divine because of the difficulties of conceiving its limits or annihilation. By and large, the criticisms revolved around three issues: the soundness of the proof itself; the problematic relation between antecedent necessity and the divine substance; and the nature of space and time and their relation to God. Clarke's replies, especially to the last one in the letter to Waterland and in the exchange with Butler, as we saw, did contribute some degree of clarification of his views. After Clarke's death, his views were defended by his brother, John Clarke (1682–1757), and by John Jackson (1686–1763) and criticized by, among others, Joseph Clarke (d. 1749) and William Law (1686–1761). An account of their controversies can be found in chapter 3 of Ferguson's *The Philosophy of Dr. Samuel Clarke and its Critics*.

After the middle of the century, interest in Clarke's book diminished, in large part because the cosmological argument fell out of fashion, being replaced by the argument from design. Certainly, if one makes the reasonable assumption that Demea presents Clarke's argument (the text is similar to Clarke's account in the letter to Waterland), David Hume (1711–76) still felt the need to criticize it in the *Dialogues on Natural Religion*. However, the criticism occurred in but a few pages within a work discussing at length the argument from design. The waning of the fortunes of *A Demonstration* at the end of the century was mostly due to the anti-metaphysical tenor of the eighteenth century. As we saw, Clarke himself was the first to admit that the argument from design (which is briefly but adequately presented in *A Demonstration*) is easier to understand; but he also believed, correctly, that only a metaphysical argument proving the necessity of God's existence could meet metaphysical attacks on natural religion, fully prove the infinity of God's attributes, and show that there is, and cannot but be, one God.

On the Continent, the fortune of *A Demonstration* was more modest, in part because there Clarke's reputation rested more on his exchanges with Collins and Leibniz than on the Boyle Lectures. Even so, in 1713 Jean Le Clerc (1657–1736), one of Clarke's admirers on the Continent, glowingly reviewed it together with Clarke's correspondence with Collins in his *Bibliothèque Choisie*. Moreover, almost certainly Leibniz read *A Demonstration* during his controversy with Clarke (a copy was sent to him by Caroline), and a French translation by Pierre Ricotier, which included the exchange with Butler and Clarke's reply to an anonymous critic, appeared in Amsterdam in 1717.

Today few people will find the cosmological argument compelling. In fact, many will find Clarke's use of the principle of sufficient reason to answer global questions like "Why is there something rather than nothing?" reckless. However, a study of *A Demonstration* can still prove rewarding on both historical and theoretical grounds. The cosmological argument was one of the standard arguments for the existence of God, and Clarke's version, when compared, for example, to Locke's or Leibniz's, is extraordinarily thorough and, as far as the nature of the argument allows, cogent. Indeed, Rowe claims that Clarke's is "the most complete, forceful, and cogent presentation of the Cosmological Argument we possess."[15]

More importantly, setting aside the argument itself, Clarke's book, together with the various pieces he wrote to clarify or defend it, contains not only the clearest and most interesting statement of the theological and metaphysical views circulating within the Newtonian circle, but also the outlines of a sophisticated metaphysical system built to show that Newtonianism, in contrast to Cartesianism, far from representing a threat to religion, could be used to support it. Furthermore, some of the issues raised in *A Demonstration* and debated in related works continue to be at the center of lively theological discussion. For example, many of Clarke's views and arguments on divine immutability, eternity, and immensity are still discussed by philosophers interested in theism.[16]

---

[15] William L. Rowe, *The Cosmological Argument* (Princeton University Press, 1975), p. 8.

[16] See, for example, N. Pike, *God and Timelessness* (London, Routledge and Kegan Paul, 1970); R. Swinburne, *The Coherence of Theism* (Oxford, Clarendon Press, 1977); A. Kenny, *The God of the Philosophers* (Oxford, Clarendon Press, 1979); B. Leftow, *Time and Eternity* (Ithaca, Cornell University Press, 1991).

Chronology

1710	Whiston, Newton's successor to the Lucasian Chair at Cambridge, loses his post because of his Arian views
1712	Publishes the *Scripture Doctrine of the Trinity* and produces a highly praised edition of Caesar's *De Bello Gallico* and *De Bello Civili*
1713	Second edition of Newton's *Principia*
1713–14	Corresponds with Butler on theological issues
1714	Is accused of Arianism and compelled to promise not to write on the Trinity; however, to the end of his life he responds to his Trinitarian critics
1715–16	With Caroline Princess of Wales as an intermediary, engages Leibniz in a famous exchange on theological, metaphysical, and physical issues
1717	Edits the correspondence with Leibniz, adding a defense of free will against Collins's *A Philosophical Enquiry concerning Human Liberty*
1728	His letter to Hoadly "On the Proportion of Force to Velocity in Bodies in Motion" is published in the *Philosophical Transactions*
1729	Edits and translates into Latin the first twelve books of the *Iliad*; dies after a short illness on May 17

Further reading

In spite of Clarke's pre-eminence in British philosophy in the generation between Locke and Berkeley, and in spite of his being Leibniz's correspondent in the most famous philosophical exchange of the eighteenth century, the only available monograph covering most of his philosophical work is J. P. Ferguson, *The Philosophy of Dr Samuel Clarke and its Critics* (New York, Vantage Press, 1974), which provides a good introduction with extensive factual information. On Clarke's ethics and its relations to his metaphysics, J. E. Le Rossignol, *The Ethical Philosophy of Samuel Clarke* (Leipzig,1892) is still useful. A much shorter alternative to the two previous books is P. Edwards (ed.), *The Encyclopedia of Philosophy* (New York, Macmillan, 1967), s.v. On Clarke's life, a good source is L. Stephen and S. Lee (eds.), *Dictionary of National Biography* (London, 1882; reprint London, Oxford University Press, 1949–50), s.v. An interesting contemporary biography, which, however, reflects the concerns of the author about the Trinitarian controversy, is W. Whiston, *Historical Memoirs of the Life of Dr. Samuel Clarke* (London, 1730). On the Boyle Lectures, see M. C. Jacob, *The Newtonians and the English Revolution 1689–1720* (Ithaca, Cornell University Press, 1976) and M. C. W. Hunter, *Science and Society in Restoration England* (Cambridge University Press, 1981).

There are very few works on specific aspects of Clarke's thought. On Clarke's version of the cosmological argument, W. R. Rowe, *The Cosmological Argument* (Princeton University Press, 1975), is very useful. On Clarke's Arian views, see J. P. Ferguson, *An Eighteenth Century Heretic: Dr Samuel Clarke* (Kineton, UK, Roundwood Press, 1976). On possible political implications of Clarke's theology, see L. Stewart, "Samuel Clarke, Newtonianism and the Factions of post-revolutionary England," *Journal of the History of Ideas*, 42 (1981), 53–71, and S. Shapin, "Of Gods and Kings: Natural Philosophy and Politics in the Leibniz-Clarke Disputes," *Isis*, 72 (1981),187–215. On space and time and their relation to divine immensity and eternity in the Newtonian circle, the best introduction remains A. Koyre's *From the Closed World to the Infinite Universe* (Baltimore, Johns Hopkins University Press, 1957); for a more detailed view of Newton's position, which was almost certainly very similar, if not identical, to Clarke's, see J. E. McGuire, "Existence, Actuality and Necessity: Newton on Space and Time," *Annals of Science*, 35 (1978), 463–508, and his more recent "Predicates of Pure Existence: Newton on God's Space and Time" and J. Carriero's comments in *Philosophical Perspectives on Newtonian Science*, eds. P. Bricker and R. I. G. Hughes (Cambridge, MA, MIT Press, 1990), pp. 91–134. See also E. Grant's *Much Ado about Nothing: Theories of Space and Vacuum from the Middle Ages to the Scientific Revolution* (Cambridge University Press, 1981), a work of great scholarship and intelligence.

Clarke's argument for the immateriality of the soul has a distinguished history which has been studied in B. L. Mijuskovic, *The Achilles of Rationalist Arguments* (The Hague, M. Nijhoff, 1974). There is neither a satisfactory nor a full-scale analysis of Clarke's version (or versions) of the argument. However, see H. Ducharme, "Personal Identity in Samuel Clarke," *Journal of the History of Philosophy*, 24 (1986), 359–83, especially 378–82; J. W. Yolton, *Thinking Matter: Materialism in Eighteenth-Century Britain* (Minneapolis, University of Minnesota Press, 1983), especially pp. 39–41, which places Clarke's views in the context of the English debate on thinking matter in the light of Locke's pronouncements on thinking matter in the *Essay*; R. Attfield, "Clarke, Collins and Compounds," *Journal of the History of Philosophy*, 15 (1977), 45–54, which investigates the issue of emergent properties in the Clarke–Collins debate. On Clarke's views about the extension of the soul and its problems, see E. Vailati, "Clarke's Extended Soul," *Journal of the History of Philosophy*, 28 (1990), 213–28.

Clarke's views on the mind–body relation, especially in connection with occasionalism, have not been satisfactorily studied. However, see Le Rossignol's *The Ethical Philosophy of Samuel Clarke*, especially pp. 29–30, and Ferguson's *The Philosophy of Dr Samuel Clarke and its Critics*, particularly pp. 244–5.

On Clarke's agent causation theory, see W. L. Rowe, "Causality and Free Will in the Controversy Between Collins and Clarke," *Journal of the*

History of Philosophy, 25 (1987), 51–67, and J. O'Higgins's introduction to *Determinism and Freewill: Anthony Collins' "A Philosophical Inquiry concerning Human Liberty"* (The Hague, M. Nijhoff, 1976). On the topic of miracles in early modern England, see R. M. Burns, *The Great Debate on Miracles: from Joseph Glanville to David Hume* (Lewisburg, Bucknell University Press, 1980). On the issue of theological voluntarism and the laws of nature in early modern thought, see F. Oakley, *Omnipotence, Covenant and Order* (Ithaca, Cornell University Press, 1984), especially chs. 3 and 4, which also deal with related political theories; A. Funkenstein, *Theology and the Scientific Imagination* (Princeton University Press, 1986), ch. 3; J. E. Force, "Newton's God of Dominion: The Unity of Newton's Theological, Scientific, and Political Thought," in *Essays on the Context, Nature, and Influence of Isaac Newton's Theology*, eds. J. E. Force and R. H. Popkin (Dordrecht, Kluwer Academic Publishers, 1990), pp. 75–102.

On the issue of the inertness of matter in eighteenth-century English thought, see J. W. Yolton, *Thinking Matter. Materialism in Eighteenth Century Britain* (Minneapolis, Minnesota University Press, 1983), chs. 5 and 6. On the general issue of the reduction of nature from a living thing to a conglomerate of lifeless particles, see C. Merchant, *The Death of Nature* (San Francisco, Harper and Row, 1980). On the Leibniz-Clarke correspondence, see E. Vailati, *Leibniz and Clarke: A Study of their Correspondence* (New York, Oxford University Press, 1997).

Note on the text

A Demonstration of the Being and Attributes of God went through seven editions during Clarke's life, with occasional significant changes. The seventh edition, *A Discourse concerning the Being and Attributes of God, the Obligations of Natural Religion, and the Truth and Certainty of the Christian Revelation* (London, James and John Knapton, 1728), at pp. 503–6 contains two addenda to the text which are appropriately inserted in the eighth edition (1732), which is that incorporated in the 1738 edition in four volumes of Clarke's works. The present edition follows the text in the four-volume *The Works of Samuel Clarke* (London, John and Paul Knapton, 1738; reprint New York, Garland Publishing Co., 1978). The supplementary material, much of which was included by Clarke himself in the later editions of his book, comes from the same source.

Following the guidelines of Cambridge Texts in the History of Philosophy, I have eliminated unnecessary capitalization, modernized spelling and punctuation, and minimized the use of italics. Occasionally, in order to improve the readability of the text, I have repeated a main clause or altered the location of a paragraph break. I have also moved footnote markers to the end of their sentences, checked Clarke's quotations against the originals, corrected them when needed, and translated them. In addition, I have completed and standardized Clarke's often scanty references and corrected them when mistaken. Clarke's own additions to quotations from other authors are in italics and bracketed. Words and translations inserted by me are in square brackets, except where I have completed and standardized Clarke's own references. I have used numbers to mark Clarke's notes, and letters to mark my few explanatory notes.

A Demonstration of the Being and Attributes of God

A Demonstration of the Being and Attributes of God.

More particularly in answer to Mr. Hobbes, Spinoza, and their followers.

Being the substance of eight sermons preached in the year 1704 at the lecture founded by the honourable Robert Boyle, Esquire.

All those who either are or pretend to be atheists, who either disbelieve the being of God or would be thought to do so or, which is all one, who deny the principal attributes of the divine nature and suppose God to be an unintelligent being which acts merely by necessity, that is, which in any tolerable propriety of speech acts not at all, but is only acted upon – all men that are atheists, I say, in this sense, must be so upon one or other of these three accounts.

Either, firstly, because, being extremely ignorant and stupid, they have never duly considered any thing at all, nor made any just use of their natural reason to discover even the plainest and most obvious truths, but have spent their time in a manner of life very little superior to that of beasts.

Or, secondly, because, being totally debauched and corrupted in their practice, they have by a vicious and degenerate life corrupted the principles of their nature and defaced the reason of their own minds. And instead of fairly and impartially enquiring into the rules and obligations of nature and the reasons and fitness of things, [they] have accustomed themselves only to mock and scoff at religion and, being under the power of evil habits and the slavery of unreasonable and indulged lusts, are resolved not to harken to any reasoning which would oblige them to forsake their beloved vices.

Or, thirdly, because in the way of speculative reasoning and upon the principles of philosophy, they pretend that the arguments used against the being and attributes of God seem to them, after the strictest and fullest enquiry, to be more strong and conclusive than those by which we endeavor to prove these great truths.

These seem the only causes which can be imagined of any man

we rationally have a longing for God.

* atheism can only be disappointed theism
* you want to believe in God

disbelieving the being and attributes of God; and no man can be supposed to be an atheist but upon one or other of these three accounts. Now to the two former of these three sorts of men, namely, to such as are wholly ignorant and stupid, or to such as through habitual debauchery have brought themselves to a custom of mocking and scoffing at all religion and will not hearken to any fair reasoning, it is not my present business to apply myself. The one of these wants to be instructed in the first principles of reason as well as religion; the other disbelieves only for a present false interest and because he is desirous that the thing should not be true. The one has not yet arrived at the use of his natural faculties; the other has renounced them and declares he will not be argued with as a rational creature. It is therefore the third sort of atheists only (namely, those who in the way of speculative reasoning and upon the principles of philosophy pretend that the arguments brought against the being and attributes of God do, upon the strictest examination, appear to them to be the more strong and conclusive than those by which these great truths are attempted to be proved) – these, I say, are the only atheistical persons to whom my present discourse can be supposed to be directed, or indeed who are capable of being reasoned with at all.

Now before I enter upon the main argument, I shall premise several concessions which these men, upon their own principles, are unavoidably obliged to make.

And, firstly, they must of necessity own that supposing it cannot be proved to be true, yet it is a thing very desirable and which any wise man would wish to be true for the great benefit and happiness of men that there was a God, an intelligent, and wise, and just, and good being to govern the world. Whatever hypothesis these men can possibly frame, whatever argument they can invent by which they would exclude God and providence out of the world, that very argument or hypothesis will of necessity lead them to this concession. If they argue that our notion of God arises not from nature and reason but from the art and contrivance of politicians, that argument itself forces them to confess that it is manifestly for the interest of human society that it should be believed there is a God. If they suppose that the world was made by chance and is every moment subject to be destroyed by chance again, no man can be so absurd as to contend that it is as comfortable and desirable to live in such an uncertain state of things, and so continually liable to ruin without any hope of renovation, as in a world that were under the preservation and conduct of a powerful, wise,

4

atheists

and good God.[1] If they argue against the being of God from the faults and defects which they imagine they can find in the frame and constitution of the visible and material world, this supposition obliges them to acknowledge that it would have been better the world had been made by an intelligent and wise being who might have prevented all faults and imperfections. If they argue against providence from the faultiness and inequality which they think they discover in the management of the moral world, this is a plain concession that it is a thing more fit and desirable in itself that the world should be governed by a just and good being than by mere chance or unintelligent necessity. Lastly, if they suppose the world to be eternally and necessarily self-existent, and consequently that every thing in it is established by a blind and eternal fatality, no rational man can at the same time deny but that liberty and choice, or the free power of acting, is a more eligible state than to be determined thus in all our actions, as a stone is to move downward by an absolute and inevitable fate.

this is far from self-evident

In a word, which way soever they turn themselves and whatever hypothesis they make concerning the original and frame of things, nothing is so certain and undeniable as that man, considered without the protection and conduct of a superior being, is in a far worse case than upon supposition of the being and government of God and of men's being under his peculiar conduct, protection, and favor. Man, of himself, is infinitely insufficient for his own happiness. "He is liable to many evils and miseries, which he can neither prevent nor redress; he is full of wants which he cannot supply; and compassed about with infirmities which he cannot remove; and obnoxious to dangers which he can never sufficiently provide against ... He is secure of nothing that he enjoys in the world, and uncertain of everything that he hopes for; he is apt to grieve for what he cannot have, and eagerly to desire what he is never able to obtain." [2] Under which evil

---

[1] "... maria ac terras coelumque ...
    ... una dies dabit exitio, multosque per annos
    sustentata ruet moles et machina mundi.
    ... dictis dabit ipsa fidem res
    forsitan et graviter terrarum motibus ortis
    omnia conquassari in parvo tempore cernes."

["... the seas, the lands and the sky ... just one day will bring to destruction, and the mass and machinery of the universe, upheld for many years, will crash to ruin ... Things themselves will perhaps give credit to my words, and in a short time you will see all things violently convulsed and shocked by earthquakes."] T. Lucretius Caro, *De Rerum Natura*, book 5, vv. 92–106.

[2] Archbishop John Tillotson's sermon on Job xxviii, 28, in John Tillotson, *The Works of the Most Reverend Dr. John Tillotson*, seventh edition (London, 1714), p. 22.

circumstances it is evident there can be no sufficient support but in the belief of a wise and good God and in the hopes which true religion affords. Whether, therefore, the being and attributes of God can be demonstrated or not, it must at least be confessed by all rational and wise men to be a thing very desirable and which they would heartily wish to be true, that there was a God, an intelligent and wise, a just and good being, to govern the world.

Now the use I desire to make of this concession is only this: that, since the men I am arguing with are unavoidably obliged to confess that it is a thing very desirable at least that there should be a God, they must of necessity upon their own principles be very willing, nay desire upon all things, to be convinced that their present opinion is an error, and sincerely hope that the contrary may be demonstrated to them to be true. And, consequently, they are bound with all seriousness, attention, and impartiality to consider the weight of the arguments by which the being and attributes of God may be proved to them.

Secondly, all such persons as I am speaking of, who profess themselves to be atheists not upon any present interest or lust but purely upon the principles of reason and philosophy, are bound by these principles to acknowledge that all mocking and scoffing at religion, all jesting and turning arguments of reason into drollery and ridicule, is the most unmanly and unreasonable thing in the world. And, consequently, they are obliged to exclude out of their number, as irrational and self-condemned persons and unworthy to be argued with, all such scoffers at religion who deride at all adventures without hearing reason, and who will not use the means of being convinced and satisfied. Hearing the reasons of the case with patience and lack of prejudice is an equity which men owe to every truth that can in any manner concern them and which is necessary to the discovery of every kind of error. How much more in things of the utmost importance!

Thirdly, since the persons I am discoursing to cannot but own that the supposition of the being of God is in itself most desirable and for the benefit of the world that it should be true, they must of necessity grant further that, supposing the being and attributes of God to be things not indeed demonstrable to be true but only possible and such as cannot be demonstrated to be false, as most certainly they cannot; and, much more, supposing them once made to appear probable and but more likely to be true than the contrary opinion; nothing is more evident, even upon these

6

suppositions only, than that men ought in all reason to live piously and virtuously in the world and that vice and immorality are, upon all accounts and under all hypotheses, the most absurd and inexcusable things in nature.

Thus much being premised, which no atheist who pretends to be a rational and fair enquirer into things can possibly avoid granting (and other atheists, I have before said, are not to be disputed with at all, as being enemies to reason no less than to religion, and therefore absolutely self-condemned), I proceed now to the main thing I at first proposed, namely, to endeavor to show to such considering persons as I have already described that the being and attributes of God are not only possible or barely probable in themselves, but also strictly demonstrable to any unprejudiced mind from the most incontestable principles of right reason.

And here, because the persons I am at present dealing with must be supposed not to believe any Revelation, nor acknowledge any authority which they will submit to but only the bare force of reasoning, I shall not, at this time, draw any testimony from Scripture, nor make use of any sort of authority, nor lay any stress on any popular arguments in the matter before us, but confine myself to the rules of strict and demonstrative argumentation.

Now many arguments there are by which the being and attributes of God have been undertaken to be demonstrated. And perhaps most of those arguments, if thoroughly understood, rightly stated, fully pursued, and duly separated from the false and uncertain reasoning which have sometimes been intermixed with them, would at length appear to be substantial and conclusive. But because I would endeavor, as far as possible, to avoid all manner of perplexity and confusion, therefore I shall not at this time use any variety of arguments, but endeavor, by one clear and plain series of propositions necessarily connected and following one from another, to demonstrate the certainty of the being of God and to deduce in order the necessary attributes of his nature, so far as by our finite reason we are enabled to discover and apprehend them. And because it is not to my present purpose to explain and illustrate things to them that believe, but only to convince unbelievers and settle them that doubt by strict and undeniable reason, therefore I shall not allege anything which, however really true and useful, may yet be liable to contradiction or dispute, but shall endeavor to urge such propositions only as cannot be denied without departing from that reason which all atheists pretend to be the foundation of their unbelief. Only it is absolutely necessary before all things that they

7

consent to lay aside all manner of prejudices, and especially such as have been apt to arrive from the too frequent use of terms of art which have no ideas belonging to them, and from the common receiving of certain maxims of philosophy as true which at bottom seem to be only propositions without any meaning or signification at all.

I

Atheist will not object to this claim.

First, then, it is absolutely and undeniably certain that *something has existed from all eternity*. This is so evident and undeniable a proposition, that no atheist in any age has ever presumed to assert the contrary, and therefore there is little need of being particular in the proof of it. For, since something now is, it is evident that something always was, otherwise the things that now are must have been produced out of nothing, absolutely and without a cause, which is a plain contradiction in terms. For, to say a thing is produced and yet that there is no cause at all for that production, is to say that something is effected when it is effected by nothing, that is, at the same time when it is not effected at all. Whatever exists has a cause, a reason, a ground of its existence, a foundation on which its existence relies, a ground or reason why it does exist rather than not exist, either in the necessity of its own nature (and then it must have been of itself eternal), or in the will of some other being (and then that other being must, at least in the order of nature and causality, have existed before it).

That something, therefore, has really existed from eternity, is one of the most certain and evident truths in the world, acknowledged by all men and disputed by no one. Yet, as to the manner how it can be, there is nothing in nature more difficult for the mind of men to conceive than this very first plain and self-evident truth. For how anything can have existed eternally, that is, how an eternal duration can be now actually past, is a thing utterly as impossible for our narrow understandings to comprehend, as anything that is not an express contradiction can be imagined to be. And yet, to deny the truth of the proposition, that an eternal duration is now actually past, would be to assert something still far more unintelligible, even a real and express contradiction.

The use I would make of this observation is this: that since in all questions concerning the nature and perfections of God (or concerning anything to which the idea of eternity or infinity is joined), though we can indeed demonstrate certain propositions to be true, yet it is impossible for

8

us to comprehend or frame any adequate or complete ideas of the manner how the things so demonstrated can be. Therefore, when once any proposition is clearly demonstrated to be true, it ought not to disturb us that there be perhaps perplexing difficulties on the other side which, merely for want of adequate ideas of the manner of the existence of the things demonstrated, are not easy to be cleared. Indeed, were it possible there should be any proposition which could equally be demonstrated on both sides of the question, or which could on both sides be reduced to imply a contradiction (as some have very inconsiderately asserted), this, it must be confessed, would alter the case. Upon this absurd supposition, all difference of true and false, all thinking and reasoning, and the use of all our faculties, would be entirely at an end. But when to demonstration on the one side there are proposed on the other only difficulties raised from our want of having adequate ideas of the things themselves, this ought not to be esteemed an objection of any real weight.

It is directly and clearly demonstrable, and acknowledged to be so even by all atheists who ever lived, that something has been from eternity. All the objections, therefore, raised against the eternity of anything, grounded merely on our want of having an adequate idea of eternity, ought to be looked upon as of no real solidity. Thus in other like instances. It is demonstrable, for example, that something must be actually infinite. All the metaphysical difficulties, therefore, which arise usually from applying the measures and relations of things finite to what is infinite and from supposing finites to be *aliquot* parts of infinite, when indeed they are not properly so but only as mathematical points to quantity, which have no proportion at all (and from imagining of infinites to be equal, when in things disparate they manifestly are not so, an infinite line being not only not equal to, but infinitely less than, an infinite surface, and an infinite surface than space infinite in all dimensions) – all metaphysical difficulties, I say, arising from false suppositions of this kind, ought to be esteemed vain and of no force. Again, it is in like manner demonstrable that quantity is infinitely divisible. All the objections, therefore, raised by supposing the sum total of all infinites to be equal when in disparate parts they manifestly are not so, and by comparing the imaginary equality or inequality of the number of the parts of unequal quantities whose parts have really no number at all (they all having parts without number), ought to be looked upon as weak and altogether inconclusive; to ask whether the parts of unequal quantities be equal in number or not, when they have no number at all, being the same thing as to ask whether two lines drawn from differently distant points, and each of them continued infinitely, be equal in length or not, that is, whether they end together, when neither of them have any end at all.

II

There has existed from eternity some one unchangeable and independent being.[3] For, since something must needs have been from eternity, as has been already proved and is granted on all hands, either there has always existed some one unchangeable and independent being from which all other beings that are or ever were in the universe have received their original, or else there has been an infinite succession of changeable and dependent beings produced one from another in an endless progression without any original cause at all. Now this latter supposition is so very absurd that, though all atheism must in its accounts of most things (as shall be shown hereafter) terminate in it, yet I think very few atheists ever were so weak as openly and directly to defend it. For it is plainly impossible and contradictory to itself. I shall not argue against it from the supposed impossibility of infinite succession, barely and absolutely considered in itself, for a reason which shall be mentioned hereafter. But, if we consider such an infinite progression as one entire endless series of dependent beings, it is plain this whole series of beings can have no cause from without of its existence because in it are supposed to be included all things that are, or ever were, in the universe. And it is plain it can have no reason within itself for its existence because no one being in this infinite succession is supposed to be self-existent or necessary (which is the only ground or reason of existence of anything that can be imagined within the thing itself, as will presently more fully appear), but every one dependent on the foregoing. And, where no part is necessary, it is manifest the whole cannot be necessary – absolute necessity of existence not being an extrinsic, relative, and accidental denomination but an inward and essential property of the nature of the thing which so exists.

An infinite succession, therefore, of merely dependent beings without any original independent cause is a series of beings that has neither neces-

---

[3] The meaning of this proposition, and all [that] the argument here requires, is that there must needs have always been some independent being, some one at least. To show that there can be no more than one is not the design of this proposition but of the seventh.

sity, nor cause, nor any reason or ground at all of its existence either within itself or from without. That is, it is an express contradiction and impossibility. It is a supposing something to be caused (because it is granted in every one of its stages of succession not to be necessarily and of itself), and yet that, in the whole, it is caused absolutely by nothing, which every man knows is a contradiction to imagine done in time; and because duration in this case makes no difference, it is equally a contradiction to suppose it done from eternity. And consequently there must, on the contrary, of necessity have existed from eternity some one immutable and independent being.

To suppose an infinite succession of changeable and dependent beings produced one from another in an endless progression without any original cause at all is only a driving back from one step to another and, as it were, removing out of sight the question concerning the ground or reason of the existence of things.[4] It is, in reality and in point of argument, the very same supposition as it would be to suppose one continued being of beginningless and endless duration neither self-existent and necessary in itself, nor having its existence founded in any self-existent cause, which is directly absurd and contradictory.

Otherwise, thus: either there has always existed some unchangeable and independent being from which all other beings have received their original, or else there has been an infinite succession of changeable and dependent beings, produced one from another in an endless progression without any original cause at all. According to this latter supposition, there is nothing

---

[4] This matter has been well illustrated by a late able writer: "Suppose a chain hung down out of the heavens from an unknown height, and though every link of it gravitated toward the Earth and what it hung upon was not visible, yet it did not descend but kept its situation; and [suppose] upon this a question should arise, what supported or kept up this chain? Would it be a sufficient answer to say that the first or lowest link hung upon the second, or that next above it, [and] the first, or rather the first and the second together, upon the third, and so on *in infinitum*? For what holds up the *whole*? A chain of ten links would fall down unless something able to bear it hindered. One of twenty, if not staid by something of a yet greater strength, [would fall] in proportion to the increase of weight, and therefore one of infinite links, certainly, if not sustained by something infinitely strong and capable to bear up an infinite weight. And thus it is in a chain of causes and effects tending or, as it were, gravitating towards some end. The last or lowest depends or, as one may say, is suspended upon the cause above it. This again, if it be not the first cause, is suspended as an effect upon something above it, etc. And if they should be infinite, unless agreeably to what has been said there is some cause upon which all hang or depend, they would be but an infinite effect without an efficient. And so to assert there is any such thing would be as great an absurdity as to say that a finite or little weight wants something to sustain it, but an infinite one, or the greatest, does not." W. Wollaston, *The Religion of Nature Delineated* (London, Samuel Palmer, 1724; reprint New York, Garland Publishing Co., 1978), p. 67.

in the universe self-existent or necessarily existing. And if so, then it was originally equally possible that from eternity there should never have existed anything at all, as that there should from eternity have existed a succession of changeable and dependent beings. Which being supposed, then, what is it that has from eternity determined such a succession of beings to exist, rather than that from eternity there should never have existed anything at all? Necessity it was not because it was equally possible, in this supposition, that they should not have existed at all. Chance is nothing but a mere word, without any signification. And other being it is supposed there was none, to determine the existence of these. Their existence, therefore, was determined by nothing; neither by any necessity in the nature of the things themselves, because it is supposed that none of them are self-existent, nor by any other being, because no other is supposed to exist. That is to say, of two equally possible things, viz., whether anything or nothing should from eternity have existed, the one is determined rather than the other absolutely by nothing, which is an express contradiction. And consequently, as before, there must on the contrary of necessity have existed from eternity some one immutable and independent being. Which, what it is, remains in the next place to be inquired.

III

That unchangeable and independent being which has existed from eternity, without any external cause of its existence, must be self-existent, that is, necessarily existing. For whatever exists must either have come into being out of nothing, absolutely without cause, or it must have been produced by some external cause, or it must be self-existent. Now to arise out of nothing absolutely without any cause has been already shown to be a plain contradiction. To have been produced by some external cause cannot possibly be true of every thing, but something must have existed eternally and independently, as has likewise been shown already. Which remains, therefore, [is] that that being which has existed independently from eternity must of necessity be self-existent. Now to be self-existent is not to be produced by itself, for that is an express contradiction, but it is (which is the only idea we can frame of self-existence, and without which the word seems to have no signification at all) – it is, I say, to exist by an absolute necessity originally in the nature of the thing itself. And this necessity must be antecedent, not indeed in time, to the existence of the being itself (because that is eternal), but it must be antecedent in the natural order of our ideas to our supposition of its being. That is, this necessity must not barely be consequent upon our supposition of the existence of such a being (for then it would not be a necessity absolutely such in itself, nor be the ground or foundation of the existence of anything, being on the contrary only a consequent of it), but it must antecedently force itself upon us whether we will or no, even when we are endeavoring to suppose that no such being exists. For example, when we are endeavoring to suppose that there is no being in the universe that exists necessarily, we always find in our minds (besides the foregoing demonstration of something being self-existent from the impossibility of every thing's being dependent) – we always find in our minds, I say, some ideas, as of infinity and eternity, which to remove (that is, to suppose that there is no being, no substance in the universe to which these attributes or modes of existence are necessarily inherent) is a contradiction in the very terms. For modes and attributes exist only by the existence of the substance to which they belong. Now he that can suppose eternity and immensity, and consequently the substance by whose existence these modes or attributes exist, removed out of the universe, may, if he please, as easily remove the relation of equality between twice two and four.

That to suppose immensity removed out of the universe, or not necessarily eternal, is an express contradiction is intuitively evident to every one who attends to his own ideas and considers the essential nature of things. To suppose any part of space removed is to suppose it removed from and out of itself; and to suppose the whole to be taken away is supposing it to be taken away from itself, that is, to be taken away while it still remains, which is a contradiction in terms.[5] There is no obscurity in the argument but what arises to those who think immense space to be absolutely nothing, which notion is itself likewise an express contradiction. For nothing is that which has no properties or modes whatsoever, that is to say, it is that of which nothing can truly be affirmed and of which every thing can truly be denied, which is not the case of immensity or space.

From this third proposition it follows, first, that the only true idea of a self-existent or necessarily existing being is the idea of a being the supposition of whose not-existing is an express contradiction. For, since it is

[5] "Moveantur partes spatii de locis suis, et movebuntur (ut ita dicam) de seipsis." ["Suppose the parts of space to be moved out of their places, and they will be moved (if I may say so) out of themselves."] *NP*, Book I, Scholium to Definition 8, p. 48.

absolutely impossible but there must be somewhat self-existing, that is, [something] which exists by the necessity of its own nature, it is plain that that necessity cannot be a necessity consequent upon any foregoing supposition (because nothing can be antecedent to that which is self-existent, no not its own will, so as to be the cause or ground of its own existence), but it must be a necessity absolutely such in its own nature. Now a necessity not relatively or consequentially, but absolutely such in its own nature, is nothing else but its being a plain impossibility or implying a contradiction to suppose the contrary. For instance, the relation of equality between twice two and four is an absolute necessity only because it is an immediate contradiction in terms to suppose them unequal. This is the only idea we can frame of an absolute necessity, and to use the word in any other sense seems to be using it without any signification at all.

If any one now asks, what sort of idea the idea of that being is, the supposition of whose not-existing is thus an express contradiction, I answer: it is that first and simplest idea we can possibly frame; an idea necessarily and essentially included or presupposed as a *sine qua non* in every other idea whatsoever; an idea which (unless we forbear thinking at all) we cannot possibly extirpate or remove out of our minds of a most simple being, absolutely eternal and infinite, original and independent. For, that he who supposes there is no original independent being in the universe supposes a contradiction, has been shown already. And that he who supposes there may possibly be no eternal and infinite being in the universe, supposes likewise a contradiction, is evident from hence (beside that these two attributes do necessarily follow from self-originate independent existence, as shall be shown hereafter), that when he has done his utmost in endeavoring to imagine that no such being exists, he cannot avoid imagining an eternal and infinite nothing.[6] That is, he will imagine eternity and immensity removed out of the universe, and yet that at the same time they still continue there, as has been above distinctly explained.

This argument the Cartesians, who supposed the idea of immensity to be the idea of matter, have been greatly perplexed with. For however in words they have contradicted themselves, yet in reality they have more easily been driven to that most intolerable absurdity of asserting matter to be a necessary being, than being able to remove out of their minds the idea

[6] See the answer to a Seventh Letter at the end of this book [Supplementary text III].

of immensity as existing necessarily and inseparably from eternity.[7] Which absurdity and inextricable perplexity of theirs, in respect of the idea of immensity, shows that they found *that* indeed to be necessary and impossible to be removed; but in respect of matter it was only a perverse applying [of] an idea to an object whereto it no ways belongs. For, that it is indeed absolutely impossible and contradictory to suppose matter necessarily existing, shall be demonstrated presently.

Secondly, from hence it follows that there is no man whatsoever who makes any use his reason but may easily become more certain of the being of a supreme independent cause than he can be of any thing else besides his own existence. For how much thought soever it may require to demonstrate the other attributes of such a being, as it may do to demonstrate the greatest mathematical certainties (of which more hereafter), yet, as to its existence, that there is somewhat eternal, infinite, and self-existing, which must be the cause and origin of all other things, this is one of the first and most natural conclusions that any man who thinks at all can frame in his mind; and no man can any more doubt of this than he can doubt whether twice two be equal to four. It is possible indeed a man may in some sense be ignorant of this first and plain truth by being utterly stupid and not thinking at all (for though it is absolutely impossible for him to imagine

---

[7] "... puto implicare contradictionem ut mundus sit finitus," i.e., "... I think it implies a contradiction for the world to be finite." R. Descartes, Letter to More of 15 April 1649, in *Oeuvres de Descartes*, eds. C. Adam and P. Tannery (Paris, 1897–1913; reprint Paris, J. Vrin, 1964–76), vol. 5, p. 345.

And his follower Mr. Regis, "Mais peut etre," says he, "que je raisonne mal" etc. "But perhaps I argue ill when I conclude that the property my idea has to represent extension {*that is, in the sense of the Cartesians, matter*} comes from extension itself as its cause. For what hinders me from believing that if this property comes not from myself yet at least it may come from some spirit {*or being*} superior to me which produces in me the idea of extension though extension does not actually exist? Yet, when I consider the thing attentively I find that my conclusion is good, and that no spirit {*or being*} how excellent soever can cause the idea which I have of extension to represent to me extension rather than anything else if extension does not actually exist, because if he should do so, the idea which I should then have of extension would not be a representation of extension but a representation of nothing, which is impossible."

"But it may be I still deceive myself when I say that the idea I have of extension supposes an object actually existing. For it seems that I have ideas which do not suppose any object. I have, for example, the idea of an enchanted castle, though no such thing really exists. Yet, when I consider the difficulty more attentively, I find there is this difference between the idea of extension and that of an enchanted castle, that the first, being natural, that is, independent of my will, supposes an object which is necessarily such as it represents, whereas the other, being artificial, supposes indeed an object, but it is not necessary that that object be absolutely such as the idea represents because my will can add to that object or diminish from it as it pleases, as I have before said and as I shall prove hereafter, when I come to treat of the origin of ideas." P. S. Regis, *Cours Entier de Philosophie ou Systeme General selon les Principes de M. Descartes* (Amsterdam, 1691; reprint New York, Johnson Reprint Corporation, 1970), Metaphysics, Book I, Part I, ch. 3 [vol. I, p. 75].

the contrary, yet he may possibly neglect to conceive this; though no man can possibly think that twice two is not four, yet he may possibly be stupid and never have thought at all whether it be so or not). But this I say: there is no man who thinks or reasons at all but may easily become more certain that there is something eternal, infinite, and self-existing than he can be certain of anything else.

Thirdly, hence we may observe that our first certainty of the existence of God does not arise from this, that in the idea our minds frame of him (or rather in the definition that we make of the word *God* as signifying a being of all possible perfections) we include self-existence, but from hence, that it is demonstrable both negatively, that neither can all things possibly have arisen out of nothing, nor can they have depended one on another in an endless succession, and also positively, that there is something in the universe actually existing without us, the supposition of whose not existing plainly implies a contradiction. The argument which has by some been drawn from our including self-existence in the *idea* of God, or our comprehending it in the *definition* or *notion* we frame of him, has this obscurity and defect in it: that it seems to extend only to the nominal idea or mere definition of a self-existent being, and does not with a sufficiently evident connection refer and apply that general nominal idea, definition, or notion which we frame in our own mind, to any real particular being actually existing without us. For it is not satisfactory that I have in my mind an idea of the proposition "there exists a being endowed with all possible perfections" or "there is a self-existent being." But I must also have some idea of the thing. I must have an idea of something actually existing without me. And I must see wherein consists the absolute impossibility of removing that idea, and consequently of supposing the non-existence of the thing before I can be satisfied from that idea that the thing actually exists. The bare having an idea of the proposition "there is a self-existent being" proves indeed the thing not to be impossible, for of an impossible proposition there can be no idea. But that it actually is, cannot be proved from the idea unless the certainty of the actual existence of a necessarily existing being follows from the possibility of the existence of such a being, which that it does in this particular case many learned men have indeed thought, and their subtle arguings upon this head are sufficient to raise a cloud not very easy to be seen through.

But it is a much clearer and more convincing way of arguing, to demonstrate that there does actually exist without us a being whose existence is necessary and of itself, by showing the evident contradiction contained in the contrary supposition (as I have before done), and at the same time the absolute impossibility of destroying or removing some ideas, as of eternity and immensity, which therefore must needs be modes or attributes of a necessary being actually existing. For if I have in my mind an idea of a thing, and cannot possibly in my imagination take away the idea of that thing as actually existing any more than I can change or take away the idea of the equality of twice two to four, the certainty of the existence of that thing is the same, and stands on the same foundation, as the certainty of the other relation. For the relation of equality between twice two and four has no other certainty but this, that I cannot, without a contradiction, change or take away the idea of that relation. We are certain, therefore, of the being of a supreme independent cause because it is strictly demonstrable that there is some thing in the universe actually existing without us, the supposition of whose not-existing plainly implies a contradiction.

Some writers have contended that it is preposterous to inquire in this manner at all into the ground or reason of the existence of the first cause, because evidently the first cause can have nothing prior to it, and consequently must needs (they think) exist absolutely without any cause at all.[8] That the first cause can have no other *being* prior to it, to be the cause of its existence, is indeed self-evident. But if originally, absolutely, and antecedently to all supposition of existence, there be no necessary ground or reason why the first cause does exist rather than not exist, if the first cause can rightly and truly be affirmed to exist absolutely without any ground or reason of existence at all, it will unavoidably follow, by the same argument, that it may as well cease likewise to exist without any ground or reason of ceasing to exist, which is absurd. The truth, therefore, plainly is: whatever is the true reason why the first cause can never possibly cease to exist, the same is and originally and always was the true reason why it always did and cannot but exist, that is, it is the true ground and reason of its existence.

Fourthly, from hence it follows that the material world cannot possibly be the first and original being, uncreated, independent, and of itself eternal. For, since it has been already demonstrated that whatever being has existed from eternity, independent, and without an external cause of

attacks. material world.

---

[8] See the answer to a Seventh Letter at the end of this book [Supplementary text III].

its existence, must be self-existent, and that whatever is self-existent must exist necessarily by an absolute necessity in the nature of the thing itself, it follows evidently that unless the material world exists necessarily by an absolute necessity in its own nature, so as that it must be an express contradiction to suppose it not to exist, it cannot be independent and of itself eternal. Now that the material world does not exist thus necessarily is very evident. For absolute necessity of existing and a possibility of not existing being contradictory ideas, it is manifest the material world cannot exist necessarily, if without a contradiction we can conceive it either not to be or to be in any respect otherwise than it now is. Than which nothing is more easy. For whether we consider the form of the world with the disposition and motion of its parts, or whether we consider the matter of it as such, without respect to its present form, every thing in it, both the whole and every one of its parts, their situation and motion, the form and also the matter, are the most arbitrary and dependent things and the farthest removed from necessity that can possibly be imagined. A necessity indeed of fitness, that is, a necessity that things should be as they are in order to the well-being of the whole, there may be in all these things; but an absolute necessity of nature in any of them (which is what the atheist must maintain), there is not the last appearance of. If any man will say in this sense (as every atheist must do) either that the form of the world, or at least the matter and motion of it, is necessary, nothing can possibly be invented more absurd.

If he says that the particular form is necessary, that is, that the world and all things that are therein exist by necessity of nature, he must affirm it to be a contradiction to suppose that any part of the world can be in any respect otherwise than it now is. It must be a contradiction in terms to suppose more or fewer stars, more or fewer planets, or to suppose their size, figure, or motion different from what it now is, or to suppose more or fewer plants and animals upon Earth or the present ones of different shape and bigness from what they now are. In all which things there is the greatest arbitrariness in respect of power and possibility that can be imagined, however necessary any of them may be in respect of wisdom and preservation of the beauty and order of the whole.

If the atheist will say that the motion in general of all matter is necessary, it follows that it must be a contradiction in terms to suppose any matter to be at rest, which is so absurd and ridiculous that I think hardly any atheists, either ancient or modern, have presumed directly to suppose it.

18

One late author indeed has ventured to assert, and pretended to prove, that motion (that is, the *conatus* to motion, the tendency to move, the power or force that produces actual motion) is essential to all matter.[9] But how philosophically, may appear from this one consideration. The essential tendency to motion of every one or of any one particle of matter in this author's imaginary infinite plenum must be either a tendency to move some one determinate way at once, or to move every way at once. A tendency to move some one determinate way cannot be essential to any particle of matter, but must arise from some external cause because there is nothing in the pretended necessary nature of any particle to determine its motion necessarily and essentially one way rather than another. And a tendency or *conatus* equally to move every way at once is either an absolute contradiction, or at least could produce nothing in matter but an eternal rest of all and every one of its parts.

If the atheist will suppose motion necessary and essential to some matter but not to all, the same absurdity as to the determination of motion still follows. And now he, moreover, supposes an absolute necessity not universal, that is, that it shall be a contradiction to suppose some certain matter at rest, though at the same time some other matter actually be at rest.

If he only affirms bare matter to be necessary, then, besides the extreme folly of attributing motion and the form of the world to chance (which senseless opinion I think all atheists have now given up, and therefore I shall not think myself obliged to take any notice of it in the sequel of this discourse), it may be demonstrated by many arguments drawn from the nature and affections of the thing itself that matter is not a necessary being. For instance, thus. Tangibility or resistance (which is what mathematicians very properly call *vis inertiae*) is essential to matter, otherwise the word *matter* will have no determinate signification. Tangibility therefore, or resistance, belonging to all matter, it follows evidently that if all space were filled with matter, the resistance of all fluids (for the resistance of the parts of hard bodies arises from another cause) would necessarily be equal. For greater or less degrees of fineness or subtility can in this case make no difference, because the smaller or finer the parts of the fluid are, where-with any particular space is filled, the greater in proportion is the number of the parts, and consequently the resistance still always equal. But

---

[9] John Toland, *Letters to Serena* (London, 1704; reprint Stuttgart-Bad Cannstatt, F. Fromann, 1964), Letter 5. [Clarke mistakenly has Letter 3.]

experience shows, on the contrary, that the resistance of all fluids is not equal, there being large spaces in which no sensible resistance at all is made to the swiftest and most lasting motion of the most solid of bodies. Therefore, all space is not filled with matter but, of necessary consequence, there must be a vacuum.

Or thus. It appears from experiments of falling bodies and from experiments of pendulums which (being of equal length and unequal gravities) vibrate in equal times, that all bodies whatsoever, in spaces void of sensible resistance, fall from the same height with equal velocities. Now it is evident that whatever force causes unequal bodies to move with equal velocities must be proportional to the quantities of the bodies moved. The power of gravity, therefore, in all bodies is (at equal distances suppose from the center of the Earth) proportional to the quantity of matter contained in each body. For if in a pendulum there were any matter that did not gravitate proportionally to its quantity, the *vis inertiae* of that matter would retard the motion of the rest, so as soon to be discovered in pendulums of equal lengths and unequal gravities in spaces void of sensible resistance. Gravity, therefore, is in all bodies proportional to the quantity of the matter.[10] And consequently, all bodies not being equally heavy, it follows again necessarily that there must be a vacuum.[11]

Now if there be a vacuum, it follows plainly that matter is not a necessary being. For if a vacuum actually be, then it is evidently more than possible for matter not to be. If an atheist will yet assert that matter may be necessary, though not necessary to be everywhere, I answer this is an express contradiction. For *absolute* necessity is absolute necessity *everywhere alike*. And if it be no impossibility for matter to be absent from one place, it is no impossibility (absolutely in the nature of the thing, for no relative or consequential necessity can have any room in this argument) – it is not absolute impossibility, I say, in the nature of the thing, that matter should be absent from any other place or from every place.

Spinoza, the most celebrated patron of atheism in our time (who thought that there is no difference of substances but that the whole and every part of the material world is a necessarily existing being, and that there is no other God but the universe), that he might seemingly avoid the manifold absurdities of that opinion, endeavors by an ambiguity of expression in the progress of his discourse to elude the arguments by which he

[10] *NP*, Book II, Section VI, Proposition 24, 432.
[11] *NP*, Book III, Proposition VI, Corollary 3, p. 575.

foresaw his assertion would be confuted.[12] For having at first plainly asserted that all substance is necessarily existing, he would afterward seem to explain it away by asserting that the reason why every thing exists necessarily, and could not possibly have been in any respect different from what it now is, is because every thing flows from the necessity of the divine nature.[13] By which, if the unweary reader understands that he means things are therefore necessarily such as they are, because infinite wisdom and goodness could not possibly make things but in that order which is fittest and wisest in the whole, he is very much mistaken. For such a necessity is not a natural, but only a moral and consequential necessity, and directly contrary to the author's true intention. Further, if the reader hereby understands that God was determined not by a necessity of wisdom and goodness but by a mere natural necessity, exclusive of will and choice, to make all things just as they now are, neither is this the whole of Spinoza's meaning. For this, as absurd as it is, is still supposing God as a substance distinct from the material world, which he expressly denies. Nay, further, if any one thinks his meaning to be that all substances in the world are only modifications of the divine essence, neither is this all. For thus God may still be supposed as an agent acting upon himself at least, and manifesting himself in different manners according to his own will, which Spinoza expressly denies.[14]

But his true meaning, therefore, however darkly and ambiguously he sometimes speaks, must be this (and if he means any thing at all consistent with himself can be no other than this): that, since it is absolutely impossible

---

[12] "Una substantia non potest produci ab alia substantia." ["A substance cannot be produced by another substance."]. *E*, Part I, Proposition 6.

"Omnis substantia est necessario infinita." ["Every substance is necessarily infinite."]. *E*, Part I, Proposition 8.

"Ad naturam substantiae pertinet existere." ["Existence pertains to the nature of substance."]. *E*, Part I, Proposition 7.

"Praeter Deum nulla dari, neque concipi potest substantia." ["Besides God no substance can be or be conceived."]. *E*, Part I, Proposition 14.

[13] "Ad naturam substantiae pertinet existere." ["Existence pertains to the nature of substance."]. *E*, Part I, Proposition 7.

"Res nullo alio modo, neque alio ordine a Deo produci potuerunt, quam productae sunt." ["Things could not have been produced by God in any other way or order than they have been produced."]. *E*, Part I, Proposition 33.

"Ex necessitate divinae naturae, infinita infinitis modis (hoc est, omnia quae sub intellectum infinitum cadere possunt) sequi debent." ["From the necessity of the divine nature there must follow infinite things in infinite ways (that is, all that can fall within the scope of infinite intellect."]. *E*, Part I, Proposition 16.

[14] "Deum non operari ex libertate voluntatis." ["God does not act from freedom of the will."]. *E*, Part I, Proposition 32, Corollary 1. [See also the] Scholium to Proposition 17.

for anything to be created or produced by another, and also absolutely impossible for God to have caused any thing to be in any respect different from what it now is, everything that exists must needs be so a part of the divine substance not as a modification caused in it by any will or good pleasure or wisdom in the whole, but as of absolute necessity in itself with respect to the manner of the existence of each part no less than with respect to the self-existence of the whole.[15] Thus the opinion of Spinoza, when expressed plainly and consistently, comes evidently to this: that the material world and every part of it, with the order and manner of being of each part, is the only self-existent or necessarily existing being. And now, consequently, he must of necessity affirm all the conclusions which I have before shown to follow demonstrably from that opinion. He cannot possibly avoid affirming that it is a contradiction (not to the perfections of God, for that is mere senseless cant and amusement in him who maintains that there is but one substance in the universe; but he must affirm that it is in itself and in terms a contradiction) for any thing to be or to be imagined in any respect otherwise than it now is. He must say it is a contradiction to suppose the number, or figure, or order of the several parts of the world could possibly have been different from what they now are. He must say motion is necessarily of itself, and consequently that it is a contradiction in terms to suppose any matter to be at rest. Or else he must affirm, which is rather the more absurd of the two (as may appear from what has been already said in proof of the second general head of this discourse, and yet he has chosen to affirm it), that motion, as a dependent being, has been eternally communicated from one piece of matter to another without having at all any original cause of its being either within itself or from without.[16] Which, with other like consequences touching the necessity of the existence of

---

[15] "Una substantia non potest produci ab alia substantia." ["A substance cannot be produced by another substance."]. *E*, Part I, Proposition 6.

"Res nullo alio modo, neque alio ordine a Deo produci potuerunt quam productae sunt." ["Things could not have been produced by God in any other way or order than they have been produced."]. *E*, Part I, Proposition 33.

"Praeter Deum nulla dari neque concipi potest substantia." ["Besides God no substance can be or be conceived."]. *E*, Part I, Proposition 14.

"Deum non operari ex libertate voluntatis." ["God does not act from freedom of the will."]. *E*, Part I, Proposition 32, Corollary 1.

"Nullo alio modo, neque ordine", etc. ["in no other way or order" etc.]. See above.

[16] "Corpus motum, vel quiescens ad motum, vel quietem determinari debuit ab alio corpore, quod etiam ad motum, vel quietem determinatum fuit ab alio, et illud iterum ab alio, et sic in infinitum." ["A body in motion or at rest must have been determined to motion or rest by another body, which itself was determined to motion or rest by another body, and that body by another, and so on *ad infinitum*."]. *E*, Part II, Proposition 13, Lemma 3.

things (the very mention of which is a sufficient confutation of any opinion they follow from) do, as I have said, unavoidably follow from the aforementioned opinion of Spinoza. And, consequently, that opinion, viz., that the universe or whole world is the self-existent or necessarily existing being, is demonstrated to be false.

I have, in this attempt to show that the material world cannot possibly be the first and original being, uncreated, independent, and self-existent, designedly omitted the argument usually drawn from the supposed absolute impossibility in the nature of the thing itself, of the world's being eternal or having existed through an infinite succession of time. And this I have done for the two following reasons.

First, because the question between us and the atheists is not whether the world can possibly have been eternal, but whether it can possibly be the original, independent, and self-existing being, which is a very different question. For many who have affirmed the one have still utterly denied the other. And almost all the ancient philosophers that held the eternity of the world, in whose authority and reasons our modern atheists do so greatly boast and triumph, defended their opinion by such arguments as show plainly that they did by no means thereby intend to assert that the material world was the original, independent, self-existing being, in opposition to the belief of the existence of a supreme all-governing mind, which is the notion of God. So that the deniers of the being of God have no manner of advantage from that opinion of the eternity of the world, even supposing it could not be disproved. Almost all the old philosophers, I say, who held the eternity of the world did not thereby mean (at least their arguments do not tend to prove) that it was independent and self-existent. But their arguments are wholly leveled either to prove barely that something must needs be eternal and that the universe could not possibly arise out of nothing absolutely and without cause (which is all that Ocellus Lucanus' arguments amount to); or else that the world is an eternal and necessary effect flowing from the essential and immutable energy of the divine nature (which seems to have been Aristotle's opinion); or else that the world is an eternal voluntary emanation from the all-wise and supreme cause (which was the opinion of many of Plato's followers).

None of which opinions or arguments will in the least help out our modern atheists, who would exclude supreme mind and intelligence out of the universe. For however the opinion of the eternity of the world is really inconsistent with the belief of its being created in time, yet so long as the defenders of that opinion either did not think it inconsistent with the belief of the world's being the effect and work of an eternal, all-wise and all powerful mind, or at least could defend that opinion by such arguments only as did not in the least prove the self-existence or independency of the world but most of them rather quite the contrary, it is with the greatest injustice and unreasonableness in the world that modern atheists (to whose purpose the eternity or non-eternity of the world would signify nothing, unless at the same time the existence and sovereignty of eternal intelligence and mind were likewise disproved), pretend either the authority or the reasons of these men to be on their side.

Ocellus Lucanus, one of the most ancient asserters of the eternity of the world (whose antiquity and authority Mr Blount opposes to that of Moses), in delivering his opinion speaks indeed like one that believed the material world to be self-existent, asserting that "it is utterly incapable either of generation or corruption, or beginning or end," that "it is of itself eternal, and perfect, and permanent forever," and that "the frame and parts of the world must needs be eternal, as well as the substance and matter of the whole."[17] But when he comes to produce his arguments or reasons for his opinion, they are either so very absurd and ridiculous that even any atheist in this age ought to be ashamed to repeat them (as when he proves that "the world must needs be eternal without beginning or end because both its figure and motion are a circle, which has neither beginning nor end"); or else they are such arguments as prove only what no man ever really denied, viz., that something must needs be eternal because it is impossible for every thing to arise out of nothing or to fall into nothing (as when he says that "the world must have been eternal because it is a contradiction for the universe to have had a beginning since, if it had a beginning, it must

---

[17] C. Blount, *The Oracles of Reason*, Letter to Mr Gildon, in *The Miscellaneous Works of Charles Blount, Esq.* (No Place, 1695; reprint New York, Garland Publishing Co., 1979), p. 218.

"... ἀγέὼνητον τὸ πᾶν." ["... the universe is uncreated."]. Ocellus Lucanus, *On the Nature of the Universe*, I, 2, in *Ocellus Lucanus: Text und Commentar*, R. Harder ed. (Berlin, 1925; reprint Dublin, Weidmann, 1966), p. 11.

"... ἄναρχον ... καὶ ἀτελεύτητον." ["... without beginning ... and without end."]. Ocellus Lucanus, *On the Nature of the Universe*, I, 2, in *Ocellus Lucanus: Text und Commentar*, p. 11.

"... κόσμοὲς ... αὐτὸς ... ἐξ ἑαυτοῦ ἀίδιός ἐστι καὶ αὐτοτελὴς καὶ διαμένων τὸν πάντα αἰῶνα." ["... the world is of itself perpetual and complete, and for ever permanent."]. Ocellus Lucanus, *On the Nature of the Universe*, I, 9, in *Ocellus Lucanus: Text und Commentar*, p. 13.

"[γὰρ] ἀεὶ ὄντος τοῦ κόσμου ἀναγκαῖον καὶ τὰ μέρη αὐτοῦ συνυπάρχειν. λεγω δὲ μέρη οὐρανόν, γῆν," etc. ["For since the world has always existed, it is necessary that its parts should coexist with it. By parts, I mean the heavens, the Earth" etc.]. Ocellus Lucanus, *On the Nature of the Universe*, III, 1, in *Ocellus Lucanus: Text und Commentar*, p. 20.

have been caused by some other thing, and then it is not the universe").[18]
To which one argument all that he says in his whole book is plainly
reducible. So that it is evident all that he really proves is only this, that
there must needs be an eternal being in the universe, and not that matter
is self-existent, in opposition to intelligence and mind. For all that he
asserts about the absolute necessity of the order and parts of the world is
confessedly most ridiculous, not at all proved by the arguments he alleges.
And in some passages of this very book, as well as in other fragments, he
himself supposes and is forced expressly to confess that, however eternal
and necessary every thing in the world be imagined to be, yet even that
necessity must flow from an eternal and intelligent mind, the necessary
perfections of whose nature are the cause of the harmony and beauty of
the world, and particularly of men's having faculties, organs of sense,
appetites, etc., fitted even to final causes.[19]

Aristotle, likewise, was a great asserter indeed of the eternity of the
world, but not in opposition to the belief of the being, or of the power,
wisdom, or goodness of God. On the contrary, he for no other reason asserted
the world to be eternal but because he fancied that such an effect must

---

[18] "[ἔτι δὲ καὶ] τὸ ἄναρχον καὶ τὸ ἀτελεύτητον [καὶ] τοῦ σχήματος καὶ τῆς κινήσεως ...
πιστοῦται, διότι ἀγένητος ὁ κόσμος καὶ ἄφθαρτος. ἥ τε γὰρ τοῦ σχήματος ἰδέα κύκλος,
οὗτος δὲ πάντοθεν ἴσος καὶ ὅμοιος, διόπερ ἄναρχος καὶ ἀδιέξοδος. ἥ τε τῆς κίνησις
[κατὰ κύκλον]," etc. Ocellus Lucanus, *On the Nature of the Universe*, III, 1, in *Ocellus Lucanus:
Text und Commentar*, p. 15. Thus translated: "... nay, that the figure, motion, etc., thereof are without beginning or end; thereby it plainly appears that the world admits neither production nor dis-
solution. For the figure is spherical, and consequently on every side equal and without beginning
or ending. Also, the motion is circular," etc. C. Blount, *The Oracles of Reason*, in *The Miscellaneous
Works of Charles Blount, Esq.* (No place, no publisher, 1695; reprint New York, Garland Publishing
Co., 1979), p. 215.
"... ἀγένητον τὸ πᾶν ... ἐξ ὅτου τε καὶ γέγονεν, ἐκεῖνο πρῶτον τοῦ παντός ἐστιν ...
τὸ δέ γε πᾶν γινόμενον σὺν πᾶσι γίνεται καὶ ... τοῦτό γε δὴ ἀδύνατον." ["... the universe
is uncreated ... [for,] had it been created from something, that would be prior to everything ... [or]
the created universe comes to be with everything ... and this, indeed, is impossible"]. Ocellus
Lucanus, *On the Nature of the Universe*, I, 2, in *Ocellus Lucanus: Text und Commentar*, p. 11.
"ἐκτὸς γὰρ τοῦ παντὸς οὐδέν." ["outside the universe there is, in fact, nothing."]. Ocellus
Lucanus, *On the Nature of the Universe*, I, 7, in *Ocellus Lucanus: Text und Commentar*, p. 12.
[19] "... τὸ [δὲ] ἀεικίνατον ... θεῖον ... καὶ λόγον ἔχον καὶ ἔμφρον." ["... the evermoving
divinity both has reason and is intelligent."]. Ocellus Lucanus, *On the Laws*, in *Ocellus Lucanus:
Text und Commentar*, p. 26.
"Συνέχει ... τὸν [δὲ] κόσμον ἁρμονία, ταύτας δ' αἴτιος ὁ θεος." ["Harmony holds together
the world; and of this, God is the cause."]. Ocellus Lucanus, *On the Laws*, in *Ocellus Lucanus: Text
und Commentar*, p. 26.
"... τὰς δυνάμεις καὶ τὰ ὄργανα καὶ τὰς ὀρεξεις ... ὑπὸ ... θεοῦ δεδομένας [τοῖς]
ἀνθρώποις οὐχ ἡδονῆς ἕνεκα δεδόσθαι συμβέβηκεν ἀλλὰ" etc. ["... the powers, and organs,
and appetites were given by God ... to men, but he did not give them for the sake of pleasure."].
Ocellus Lucanus, *On the Nature of the Universe*, IV, 2, in *Ocellus Lucanus: Text und Commentar*, p. 22.

needs eternally proceed from such an eternal cause. And so far was he from teaching that matter is the first and original cause of all things that, on the contrary, he everywhere expressly describes God to be an intelligent being, incorporeal, the first mover of all things, himself immovable, and affirms that if there were nothing but matter in the world, there would be no original cause but an infinite progression of causes, which is absurd.[20]

As to those philosophers who taught plainly and expressly that matter was not only eternal but also self-existent and entirely independent, co-existing from eternity with God independently as a second principle, I have already shown the impossibility of this opinion at the entrance upon the present head of discourse, where I proved that matter could not possibly be self-existent. And I shall further demonstrate it to be false when I come to prove the unity of the self-existent being.

Plato, whatever his opinion was about the original matter, very largely and fully declares his sentiments about the formation of the world, viz., that it was composed and framed by an intelligent and wise God. And there is no one of all the ancient philosophers who does in all his writings speak so excellently and worthily as he concerning the nature and attributes of God.[21] Yet, as to the time of the world's beginning to be formed, he seems to make it indefinite when he says the world must needs be an eternal resemblance of the eternal idea.[22] At least his followers afterwards so

---

[20] "... Νοῦς." ["... Intelligence." Clarke provides no reference; see, however, Aristotle, *Metaphysics*, XII, 7 *passim*.].

"... θεὸν ἀσώματον ἀπέφαινε." ["... he held that God is incorporeal."]. Diogenes Laertius, *Lives of Eminent Philosophers*, Book 5, Section 32.

"... τὸ πρῶτον κινοῦν ἀκίνητον." ["... the prime mover is unmoved."]. Aristotle, *Metaphysics*, 1073a26–7.

"ἔτι εἰ μὴ ἔσται παρὰ τὰ αἰσθητὰ ἄλλα, οὐκ ἔσται ἀρχὴ καὶ τάξις ... ἀλλ᾽ ἀεὶ τῆς ἀρχῆς ἀρχή." ["Further, if there is to be nothing besides sensible things, there will be no first principle nor order ... but every principle will be based on another."]. Aristotle, *Metaphysics*, 1075b24–6.

[21] "... οὖν ποιητὴ καὶ πατέρα τοῦδε τοῦ παντός." ["... the maker and father of this universe."]. Plato, *Timaeus*, 28c4–5.

"... γῆν καὶ οὐρανὸν καὶ θεοὺς καὶ πάντα τὰ ἐν οὐρανῷ καὶ τὰ ἐν Ἅιδου ὑπὸ γῆς ἅπαντα ἐργάζεται." ["... He makes the Earth, the heavens and the gods, all things in heaven and in Hades below the earth."]. Plato, *Republic*, 596c7–9.

[22] "... πᾶσα ἀνάγκη τόνδε τὸν κόσμον εἰκόνα τινὸς εἶναι." ["... it is necessary that this cosmos should be a copy of something."]. Plato, *Timeus*, 29b1–2. Which words, being very imperfect in our copies of the original, are thus translated by Cicero: "Si ergo generatus {est mundus}, ad id effectus est quod ratione sapientiaque comprehenditur atque immutabili aeternitate continetur. Ex quo efficitur ut sit necesse hunc quem cernimus mundum simulachrum aeternum esse alicuius aeterni." ["If then {the world} was generated, then it was made so that it is comprehended by reason and knowledge and contained by an immutable eternity. From which it follows that necessarily this world we see is the eternal image of something eternal."]. M. T. Cicero, *Timaeus ex Platone*, ch. 3, section 7.

understood and explained it as if by the creation of the world was not to be understood a creation in time but only an order of nature.[23] Causality and dependence, that is, the will of God and his power of acting, being necessarily as eternal as his essence, the effects of that will and power might be supposed coeval to the will and power themselves in the same manner as light would eternally proceed from the sun, or a shadow from the interposed body, or an impression from an imposed seal, if the respective causes of these effects were supposed eternal.[24]

From all which it plainly appears how little reason modern atheists have to boast of the authority or reasons of those ancient philosophers who held

---

[23] "... νοῦν πρὸ... {κόσμου} εἶναι οὐχ ὡς χρόνῳ πρότερον {αὐτοῦ} ὄντα, ἀλλ᾽ ὅτι {ὁ κόσμος} παρὰ νοῦ ἐστι καὶ φύσει πρότερος ἐκεῖνος καὶ αἴτιος τούτου." ["... Intellect is prior to it {*the universe*}, not in the sense of being prior in time, but in the sense that it is from Intellect, and Intellect is prior in nature and the cause of it."]. Plotinus, *Enneads*, III, 2, 1, 18–20.

"Qui autem a Deo quidem factum fatentur, non tamen eum volunt *temporis* habere, sed suae *creationis* initium ut modo quodam vix intelligibili *semper* sit factus ..." ["But there are those who hold that the universe was created by God, and refuse to allow it had a *temporal* beginning, but allow it to have a beginning of its *creation*, so that in a hardly intelligible way it is *always* created." Clarke's italics.]. St. Augustine, *The City of God against the Pagans*, Book 11, Chapter 4.

"... de mundo et de his quos in mundo deos a Deo factos scribit Plato, apertissime dicit eos esse coepisse, et habere initium ... Verum id quomodo intelligant invenerunt {*Platonici*}, non esse hoc videlicet *temporis*, sed *substitutionis* initium." ["... Plato speaks of the world and of those gods in the world made by God, and he very clearly says that they came into being and had a beginning ... But {*the Platonists*} have found a way to understand this by saying that he meant not a beginning of time but of dependence."]. St. Augustine, *The City of God against the Pagans*, Book 10, Chapter 31.

"Sed mundum quidem fuisse semper philosophia auctor est, conditore quidem deo, sed non ex tempore." ["Yet philosophy teaches that the world has always existed and that God made it, but not in time."]. A. A. T. Macrobius, *Commentaria in Somnium Scipionis*, Book 2, Chapter 10.

[24] "... καὶ εἰ βούλει, παραδείγματί σέ τινι τῶν γνωρίμων ξεναγήσω πρὸς τὸ ζητούμενον. Φασὶ γὰρ ὅτι, καθάπερ αἴτιον τὸ σῶμα τῆς ἑκάστου σκιᾶς γίνεται, ὁμόχρονος δὲ τῷ σώματι ἡ σκιὰ καὶ οὐχ ὁμότιμος· οὕτω δὲ καὶ ὅδε ὁ κόσμος παρακολούθημά ἐστι τοῦ Θεοῦ, αἰτίου ὄντος αὐτῷ τοῦ εἶναι· καὶ συναΐδιός ἐστι τῷ Θεῷ, οὐκέτι δὲ καὶ ὁμότιμος." ["... if you wish, I will lead you to what we are searching for with a familiar model. For, they say that just as the body is the cause of the shadow that comes to be from it, and the shadow is contemporaneous with it but not of equal worth; so, this world follows closely beside God, who is the cause of its being, and is coeternal with God but not of equal worth."]. Zacharias of Mitylene, *Disputatio de Mundi Opificio*, in *Patrologia Cursus Completus: Patrologia Graeca*, ed. J. P. Migne (Paris, 1864), vol. LXXXV, p. 1078.

"Sicut enim," inquiunt {*Platonici*} "si pes ex aeternitate semper fuisset in pulvere, semper ei subesset vestigium, quod tamen vestigium a calcante factum nemo dubitaret, nec alterum altero prius esset, quamvis alterum ab altero factum esset, sic" inquiunt "et mundus atque in illo Dii creati, et semper fuerunt semper existente qui fecit; et tamen facti sunt." ["For," say {*the Platonists*}, "if from all eternity a foot were standing on the dust, then its imprint would always be underneath it; yet nobody would doubt that the imprint was made by the planter of the foot, and the one would not be earlier than the other, although it would be made by the other. So," they say, "the world and the gods created in it always existed during the eternal existence of him who made them, and yet, they were made."]. St. Augustine, *The City of God against the Pagans*, Book 10, Chapter 31.

the eternity of the world. For since these men neither proved nor attempted to prove that the material world was original to itself, independent or self-existing, but only that it was an eternal effect of an eternal cause, which is God, it is evident that this their opinion, even supposing it could by no means be refuted, could afford no manner of advantage to the cause of atheists in our days who, excluding supreme mind and intelligence out of the universe, would make mere matter and necessity the original and eternal cause of things.

Secondly, the other reason why (in this attempt to prove that the material world cannot possibly be the first and original being, uncreated, independent and self-existent) I have omitted the argument usually drawn from the supposed absolute impossibility of the world being eternal or having existed through an infinite succession of time, is because that argument can never be so stated as to be of any use in convincing or affecting the mind of an atheist, who must not be supposed to come prepared beforehand with any transcendent idea of the eternity of God. For, since an atheist cannot be supposed to believe the nice and subtle (and indeed unintelligible) distinction of the schools, it is impossible by this argument so to disprove the possibility of the eternity of the world but that an atheist will understand it to prove equally against the possibility of any thing's being eternal, and, consequently, that it proves nothing at all but is only a difficulty arising from our not being able to comprehend adequately the notion of eternity. That the material world is not self-existent or necessarily existing but the product of some distinct superior agent may, as I have already shown, be strictly demonstrated by bare reason against the most obstinate atheist in the world. But the time *when* the world was created, or whether its creation was properly speaking *in time*, is not so easy to demonstrate strictly by bare reason (as appears from the opinions of many of the ancient philosophers concerning that matter), but the proof of it can be taken only from Revelation.

To endeavor to prove that there cannot possibly be any such thing as infinite time or space, from the impossibility of an addition of finite parts ever composing or exhausting an infinite, or from the imaginary inequality of the number of years, days, and hours, that would be contained in the one, or of the miles, yards, and feet that would be contained in the other, is supposing infinites to be made up of numbers of finites.[25] That is, it is

---

[25] R. Cudworth, *The True Intellectual System of the Universe* (London, 1678; reprint New York, Garland Publishing Co., 1978), pp. 643–4.

supposing finite quantities to be *aliquot* or *constituent* parts of infinite when indeed they are not so, but do all equally, whether great or small, whether many or few, bear the very same proportion to an infinite as mathematical points do to a line, or lines to a superficies, or as moments do to time, that is, none at all. So that, to argue absolutely against the impossibility of infinite space or time merely from the imaginary inequality of the numbers of their finite parts, which are not properly constituent parts but mere nothings in proportion, is the very same thing as it would be to argue against the possibility of the existence of any determinate *finite* quantity from the imaginary equality or inequality of the number of the mathematical lines and points contained therein, when indeed neither the one nor the other have (in property of speech) any number at all, but they are absolutely without number; neither can any given number or quantity be any *aliquot* or *constituent* part of infinite or be compared at all with it, or bear any kind of proportion to it, or be the foundation of any argument in any question concerning it.

IV

What the substance or essence of that being which is self-existent or necessarily existing is, we have no idea, neither is it at all possible for us to comprehend it. That there is such a being actually existing without us we are sure (as I have already shown) by strict and undeniable demonstration. Also what it is not, that is, that the material world is not it, as modern atheists would have it, has been already demonstrated. But what it is, I mean as to its substance and essence, this we are infinitely unable to comprehend. Yet this does not in the least diminish the certainty of the demonstration of its existence. For it is one thing to know certainly that a being exists, and another to know what the essence of that being is. And the one may be capable of the strictest demonstration when the other is absolutely beyond the reach of all our faculties to understand. A blind or deaf man has infinitely more reason to deny the being, or the possibility of the being, of light or sound than an atheist can have to deny or doubt of the existence of God. For the one can, at the utmost, have no other proof but credible testimony of the existence of certain things, whereof it is absolutely impossible that he himself should frame any manner of idea, not only of their essence but even of their effects or properties; but the other may, with the least use of his reason, be assured of the existence of a supreme being by undeniable demonstration, and may also certainly know abundance of its attributes (as shall be made appear in the following propositions), though its substance or essence be entirely incomprehensible. Wherefore, nothing can be more unreasonable and weak than for an atheist, upon this account, to deny the being of God merely because his weak and finite understanding cannot frame to itself any adequate notion of the substance or essence of that first and supreme cause. We are utterly ignorant of the substance or essence of all other things, even of those things which we converse most familiarly with and think we understand best. There is not so mean and contemptible a plant or animal that does not confound the most enlarged understanding upon Earth; nay, even the simplest and plainest of all inanimate beings have their essence or substance hidden from us in the deepest and most impenetrable obscurity. How weak, then, and foolish is it to raise objections against the being of God from the incomprehensibleness of his essence, and to represent it as a strange and incredible thing that there should exist any incorporeal substance the essence of which we are not able to comprehend! As if it were not far more strange that there should exist numberless objects of our senses, things subject to our daily inquiry, search, and examination, and yet we not be able, no not in any measure, to find out the real essence of any one even of the least of these things.

Nevertheless, it is very necessary to observe here, by the way, that it does not at all from hence follow that there can possibly be in the unknown substance or essence of God anything contradictory to our clear ideas. For as a blind man, though he has no idea of light and colors, yet knows certainly and infallibly that there cannot possibly be any kind of light which is not light or any sort of color which is not a color, so, though we have no idea of the substance of God nor indeed of the substance of any other being, yet we are as infallibly certain that there cannot possibly be either in the one or in the other any contradictory modes or properties, as if we had the clearest and most distinct idea of them.

For what has been said upon this head, we may observe, firstly, the weakness of such as have presumed to imagine infinite space to be a just representation or adequate idea of the essence of the supreme cause. This is a weak imagination arising from hence, that men, using themselves to judge of all things by their sense only, fancy spiritual or immaterial substances, because they are not objects of their corporeal sense, to be, as it were, mere nothings, just as children imagine air, because they cannot see it, to be mere emptiness and nothing. But the fallacy is too gross to deserve being insisted upon. There are, perhaps, numberless substances in the world whose essences are as entirely unknown and impossible to be represented to our imagination, as colors are to a man that was born blind, or sound to one that has been always deaf. Nay, there is no substance in the world of which we know anything further than only a certain number of its properties or attributes, of which we know fewer in some things and in others more. Infinite space is nothing else but abstract immensity or infinity, even as infinite duration is abstract eternity. And it would be just as proper to say that eternity is the essence of the supreme cause as to say that immensity is so. Indeed, they seem both to be but modes of an essence or substance incomprehensible to us, and when we endeavor to represent the real substance of any being whatsoever in our weak imaginations, we shall find ourselves in like manner deceived.

Secondly, from hence appears the vanity of the Schoolmen who, as in other matters, so in their disputes about the self-existing being, when they come at what they are by no means able to comprehend or explain (lest they should feel ignorant of anything) they give us terms of art and words of amusement, mere empty sounds which, under pretence of explaining the matter before them, have really no manner of idea or signification at all. Thus, when they tell us concerning the essence of God that he is *purus actus* [pure act], *mera forma* [pure form] and the like, either the words have no meaning and signify nothing, or else they express only the perfection of his power and other attributes, which is not what these men intend to express by them.

V

Though the substance or essence of the self-existent being is itself absolutely incomprehensible to us, yet many of the essential attributes of his nature are strictly demonstrable as well as his existence. Thus, in the first place the self-existent being must of necessity be eternal. The ideas of eternity and self-existence are so closely connected, that because something must of necessity be eternal independently and without any outward cause of its being, therefore it must necessarily be self-existent. And because it is impossible but something must be self-existent, therefore it is necessary that it must likewise be eternal. To be self-existent is (as has been already shown) to exist by an absolute necessity in the nature of the thing itself.

Now this necessity, being absolute and not depending upon anything external, must be always unalterably the same, nothing being alterable but what is capable of being affected by somewhat without itself. That being, therefore, which has no other cause of its existence but the absolute necessity of its own nature must of necessity have existed from everlasting, without beginning, and must of necessity exist to everlasting without end.

As to the *manner* of this eternal existence, it is manifest it herein infinitely transcends the manner of the existence of all created beings, even of such as shall exist forever. [It is manifest] that whereas it is not possible for their finite minds to comprehend all that is past or to understand perfectly all things that are at present, much less to know all that is future, or to have entirely in their power anything that is to come (but their thoughts, and knowledge, and power must of necessity have degrees and periods, and be successive and transient as the things themselves), the eternal supreme cause, on the contrary, (supposing him to be an intelligent being, which will hereafter be proved in the sequel of this discourse) must of necessity have such a perfect, independent, and unchangeable comprehension of all things, that there can be no one point or instant of his eternal duration wherein all things that are past, present, or to come, will not be as entirely known and represented to him in one single thought or view, and all things present and future be equally entirely in his power and direction, *as if* there was really no succession at all but all things were actually present at once. Thus far we can speak intelligibly concerning the eternal duration of the self-existent being, and no atheist can say this is an impossible, absurd, or insufficient account. It is, in the most proper and intelligible sense of the words, to all the purposes of excellency and perfection *interminabilis vitae tota simul et perfecta possessio*, the *entire and perfect possession of an endless life*.

Others have supposed that the difference between the manner of the eternal existence of the supreme cause and that of the existence of created beings is this, that whereas the latter is a continual transient succession of duration, the former is one point or instant comprehending eternity and wherein all things are really coexistent. But this distinction I shall not now insist upon as being of no use in the present dispute because it is impossible to prove and explain it in such a manner as ever to convince an atheist that there is anything in it. And besides, as on the one hand the Schoolmen have indeed generally chosen to defend it, so on the other hand there are many learned men of far better understanding and judgment who have rejected and opposed it.[26]

VI

The self-existent being must of necessity be infinite and omnipresent. The idea of infinity or immensity, as well as of eternity, is so closely connected with that of self-existence that because it is impossible but something must be infinite independently and of itself (for else it would be impossible there should be any infinite at all unless an effect could be more perfect than its cause), therefore it must of necessity be self-existent; and because something must of necessity be self-existent, therefore it is necessary that it must likewise be infinite. To be self-existent (as has been already shown) is to exist by an absolute necessity in the nature of the thing itself. Now this necessity being absolute in itself and not depending on any outward cause, it is evident it must be *everywhere* as well as *always* unalterably the same. For a necessity which is not everywhere the same is plainly a consequential necessity only, depending upon some external cause, and not an absolute one in its own nature. For a necessity absolutely such in itself has no relation to time or place or anything else. Whatever, therefore, exists by an absolute necessity in its own nature must needs be infinite as well as eternal. To suppose a finite being to be self-existent is to say that it is a

---

[26] "Crucem ingegno fingere, ut rem capiat fugientem captum ... Tam fieri non potest ut instans {*temporis*} coexistat rei successivae quam impossibile est punctum coexistere {*coextendi*} lineae ... Lusus merus non intellectorum verborum." ["To construct a crux for the intellect in order to capture the matter fleeing one's grasp ... In fact it is no more possible for an instant {*of time*} to coexist with a subsequent thing than for a point to coexist {*coextend*} with a line ... A mere play of non-understood words."]. P. Gassendi, *Syntagma Philosophicum*, Second Part, Section I, Book 2, Chapter vii. [Clarke's original reference is incorrect.]

"I shall not trouble you with the inconsistent and unintelligible notions of the Schoolmen, [namely] that it {*the eternity of God*} is *duratio tota simul*, in which we are not to conceive any succession but to imagine it an instant. We may as well conceive the immensity of God to be a point as his eternity to be an instant... And how that can be together which must necessarily be imagined to be coexistent to successions, let them that can, conceive." Archbishop John Tillotson, *Sermons*, fourth edition (London: Chiswell, 1704), vol. VII, Sermon 13, pp. 359–60.

"Others say ... God sees and knows future things by the presentiality and coexistence of all things in eternity, for they say that future things are actually present and existing to God, though not *in mensura propria*, yet in *mensura aliena*. The Schoolmen have much more of this jargon and canting language. I envy no man the understanding [of] these phrases. But to me they seem to signify nothing but to have been words invented by idle and conceited men which a great many ever since, lest they should seem to be ignorant, would seem to understand. But I wonder most that men, when they have amused and puzzled themselves and others with hard words, should call it *explaining* things." Archbishop John Tillotson, *Sermons*, fourth edition (London, Chiswell, 1704), vol. VI, Sermon 6, pp. 156–7.

contradiction for that being not to exist, the absence of which may yet be conceived without a contradiction, which is the greatest absurdity in the world. For if a being can without a contradiction be absent from one place, it may without a contradiction be absent likewise from another place, and from all places. And whatever necessity it may have of existing must arise from some external cause and not absolutely from itself, and consequently the being cannot be self-existent.

From hence it follows, firstly, that the infinity of the self-existent being must be an infinity of fullness as well as of immensity; that is, it must not only be without limits but also without diversity, defect, or interruption. For instance, could matter be supposed boundless, it would not therefore follow that it was in this complete sense infinite because, though it had no limits, yet it might have within itself many assignable vacuities. But whatever is self-existent must of necessity exist absolutely in every place alike and be equally present everywhere, and consequently must have a true and absolute infinity both of immensity and wholeness.

Secondly, from hence it follows that the self-existent being must be a most simple, unchangeable, incorruptible being without parts, figure, motion, divisibility, or any other such properties as we find in matter. For all these things do plainly and necessarily imply finiteness in their very notion, and are utterly inconsistent with complete infinity. Divisibility is a separation of parts real or mental, meaning by "mental separation" not barely a partial apprehending (for space, for instance, which is absolutely indivisible and inseparable either really or mentally may yet be partially apprehended), but a removing, disjoining, or separation of parts one from another, even so much as in the imagination.[27] And any such separation or removing of parts one from another is really or mentally a setting of bounds, either of which destroys infinity. Motion, for the same reason, implies finiteness; and to have parts, properly speaking, signifies either difference and diversity of existence, which is inconsistent with necessity, or else it signifies divisibility real or mental as before, which is inconsistent with complete infinity. Corruption, change, or any alteration whatsoever, implies motion, separation of parts, and finiteness. And any manner of composition, in opposition to the most perfect simplicity, signifies

---

[27] "Ordo partium spatii est immutabilis: moveantur hae de locis suis, et movebuntur (ut sic dicam) de seipsis." ["The order of the parts of space is immutable: suppose the parts of space to be moved out of their places, and they will be moved (if I may say so) out of themselves."]. *NP*, Scholium to Definition 8, p. 48.

difference and diversity in the manner of existence, which is inconsistent with necessity.

It is evident, therefore, that the self-existent being must be infinite in the strictest and most complete sense. But as to the particular manner of his being infinite or everywhere present, in opposition to the manner of created things being present in such or such finite places, it is as impossible for our finite understandings to comprehend or explain as it is for us to form an adequate idea of infinity. Yet that the thing is true, that he *is* actually omnipresent, we are as certain as we are that there must be something infinite, which no man who has thought upon these things at all ever denied. The Schoolmen indeed have presumed to assert that the immensity of God is a point, as his eternity (they think) is an instant. But this being altogether unintelligible, that which we can more safely affirm and which no atheist can say is absurd, and which nevertheless is sufficient to all wise and good purposes, is this: that whereas all finite and created beings can be present but in one definite place at once, and corporeal beings even in that one place very imperfectly and unequally, to any purpose of power or activity only by the successive motion of different members and organs, the supreme cause, on the contrary, being an infinite and most simple essence and comprehending all things perfectly in himself, is at all times equally present both in his simple essence and by the immediate and perfect exercise of all his attributes to every point of the boundless immensity as if it were really all but one single point.

VII

The self-existent being must of necessity be but one. This evidently follows from his being necessarily existent. For necessity absolute in itself is simple, and uniform, and universal, without any possible difference, difformity, or variety whatsoever. And all variety or difference of existence must needs arise from some external cause and be dependent upon it, and proportionable to the efficiency of that cause, whatsoever it be. Absolute necessity, in which there can be no variation in any kind or degree, cannot be the ground of existence of a number of beings, however similar and agreeing, because without any other difference even number is itself a manifest difformity or inequality (if I may so speak) of efficiency or causality.

Again, to suppose two or more distinct beings existing of themselves necessarily and independent from each other implies this plain contradiction, that each of them being independent from the other, they may either of them be supposed to exist alone, so that it will be no contradiction to imagine the other not to exist, and consequently neither of them will be necessarily existing.[28] Whatsoever, therefore, exists necessarily is the one simple essence of the self-existent being; and whatsoever differs from that is not necessarily existing because in absolute necessity there can be no difference or diversity of existence. Other beings there may be innumerable besides the one infinite self-existent. But no other being can be self-existent because [if] so it would be individually the same at the same time that it is supposed to be different.

From hence it follows, firstly, that the unity of God is a true and real, not figurative unity. With which prime foundation of natural religion, how the Scripture-doctrine of the Trinity perfectly agrees, I have elsewhere endeavored to show particularly in its proper place.

Secondly, from hence it follows that it is impossible there should be two different self-existent independent principles as some philosophers have imagined, such as God and matter. For since self-existence is necessary-existence, and, since it is an express contradiction (as has already been shown) that two different beings should be each necessarily existing, it evidently follows that it is absolutely impossible there should be two independent self-existing principles such as God and matter.

Thirdly, from hence we may observe the vanity, folly, and weakness of Spinoza who, because the self-existent being must necessarily be but one, concludes from thence that the whole world and everything contained therein is one uniform substance, eternal, uncreated, and necessary.[29] Whereas, just on the contrary he ought to have concluded that, because all things in the world are very different from one another and have all manner of variety, and all the marks of will, and arbitrariness, and changeableness (and not of necessity) in them, being plainly fitted with very different powers to very different ends and distinguished one from another by a diversity not only of modes but also of essential attributes, and con-

---

[28] See this farther explained in the answer to the *First Letter*, at the end of this book. [Supplementary text I]

[29] "Una substantia non potest produci ab alia." ["A substance cannot be produced by another."]. *E*, Part I, Proposition 6.

"Ad naturam substantiae pertinet existere." ["Existence pertains to the nature of substance."]. *E*, Part I, Proposition 7.

"Praeter Deum nulla dari, neque concipi potest substantia." ["Besides God no substance can be or be conceived."]. *E*, Part I, Proposition 14.

sequently (so far as it is possible for us by the use of our present faculties to attain any knowledge at all of them) of their substances themselves also – therefore none of these beings are necessary or self-existent but must needs depend all upon some external cause, that is, on the one supreme, unchangeable, self-existent being.

That which led Spinoza into his foolish and destructive opinion, and on which alone all his argumentation is entirely built, is that absurd definition of substance, that it is something the idea of which does not depend on or presuppose the idea of any other thing from which it might proceed but includes in itself necessary existence.[30] Which definition is either false and signifies nothing (and then his whole doctrine built upon it falls at once to the ground) or, if it be true, then neither matter nor spirit nor any finite being whatsoever (as has been before shown) is in that sense properly a substance but (the ὁ ὤν) the self-existent being alone. And so it will prove nothing (notwithstanding all his show and form of demonstration) to his main purpose, which was to make us believe that there is no such thing as power or liberty in the universe, but that every particular thing in the world is by an absolute necessity just what it is and could not possibly have been in any respect otherwise.[31] Supposing, I say, his definition of substance to be true, yet even that really concludes nothing to his main purpose concerning the necessity of all things. For since according to that definition neither matter nor spirit, nor any finite beings whatsoever, are substances but only modes, how will it follow that because substance is self-existent, therefore all these modes are so too? Why, because from an infinite cause infinite effects must needs follow.[32] Very true, supposing that infinite self-existent cause not to be a voluntary but a mere necessary agent, that is, no agent at all, and supposing also that in mere necessity there could and must

---

[30] "Per substantiam intelligo id, quod in se est, et per se concipitur: hoc est, id cuius conceptus non indiget conceptu alterius rei, a quo formari debeat." ["By substance I understand that which is in itself and is conceived through itself, that is, that the concept of which does not require the concept of any other thing from which it must be formed."]. *E*, Definition 3. Which presently after he thus explains: "Ad naturam substantiae pertinet existere ... hoc est, ipsius essentia involvit necessario existentiam." ["Existence pertains to the nature of substance ... that is, its essence necessarily involves existence."]. *E*, Part I, Proposition 7 and Proof.

[31] "Res nullo alio modo, neque alio ordine a Deo produci potuerunt, quam productae sunt." ["Things could not have been produced by God in any other way or order than they have been produced."]. *E*, Part I, Proposition 33.

[32] "Ex necessitate divinae naturae, infinita infinitis modis (hoc est, omnia, quae sub intellectum infinitum cadere possunt) sequi debent." ["From the necessity of the divine nature there must follow infinite things in infinite ways (that is, all that can fall within the scope of infinite intellect.")]. *E*, Part I, Proposition 16.

37

be all or any variety. Both which suppositions (in the present arguments) are the question begged; and what he afterwards attempts to allege in proof of them shall afterwards be considered in its proper place.

VIII

The *self-existent and original cause of all things must be an intelligent being.* In this proposition lies the main question between us and the atheists. For that something must be self-existent and that that which is self-existent must necessarily be eternal and infinite and the original cause of all things, will not bear much dispute. But all atheists, whether they hold the world to be of itself eternal both as to the matter and form, or whether they hold the matter only to be necessary and the form contingent, or whatever hypothesis they frame, have always asserted and must maintain, either directly or indirectly, that the self-existent being is not an intelligent being but either pure inactive matter, or, which in other words is the very same thing, a mere necessary agent. For a mere necessary agent must of necessity either be plainly and directly in the grossest sense unintelligent (which was the ancient atheists' notion of the self-existent being), or else its intelligence (which is the assertion of Spinoza and some moderns) must be wholly separate from any power of will and choice, which in respect of any excellency and perfection, or indeed to any common sense, is the very same thing as no intelligence at all.

Now that the self-existent being is not such a blind and unintelligent necessity, but in the most proper sense an understanding and really active being, does not indeed so obviously and directly appear to us by considerations *a priori*, because through the imperfection of our faculties we know not wherein intelligence consists, nor can [we] see the immediate and necessary connection of it with self-existence, as we can that of eternity, infinity, unity, etc. But *a posteriori*, almost every thing in the world demonstrates to us this great truth and upholds undeniable arguments to prove that the world and all things therein are the effects of an intelligent and knowing cause.

And first, since in general there are manifestly in things various kinds of powers and very different excellencies and degrees of perfection, it must needs be that in the order of causes and effects the cause must always be more excellent than the effect. And consequently, the self-existent being, whatever that be supposed to be, must of necessity (being the original of all things) contain in itself the sum and highest degree of all the perfections of all things. Not because that which is self-existent must therefore have all possible perfections (for this, though most certainly true in itself, yet cannot be so easily demonstrated *a priori*), but because it is impossible that any effect should have any perfection which was not in the cause. For if it had, then that perfection would be caused by nothing, which is a plain contradiction. Now an unintelligent being, it is evident, cannot be endowed with all the perfections of all things in the world because intelligence is one of those perfections. All things, therefore, cannot arise from an unintelligent original, and consequently the self-existent being must of necessity be intelligent.

There is no possibility for an atheist to avoid the force of this argument any other way than by asserting one of these two things: either that there is no intelligent being at all in the universe, or that intelligence is no distinct perfection but merely a composition of figure and motion, as color and sound are vulgarly supposed to be. Of the former of these assertions every man's own consciousness is an abundant confutation. For they who contend that beasts are mere machines have yet never presumed to conjecture that men are so too.[a] And that the latter assertion, in which the main strength of atheism lies, is most absurd and impossible shall be shown presently. Though if that assertion could be supposed to be true, yet even still it would unavoidably follow that the self-existent being must needs be intelligent, as shall be proved in my fourth argument upon this present head. In the meantime, that the assertion itself, viz., that intelligence is not any distinct perfection properly speaking but merely a composition of unintelligent figure and motion – that this assertion, I say, is most absurd and impossible will appear from what shall be said in the ensuing argument.

Secondly, since in men in particular there is undeniably that power which we call thought, intelligence, consciousness, perception, or knowledge, there must of necessity either have been from eternity, without any original cause at all, an infinite succession of men whereof no one has had a necessary but everyone a dependent and communicated being; or else these beings endowed with perception and consciousness must at some time or other have arisen merely out of that which had no such quality as

---

[a] Here Clarke was thinking of the Cartesians, who followed Descartes' view that animals, in contrast with humans, are mere machines devoid of thought and sensations in so far as they involve thought. For Descartes, see, for example, his *Discourse on Method*, part 5.

sense, perception, or consciousness; or else they must have been produced by some intelligent superior being. There never was nor can be any atheist whatsoever that can deny but one of these three suppositions must be the truth. If, therefore, the two former can be proved to be false and impossible, the latter must be owned to be demonstrably true. Now, that the first is impossible is evident from what has been already said in proof of the second general head of this discourse. And that the second is likewise impossible may be thus demonstrated. If perception or intelligence be a distinct quality or perfection and not a mere effect or composition of unintelligent figure and motion, then being endowed with perception or consciousness can never have arisen purely out of that which had no such quality as perception or consciousness, because nothing can ever give to another any perfection which it has not actually either in itself or at least in a higher degree. But perception or intelligence is a distinct quality or perfection, and not a mere effect or composition of unintelligent figure and motion.

Firstly, if perception or intelligence be any real distinct quality or perfection and not a mere effect or composition of unintelligent figure and motion, then being endowed with perception or consciousness can never possibly have arisen purely out of that which itself had no such quality as perception or consciousness, because nothing can ever give to another any perfection which it has not either actually *in itself* or at least *in a higher degree*. This is very evident because if anything could give to another any perfection which it has not itself, that perfection would be caused absolutely by nothing, which is a plain contradiction. If anyone here replies (as Mr. Gildon has done in a letter to Mr. Blount) that colors, sounds, tastes, and the like, arise from figure and motion, which have no such qualities in themselves, or that figure, divisibility, mobility, and other qualities of matter are confessed to be given from God, who yet cannot without extreme blasphemy be said to have any such qualities himself, and that therefore in like manner perception or intelligence may arise out of that which has no intelligence itself, the answer is very easy.[33]

---

[33] C. Blount, *The Oracles of Reason*, pp. 187–92. See also my letter to Mr. Dodwell with several answers and replies concerning the immortality of the soul.

If with one of Cicero's dialogists they should infer that the whole of the world must have understanding because some portions of it are intelligent, we may retort with the other speaker in Cicero that by the same argument the whole must be a courtier, a musician, a dancing master or a philosopher because many of the parts are such [M. T. Cicero, *De Natura Deorum*, III, 9].

Mr. Toland's letter *Motion essential to matter*, in *Letters to Serena* (London, 1704; reprint Stuttgart-Bad Cannstatt, F. Fromann, 1964), Letter 5.

Firstly, that colors, sounds, tastes, and the like, are by no means effects arising from mere figure and motion (there being nothing in the bodies themselves, the objects of the senses, that has any manner of similitude to any of the qualities), but they are plainly thoughts or modifications of the mind itself, which is an intelligent being, and are not properly caused but only *occasioned* by the impressions of figure and motion. Nor will it at all help an atheist, as to the present question, though we should here make for him (that we may allow him the greatest possible advantage) even that most absurd supposition, that the mind itself is nothing but mere matter and not at all an immaterial substance. For even supposing it to be mere matter, yet he must needs confess it to be such matter as is endowed not only with figure and motion, but also with the quality of intelligence and perception. And, consequently, as to the present question, it will still come to the same thing, that colors, sounds, and the like, which are not qualities of unintelligent bodies but perceptions of mind, can no more be caused by or arise from mere unintelligent figure and motion, than color can be a triangle, or sound a square, or something be caused by nothing. Secondly, as to the other part of the objection, that figure, divisibility, mobility, and other qualities of matter are, as we ourselves acknowledge, given it from God, who yet cannot without extreme blasphemy be said to have any such qualities himself, and that therefore in like manner perception or intelligence may arise out of that which has no intelligence itself – the answer is still easier, that figure, divisibility, mobility, and other such like qualities of matter, have not real, proper, distinct, and positive powers, but only negative qualities, deficiencies, or imperfections. And though no cause can communicate to its effect any real perfection which it has not itself, yet the effect may easily have many imperfections, deficiencies, or negative qualities, which are not in the cause. Though, therefore, figure, divisibility, mobility, and the like (which are mere negations, as all limitations and all defects of powers are) may be in the effect and not in the cause, yet intelligence (which I now suppose and shall prove immediately to be a distinct quality and which no man can say is a mere negation) cannot possibly be so.

Having, therefore, thus demonstrated that if perception or intelligence be supposed to be a distinct quality or perfection (though even but of matter only, if the atheist pleases) and not a mere effect or composition of unintelligent figure and motion, then beings endowed with perception or consciousness can never have arisen purely out of that which had no such quality as perception or consciousness (because nothing can ever give to another any perfection which it has not itself), it will easily appear, secondly, that perception or intelligence is really such a distinct quality or perfection, and not possibly a mere effect or composition of unintelligent figure and motion; and that for this plain reason, because intelligence is not figure and consciousness is not motion. For whatever can arise from, or be compounded of, anything is still only those very things of which it was compounded. And if infinite compositions or divisions be made eternally, the things will still be but eternally the same, and all their possible effects can never be anything but repetitions of the same. For instance, all possible changes, compositions, or divisions of figure are still nothing but figure, and all possible compositions or effects of motion can eternally be nothing but mere motion. If, therefore, there ever was a time when there was nothing in the universe but matter and motion, there never could have been anything else therein but matter and motion. And it would have been as impossible there should ever have existed any such thing as intelligence, or consciousness, or even any such thing as light, or heat, or sound, or color, or any of those we call secondary qualities of matter, as it is now impossible for motion to be blue or red, or for a triangle to be transformed into a sound.

That which has been apt to deceive men in this matter is this, that they imagine compounds to be somewhat really different from that of which they are compounded, which is a very great mistake. For all the things of which men so judge, either, if they be *really different*, are not compounds nor effects of what men judge them to be but are something totally distinct, as when the vulgar thinks colors and sounds to be properties inherent in bodies when indeed they are purely thoughts of the mind; or else, if they be really compounds and effects, then they are *not different* but exactly the same that ever they were (as when two triangles put together make a square, that square is still nothing but two triangles; or when a square cut in halves makes two triangles those two triangles are still the two halves of a square; or when the mixture of blue and yellow powder makes a green, that green is still nothing but blue and yellow intermixed, as is plainly visible by the help of microscopes). And in short, everything by composition, division, or motion, is nothing else but the very same it was before, taken either in whole or in parts, or in different place or order. He, therefore, that will affirm intelligence to be the effect of a system of unintelligent matter in motion, must either affirm intelligence to be a mere name or external denomination of certain figures and motions, and that it differs from unintelligent figures and motions no otherwise than as a circle or triangle differs from a square (which is evidently absurd); or else he must suppose it to be a real distinct quality arising from certain motions of a system of matter not in itself intelligent, and then this no less evidently absurd consequence would follow, that one quality inhered in another. For in that case not the substance itself, the particles of which the system consists, but the mere mode, the particular mode of motion and figure, would be intelligent. Mr. Hobbes seems to have been aware of this, and therefore though he is very sparing and, as it were, ashamed to speak out, yet, finding himself pressed in his own mind with the difficulty arising from the impossibility of sense or consciousness being merely the effect of figure and motion, and it not serving his purpose at all (were the thing never so possible) to suppose that God by an immediate and voluntary act of his almighty power endows certain systems of matter with consciousness and thought (of which opinion I shall have occasion to speak something more hereafter), he is forced to have recourse to that prodigiously absurd supposition, that all matter as matter is endowed not only with figure and a capacity of motion but also with an actual sense or perception, and wants only the organs and memory of animals to express its sensation.[34]

Thirdly, that the self-existent and original cause of all things is an intelligent being appears abundantly from the excellent variety, order, beauty, and wonderful contrivance and fitness of all things in the world to their proper and respective ends. This argument has been so learnedly and fully handled both by ancient and modern writers that I do but just mention it, without enlarging at all upon it. I shall only at this time make this one observation, that whereas Descartes and others have endeavored to give a possible account (*possible* did I say? Nay, indeed, a most impossible and

---

[34] "Scio fuisse philosophos quosdam, eosdemque viros doctos, qui corpora omnia sensu praedita esse sustinuerunt; nec video, si natura sensionis in reactione sola collocaretur, quomodo refutari possint. Sed etsi ex reactione etiam corporum aliorum, phantasma aliquod nasceretur, illud tamen, remoto obiecto, statim cessaret. Nam, nisi ad retinendum motum impressum, etiam remoto obiecto, apta habent organa, ut habent animalia, ita tantum sentient ut nunquam sensisse se recordentur ... Sensioni ergo ... quae vulgo ita appellatur, necessario adhaeret memoria aliqua" etc. ["I know that there have been philosophers, and those learned men, who have maintained that all bodies are endowed with sense. Nor do I see how they can be refuted, if the nature of sense be placed in reaction only. However, though by the reaction of other bodies a phantasm might arise, it would nevertheless cease as soon as the object were removed. For unless those bodies had organs fit for the retaining of motion made in them, as animals have, their sense would be such that they would never remember they sensed... Hence, some memory necessarily pertains to sense as it is commonly understood."]. T. Hobbes, *De Corpore*, Part IV, Chapter 25, Section 5.

See also Numbers 2 and 11 of the appendix to a collection of papers which passed between Mr Leibniz and Dr Clarke. [Supplementary text IX].

ridiculous account) how the world might be formed by the necessary laws of motion alone, they have by so seemingly vast an undertaking really meant no more than to explain philosophically how the inanimate part, that is infinitely the least considerable part of the world, might possibly have been framed. For as to plants and animals, in which the wisdom of the creator principally appears, they have never in any tolerable manner or with any the least appearance of success pretended to give an account how they were originally formed. In these things matter and the laws of motion are able to do nothing at all. And how ridiculous the Epicurean hypothesis is, of the earth producing them all at first by chance (besides that, I think, it is now given up even by all atheists), appears from the late discovery made in philosophy that there is no such thing as equivocal generation of any the meanest animal or plant (the Sun and earth and water and all the powers of nature in conjunction being able to do nothing at all towards the producing [of] anything endowed with so much as even a vegetable life); from which most excellent discovery we may, by the way, observe the usefulness of natural and experimental philosophy sometimes even in matters of religion. Since, therefore, things are thus, it must unavoidably be granted, even by the most obstinate atheist, either that all plants and animals are originally the work of an intelligent being and created by him in time; or that, having been from eternity in the same order and method they now are in, they are an eternal effect of an eternal intelligent cause continually exerting its infinite power and wisdom; or else, that without any self-existent original at all they have been derived one from another in an eternal succession by an infinite progress of dependent causes. The first of these three ways is the conclusion we assert; the second, so far as the cause of atheism is concerned, comes to the very same thing; and the third I have already shown in my proof of the second general head of this discourse to be absolutely impossible and a contradiction.

Fourthly, supposing it was possible that the form of the world and all the visible things contained therein, with the order, beauty, and exquisite fitness of their parts, nay, supposing that even intelligence itself with consciousness and thought in all the beings we know could possibly be the result or effect of mere unintelligent matter, figure, and motion (which is the most unreasonable and impossible supposition in the world), yet even still there would remain an undeniable demonstration that the self-existent being, whatever it be supposed to be, must be intelligent. For even these principles themselves, unintelligent figure and motion, could never have possibly existed without there had been before them an intelligent cause. I instance in motion. It is evident there is now such a thing as motion in the world which either began at some time or other or was eternal. If it began at any time, then the question is granted that the first cause is an intelligent being, for mere unintelligent matter, and that at rest, it is manifest could never of itself begin to move. On the contrary, if motion was eternal, it was either eternally caused by some eternal intelligent being, or it must of itself be necessary and self-existent, or else, without any necessity in its own nature and without any external necessary cause, it must have existed from eternity by an endless successive communication. If motion was eternally caused by some eternal intelligent being, this also is granting the question as to the present dispute. If it was of itself necessary and self-existent, then it follows that it must be a contradiction in terms to suppose any matter to be at rest. And yet, at the same time, because the determination of this self-existent motion must be every way at once, the effect of it could be nothing else but a perpetual rest. Besides (as there is no end of absurdities when they once begin), it must also imply a contradiction to suppose that there might possibly have been originally more or less motion in the universe than there actually was, which is so very absurd a consequence that Spinoza himself, though he expressly asserts all things to be necessary, yet seems ashamed here to speak out his opinion, or rather plainly contradicts himself in the question about the original of motion.[35] But if it be said, lastly, that motion, without any necessity in its own nature and without any external necessary cause, has existed from eternity merely by an endless successive communication as Spinoza inconsistently enough seems to assert, this I have before shown in my proof of the second general proposition of this discourse to be a plain contradiction.[36] It remains, therefore, that a motion must of necessity be originally caused by something that is intelligent, or else there never could have been any such thing as motion in the world, and consequently the self-existent being, the original cause of all things, whatever it be supposed to be, must of necessity be an intelligent being.

From hence it follows again that the material world cannot possibly

[35] *E*, Part I, Proposition 33, compared with *E*, Part II, Proposition 13, Lemma 3.

[36] "Corpus motum, vel quiescens ad motum, vel quietem determinari debuit ab alio corpore, quod etiam ad motum, vel quietem determinatum fuit ab alio, et illud iterum ab alio, et sic in infinitum." ["A body in motion or at rest must have been determined to motion or rest by another body, which itself was determined to motion or rest by another body, and that body by another, and so on *ad infinitum*."]. *E*, Part II, Proposition 13, Lemma 3.

be the original self-existent being. For since the self-existent being is demonstrated to be intelligent, and the material world plainly is not so, it follows that the material world cannot possibly be self-existent. What some have fondly imagined concerning a soul of the world, if thereby they mean a created, dependent being, signifies nothing in the present argument. But if they understand thereby something necessary and self-existent, then it is nothing else but a false, corrupt, and imperfect notion of God.

IX

The self-existent and original cause of all things is not a necessary agent but a being endowed with liberty and choice. The contrary to this proposition is the foundation and the sum of what Spinoza and his followers have asserted concerning the nature of God. What reasons or arguments they have offered for their opinion, I shall have occasion to consider briefly in my proof of the proposition itself.

The truth of which appears first, in that it is a necessary consequence of the foregoing proposition. For intelligence without liberty, as I there hinted, is really (in respect of any power, excellence, or perfection) no intelligence at all. It is indeed a consciousness, but it is merely a passive one, a consciousness not of acting but purely of being acted upon. Without liberty, nothing can in any tolerable propriety of speech be said to be an agent or cause of anything. For to act necessarily is really and properly not to act at all but only to be acted upon. What, therefore, Spinoza and his followers assert concerning the production of all things from the necessity of the divine nature, is mere jargon and words without any meaning at all.[37] For if by the necessity of the divine nature they understand not the perfection and rectitude of his will, whereby God is unalterably determined to do always what is best in the whole (as confessedly they do not, because this is consistent with the most perfect liberty and choice) but, on the contrary, mean an absolute and strictly natural necessity, it follows evidently that when they say [that] God by the necessity of his nature is the cause and author of all things, they understand him to be a cause or agent in no other sense than as if a man should say that a stone, by the necessity of its nature, is the cause of its own falling and striking the ground, which is really not to be an agent or cause at all. But their opinion amounts to

---

[37] "Ex necessitate divinae naturae infinita infinitis modis . . . sequi debent." ["From the necessity of the divine nature there must follow infinite things in infinite ways."]. *E*, Part I, Proposition 16.

46

this, that all things are equally self-existent, and, consequently, that the material world is God, which I have before proved to be a contradiction. In like manner, when they speak of the intelligence and knowledge of God, they mean to attribute these powers to him in no other sense than the ancient hylozoicks attributed them to all matter, that is, that a stone, when it falls, has a sensation and consciousness but that that consciousness is no cause at all, or power of acting, which kind of intelligence in any tolerable propriety of speech is no intelligence at all. And, consequently, the arguments that proved the supreme cause to be properly an intelligent and active being, do also undeniably prove that he is likewise endowed with liberty and choice, which alone is the power of acting.

Secondly, if the supreme cause is not a being endowed with liberty and choice, but a mere necessary agent whose actions are all as absolutely and naturally necessary as his existence, then it will follow that nothing which is not, could possibly have been; and that nothing which is, could possibly not have been; and that no mode or circumstance of the existence of anything could possibly have been in any respect otherwise than it now actually is. All [of] which being evidently most false and absurd, it follows on the contrary that the supreme cause is not a mere necessary agent, but a being endowed with liberty and choice.

The consequence, viz., that if the supreme cause be a necessary agent then nothing which is not could possibly have been, and nothing which is could possibly either not have been or have been different from what it is – this, I say, is expressly owned by Spinoza to be the unavoidable consequence of his own opinion.[38] And accordingly, he endeavors to maintain

[38] "Alii putant, Deum esse causam liberam, propterea quod potest, ut putant, efficere ut ea, quae ex eius natura sequi diximus, hoc est, quae *in eius potestate sunt*, non fiant ... Sed hoc idem est, ac si dicerent, quod Deus potest efficere, ut ex natura trianguli non sequatur eius tres angulos aequales esse duobus rectis ... Ego me satis clare ostendisse puto ... a summa Dei potentia ... *omnia* necessario effluxisse, vel semper eadem necessitate sequi, eodem modo, ac ex natura trianguli ab aeterno, et in aeternum sequitur, eius tres angulos aequari duobus rectis." ["Others think that God is a free cause because, as they think, he can bring it about that those things which we said follow from his nature, that is, *which are in his power*, should not come about... But this is the same as if they said that God can bring it about that it should not follow from the nature of a triangle that its three angles are equal to two right ones... I think I have shown quite clearly ... that from God's supreme power ... *all things* have necessarily flowed or always flow with the same necessity in the same way in which, from the nature of a triangle, from eternity and to eternity it follows that its three angles equal two right angles." Italics by Clarke]. *E*, Part I, Proposition 17, Scholium.

"... omnia ex necessitate naturae divinae determinata sunt, non tantum ad existendum, sed etiam ad certo modo existendum, et operandum, nullumque datur contingens." ["... all things are determined from the necessity of the divine nature not only to exist but also to exist and act in a definite way, and there is no contingency."]. *E*, Part I, Proposition 29, Proof.   *Cont'd*

47

that no thing or mode of existence of any thing could possibly have been in any respect different from what now actually is. His reasons are: (1) because from an infinitely perfect nature infinite things in infinite manners must needs proceed; and (2) because if any thing could possibly be otherwise than it is, the will and nature of God must be supposed capable of change; and (3) because if all possible things in all possible manners do not always necessarily exist, [then] they never can all exist, but some things that do not exist will still always be possible only and never can actually exist; and so the actual omnipotence of God is taken away.³⁹ The first of these arguments is a plain begging of the question. For, that an infinitely perfect nature is able indeed to produce infinite things in infinite manners is certainly true. But that it must always actually do so by an absolute necessity of nature, without any power of choice either as to time or manner of circumstances, does by no means follow from the perfection of its nature, unless it be first supposed to be a necessary agent, and also that in mere

Footnote 38 continued

"Si ... res alterius naturae potuissent esse, vel alio modo ad operandum determinari, ut naturae ordo alius esset; ergo Dei etiam natura alia posset esse, quam iam est." ["If ... things could have been of a different nature or been determined to act differently so that the order of nature would have been different, then also God's nature could have been different from what it is."]. *E*, Part I, Proposition 33, Proof.

"Quicquid concipimus in Dei potestate esse, id necessario est." ["Whatever we conceive to be in God's power necessarily exists."]. *E*, Part I, Proposition 35.

"...Deum non operari ex libertate voluntatis." ["... God does not act from freedom of the will."]. *E*, Part I, Proposition 32, Corollary I.

"Res nullo alio modo, neque alio ordine a Deo produci potuerunt, quam productae sunt." ["Things could not have been produced by God in any other way or order than they have been produced."]. *E*, Part I, Proposition 33.

³⁹ "Ex necessitate divinae naturae, infinita infinitis modis ... sequi debent." ["From the necessity of the divine nature there must follow infinite things in infinite ways ..."]. *E*, Part I, Proposition 16.

"Si ... res alterius naturae potuissent esse, vel alio modo ad operandum determinari, ut naturae ordo alius esset; ergo Dei etiam natura alia posset esse, quam iam est." ["If ... things could have been of a different nature or been determined to act differently so that the order of nature would have been different, then also God's nature could have been different from what it is."]. *E*, Part I, Proposition 33, Proof.

"Immo adversarii {*qui negant ex necessitate divinae naturae omnia necessario fluere*} Dei omnipotentiam ... negare videntur. Coguntur enim fateri, Deum infinita creabilia intelligere, quae tamen nunquam creare poterit. Nam alias, si scilicet omnia, quae intelligit, crearet, suam, juxta ipsos, exhauriret omnipotentiam, et se imperfectum redderet. Ut igitur Deum perfectum statuant, eo rediguntur, ut simul statuere debeant, ipsum non posse omnia efficere, ad quae eius potentia se extendit ..." ["Indeed my opponents {*who deny that all things flow necessarily from the necessity of the divine nature*} seem to deny ... God's omnipotence. In fact, they are compelled to admit that God understands an infinite number of creatable things which nevertheless he can never create. For if it were not so, that is, if he were to create all that he understands, according to them he would exhaust his omnipotence and make himself imperfect. Thus, in order to affirm that God is perfect, they are reduced to affirm at the same time that he cannot bring about all that is within the bounds of his power ..."]. *E*, Part I, Proposition 17, Corollary.

necessity there must be all, or can be any, variety. Both which suppositions are the very question begged that was to be proved. The second argument is, if possible, still weaker. For how does it follow, if God according to his eternal unerring purpose and infinite wisdom produces different things at different times and in different manners, that therefore the will and nature of God is changeable? It might exactly as well be argued that if God, according to Spinoza's supposition, does always necessarily produce all possible differences and varieties of things, therefore his will and nature is always necessarily infinitely various, unequal, and dissimilar to itself. And as to the third argument, which is mere metaphysical trifling, it is just such reasoning as if a man should argue that if all possible eternal duration be not always actually exhausted, it never can be all exhausted, and that therefore so the eternity of God is taken away. Which sort of arguing, everyone at first sight discerns the weakness of.

But whatever the arguments were, and if they were never so much more plausible than they really are, yet the assertion itself, viz., that no thing or mode of existence of anything could possibly have been made in any respect different from what it actually is, is so palpably absurd and false, so contradictory to experience and the nature of things, and to the most obvious and common reasons of mankind, that of itself it immediately and upon the first hearing sufficiently confutes any principle of which it is a consequence. For all things in the world appear plainly to be the most arbitrary that can be imagined, and to be wholly the effects not of necessity but of wisdom and choice. A necessity indeed of *fitness*, that is, that things could not have been otherwise than they are without diminishing the beauty, order, and well-being of the whole, there may be and, as far as we can apprehend, there certainly is. But this is so far from serving our adversaries' purpose, that on the contrary it is direct demonstration that all things were made and ordered by a free and wise agent.

That, therefore, which I affirm, contradictory to Spinoza's assertion, is that there is not the least appearance of an absolute necessity of nature (so as that any variation would imply a contradiction) in many of these things. Motion itself and all its quantities and directions with the laws of gravitation are entirely arbitrary, and might possibly have been altogether different from what they now are. The number and motion of the heavenly bodies have no manner of necessity in the nature of the things themselves. The number of the planets might have been greater or less. Their motion about their own axis might have been in any proportion swifter or slower that it now is. And the direction of all their progressive motions, both of the primary and secondary planets, uniformly from west to east (when by the motion of comets it appears there was no necessity, but that they might as easily have moved in all imaginable transverse directions), is an evident proof that these things are solely the effect of wisdom and choice.[40] There is not the least appearance of necessity, but that all these things might possibly have been infinitely varied from their present constitution and, as the late improvements in astronomy discover, they are actually liable to very great changes. Everything upon Earth is still more evidently arbitrary and plainly the product not of necessity, but will. What absolute necessity for just such a number of species of animals or plants? Or who without blushing dare affirm that neither the form, nor order, not any the minutest circumstance or mode of existence of any of these things, could possibly have been in the least diversified by the supreme cause?[41]

To give but one instance, in all the greater species of animals where was the necessity for that conformity we observe in the number and likeness of all their principal members?[42] And how would it have been a contradiction to suppose any or all of them varied from what they now are? To suppose indeed the continuance of such monsters, as Lucretius imagines to have perished for want of the principal organs of life, is really a contradiction. But how would it have been a contradiction for a whole species of horse or oxen to have subsisted with six legs or four eyes? But it is a shame to insist longer upon so plain an argument.

It might have been objected with much more plausibility that the

---

40 "... Nam dum cometae moventur in orbibus valde eccentricis undique et quoquoversum in omnes caeli partes, utique nullo modo fieri potuit ut caeco fato tribuendum sit quod planetae in orbibus concentricis motu consimili ferantur eodem omnes ... Tam miram uniformitatem in planetarum systemate necessario fatendum est intelliegentia et consilio fuisse effectam." ["... For while comets move in very eccentric orbits in all manner of positions in all parts of the heavens, blind fate could never make all the planets move one and the same way in concentric orbits ... Such a wonderful uniformity in the planetary system must be allowed the effect of intelligence and choice."]. I. Newton, *Optice: sive de Reflexionibus, Refractionibus & Coloribus Lucis libri tres*, trans. S. Clarke. (London, 1706), Quaestio 23, p. 345.

41 "Res nullo alio modo, neque alio ordine a Deo produci potuerunt, quam productae sunt." ["Things could not have been produced by God in any other way or order than they have been produced."]. See above [note 38].

42 "... idemque dici possit de *uniformitate* illa quae est in corporibus animalium ... viz., necessario fatendum est intelligentia et consilio fuisse effectam." ["... the same can be said of the *uniformity* in the bodies of animals ... viz., that it must be allowed the effect of intelligence and choice." Italics by Clarke.]. I. Newton, *Optice: sive de Reflexionibus, Refractionibus & Coloribus Lucis libri tres*, trans. S. Clarke. (London, 1706), Quaestio 23, p. 346. [In *Optice*, the part starting with "viz.," comes earlier than the part starting with "Idemque"; however, Clarke captures Newton's sense correctly.]

supreme cause cannot be free because he must needs do always what is best in the whole. But this would not at all serve Spinoza's purpose. For this is a necessity not of nature and fate, but of fitness and wisdom, a necessity consistent with the greatest freedom and most perfect choice. For the only foundation of this necessity is such an unalterable rectitude of will and perfection of wisdom as makes it impossible for a wise being to resolve to act foolishly, or for a nature infinitely good to choose to do that which is evil. Of which I shall have occasion to speak more hereafter, when I come to deduce the moral attributes of God.

Thirdly, if there be any final cause of anything in the universe, then the supreme cause is not a necessary but a free agent. This consequence also Spinoza acknowledges to be unavoidable. And therefore he has no other way left but with a strange confidence to expose all final causes as the fictions of ignorant and superstitious men, and to laugh at those who are so foolish and childish as to fancy that eyes were designed and fitted to see with, teeth to chew with, food to be eaten for nourishment, the sun to give light, etc.[43] I suppose it will not be thought that when once a man comes to this, he is to be disputed with any longer. Whosoever pleases, may for satisfaction under this head consult Galen, *De Usu Partium*, Tully, *De Natura Deorum*, Mr. Boyle, *Of Final Causes*, and Mr. Ray, *Of the Wisdom of God in the Creation*. I shall only observe this one thing, that the larger the improvements and discoveries are which are daily made in astronomy and natural philosophy, the more clearly is this question continually determined to the shame and confusion of atheists.

Fourthly, if the supreme cause be a mere necessary agent, it is impossible any effect or product of that cause should be finite. For since that which acts necessarily cannot govern or direct its own actions, but must necessarily produce whatever can be the effect or product of its nature, it is plain every effect of such an infinite uniform nature acting everywhere

---

[43] "Naturam finem nullum sibi praefixum habere, et omnes causas finales nihil nisi humana esse figmenta." ["Nature has no fixed goal, and all final causes are but figments of human imagination."]. *E*, Part I, Proposition 36, Appendix.

"Oculos ad videndum, dentes ad masticandum, herbas, et animantia ad alimentum, solem ad illuminandum, marem ad alendum pisces" etc. ["Eyes for seeing, teeth for chewing, plants and animals for food, the Sun for giving light, the sea for breeding fishes," etc.]. *E*, Part I, Proposition 36, Appendix.

"Nullas unquam rationes circa res naturales, a *fine* quem Deus aut natura in iis faciendas sibi proposuit, desumemus ..." ["When dealing with natural things we will, then, never derive any explanations from the *purpose* which God or nature may have had in making them ..." Italics by Clarke.]. R. Descartes, *Principles of Philosophy*, Part I, Principle 28.

necessarily alike must of necessity be immense or infinite in extension. And so, no creature in the universe could possibly be finite, which is infinitely absurd and contrary to experience. Spinoza, to shuffle off this absurdity, expresses the consequence of his doctrine thus: that "from the necessity of the divine nature, infinite things (meaning infinite in number) in infinite manners must needs follow."[44] But whoever reads his demonstration of this proposition can hardly fail to observe (if he be at all used to such speculations) that if it proved anything at all, it would equally prove that "from the necessity of the divine nature, only infinite things (meaning infinite in extension) can possibly arise." Which demonstration alone is a sufficient confutation of the opinion it was devised to establish.

Fifthly, if the supreme cause be not a free and voluntary agent, then in every effect, for instance in motion, there must have been a progression of causes *in infinitum*, without any original cause at all. For if there be no liberty anywhere, then there is no agent, no cause, mover, principle, or beginning of motion anywhere. Everything in the universe must be passive and nothing active, everything moved and no mover, everything effect and nothing cause. Spinoza, indeed, as has been already observed, refers all things to the necessity of the divine nature as their real cause and original; but this is mere jargon and words without any signification, and will not at all help him over the present difficulty. For if by things existing through the necessity of the divine nature, he means "absolutely a necessity of existence" so as to make the world and everything in it self-existent, then it follows (as I have before shown) that it must be a contradiction in terms to suppose motion etc. not to exist, which Spinoza himself is ashamed to assert. But if, therefore, by the "necessity of the divine nature" he means only the "necessary following of an effect from its cause" or the cause necessarily producing its effect, this necessity must still always be determined by something antecedent, and so on infinitely. And this, Spinoza (though sometimes he seems to mean the other and equally absurd sense) expressly owns in some places to be his meaning. There can be no volition, says he, but from some cause, which cause must likewise be caused by some other cause, and so on infinitely.[45] Again, will, says he, belongs to the nature of God no otherwise than motion and rest do, so that God can no more properly

---

[44] "Ex necessitate divinae naturae, infinita infinitis modis. . .sequi debent." *E*, Part I, Proposition 16.
[45] ". . . unaquaeque volitio non potest existere, neque ad operandum determinari, nisi ab alia causa determinetur, et haec rursus ab alia, et sic porro in infinitum." [". . . no volition can exist or be determined to act but by being determined by another cause, and this cause again by another, and so on *ad infinitum*."]. *E*, Part I, Proposition 32, Proof.

be said to act by the liberty of his will than by the liberty of motion and rest.[46] And what the original of motion and rest is, he tells us in these words: "Every body in motion or at rest must have been determined to that motion or rest by some other body, which must itself likewise have been determined by a third, and so on in infinitum."[47] And thus, since motion is not in any one of its stages of communication a necessary self-existent being (because the body moved may always without a contradiction have been imagined to be at rest, and is supposed not to have motion from itself but from another), the opinion of Spinoza plainly recurs to an infinite succession of dependent beings produced one from another in an endless progression, without any original cause at all. Which notion I have already, in the proof of the second general head of this discourse, demonstrated to imply a contradiction. And since, therefore, there is no other possible way to avoid this absurdity but by granting that there must be somewhere a principle of motion and action, which is liberty, I suppose it by this time sufficiently proved that the supreme cause must be a being endowed with liberty and choice.

From what has been said upon this head it sufficiently appears that liberty is not in itself, and in the very notion of the thing, an absolute contradiction and impossibility, as the pleaders for necessity and fate contend it is and place the chief strength of their argument in that supposition. For that which actually is, is certainly not impossible. And it has already been proved that liberty actually is; nay, that it is impossible for it not to be in the first and supreme cause. The principal argument used by the maintainers of fate against the possibility of liberty is this: that, since everything must have a cause, every volition or determination of the will of an intelligent being must, as all other things, arise from some cause, and that cause from some other cause, and so on infinitely.[48] But now (besides that in this

---

[46] "... voluntas ad Dei naturam non magis pertinet, quam reliqua naturalia; sed ad ipsam eodem modo sese habet ut, motus, et quies ..." ["... will pertains to God's nature no more than other natural things do; it has the same relation to God's nature as motion and rest ..."]. *E*, Part I, Proposition 32, Corollary 2.

"... Deus non magis dici potest ex libertate voluntatis agere, quam ... dici potest ex libertate motus et quietis agere." ["... God cannot be said to act from freedom of the will any more than...from freedom of motion and rest."]. *E*, Part I, Proposition 32, Corollary 2.

[47] "Corpus motum, vel quiescens ad motum, vel quietem determinari debuit ab alio corpore, quod etiam ad motum, vel quietem determinatum fuit ab alio, et illud iterum ab alio, et sic in infinitum." *E*, Part II, Proposition 13, Lemma 3.

[48] "... mens ad hoc, vel illud volendum determinatur a causa, quae etiam ab alia determinata est, et haec iterum ab alia et sic in infinitum." ["... the mind is determined to will this or that by a cause, which is itself determined by another cause, and this again by another, and so on to infinity."]. *E*, Part II, Proposition 48.

sort of reasoning these men always ignorantly confound moral motives with physical efficients, between which two things there is no manner of relation) – besides this, I say, this very argument really proves the direct contrary to what they intend. For since everything must indeed have a cause of its being, either from without or in the necessity of its own nature, and it is a plain contradiction (as has already been demonstrated) to suppose an infinite series of dependent effects none of which are necessary in themselves or self-existent, therefore it is impossible but there must be in the universe some being whose existence is founded in the necessity of its own nature and which, being acted upon by nothing beyond itself, must of necessity have *in itself* a principle of acting, or power of beginning motion, which is the idea of liberty. It is true this argument proves only the liberty of the first and supreme cause and extends not indeed to any created being. But it evinces in general (which is sufficient to my present purpose) that liberty is so far from being impossible and contradictory in itself, that on the contrary it is impossible but that it must really be somewhere. And this being once established, it will be easy to show hereafter that it is a power capable of being communicated to created beings. Of which, in its proper place.

X

The *self-existent being, the supreme cause of all things, must of necessity have infinite power*. This proposition is evident and undeniable. For since nothing (as has been already proved) can possibly be self-existent besides himself, and consequently all things in the universe were made by him and are entirely dependent upon him, and all the powers of all things are derived from him and must therefore be perfectly subject and subordinate to him, it is manifest that nothing can make any difficulty and resistance to the execution of his will, but he must of necessity have absolute power to do everything he pleases with the most perfect ease and in the most perfect manner at once and in a moment, whenever he wills it. The descriptions the Scripture gives of this power are so lively and emphatic that I cannot forbear mentioning one or two passages. Thus *Job*, ix, 4 [ff.]: "He is wise in heart and mighty in strength ... {*which*} removeth the mountains, and they know it not; which overturneth them in his anger. Which shaketh the Earth out of her place and the pillars thereof tremble. Which commandeth the Sun, and it raiseth not; and sealeth up the stars. Which alone spreadeth out the heavens and treadeth upon the waters of the sea ... Which doth great things past finding out, yea and wonders without number." Again, "Hell is naked before him and destruction hath no covering ... He stretcheth out the North over the empty place, and hangeth the Earth upon nothing ... He bindeth up the waters in his thick clouds, and the cloud is not rent under them ... The Pillars of heaven tremble and are astonished at his reproof. He divideth the sea with his power and by his understanding he smiteth through the proud ... Lo, these are part of his ways, but how little a portion is heard of him? But the thunder of his power, who can understand?" *Job*, xxvi, 6 [ff.]. So likewise, *Isaiah*, xl, 12 [ff.]. "Who has measured the waters in the hollow of his hand, and meted out heaven with the span, and comprehended the dust of the earth in a measure, and weighed the mountains in scales, and the hills in a balance ... Behold, the nations are as a drop of the bucket and are counted as the small dust of the balance; behold, he taketh up the isles as a very little thing ... All nations before him are nothing, and they are counted to him less than nothing, and vanity. To whom then will ye liken God, or what likeness will ye compare unto him?" But I do not urge authority to the persons I am at present speaking to. It is sufficiently evident from reason that the supreme cause must of necessity be infinitely powerful. The only question is what the true meaning of what we call infinite power is, and to what things it must be understood to extend, or not to extend.

Now in determining this question, there are some propositions about which there is no dispute, which therefore I shall but just mention, as:

Firstly, that infinite power reaches to all possible things, but cannot be said to extend to the working [of] anything which implies a contradiction, as that a thing should be and not be at the same time; that the same things should be made and not be made, or have been and not have been; that twice two should not make four, or that that which is necessarily false should be true. The reason whereof is plain, because the power of making a thing to be at the same time that it is not, is only a power of doing that which is nothing, that is no power at all.

Secondly, infinite power cannot be said to extend to those things which imply natural imperfection in the thing to whom such power is ascribed, as that it should destroy its own being, weaken itself or the like. These things imply natural imperfection, and are by all men confessed to be such as cannot possibly belong to the necessary self-existent being. There are also other things which imply imperfection of another kind, viz., moral imperfection, concerning which atheism takes away the subject of the question by denying wholly the difference of moral good and evil, and therefore I shall omit the consideration of them untill I come to deduce the moral attributes of God.

But some other instances there are in the question about the extent of infinite power wherein the principal difference between us and the atheists (next to the question whether the supreme cause be an intelligent being or not) does in great measure consist. As:

Firstly, that infinite power includes a power of creating matter. This has been constantly denied by all atheists both ancient and modern, and as constantly affirmed by all who believe the being, and have just notions of the attributes, of God. The only reason why the atheists have or can pretend to allege for their opinion is that the thing is in its own nature absolutely impossible. But how does it appear to be impossible? Why, only because they are not able to comprehend how it can be. For to reduce it to a contradiction, which is the alone real impossibility, this they are by no means able to do. For to say that something which once was not may since have begun to exist is neither directly, nor by any consequence what-soever, to assert that that which is not can be while it is not; or that that which is can not-be while it is. It is true; we, who have been used to con-verse only with generations and corruptions and never saw anything made or created but only formed or framed, are apt to endeavor to conform our idea of creation to that of formation, and to imagine that, as in all formations there is some pre-existing matter out of which a thing is formed, so in creation there must be considered a pre-existing nothing out of which, as out of a real material cause, a thing is created; which looks indeed very like a contradiction. But this is only a confusion of ideas, just like children's imagining that darkness is some real thing which, in the morning, is driven away by the light or transformed into it. Whereas the true notion of creation is not a forming something out of nothing as out of a material cause, but only a bringing something into being that before had no being at all, or a causing something to exist now that did not exist before, or which, without this cause, would not have existed. Which no man can ever reduce to a contradiction any more than the formation of anything into a shape which it had not before can be reduced to a contradiction.

But further, the creation of matter is a thing not only not impossible in itself but what moreover, even by bare reason, is demonstrated to be true.

For it is a contradiction, as I have shown above, to suppose matter necessarily existing.

Secondly, it is possible to infinite power to create an immaterial cogitative substance endowed with a power of beginning motion, and with a liberty of will or choice. This also has been always denied by all atheists. And because it is a proposition of the greatest consequence to religion and morality, therefore I shall be particular in endeavoring the proof of the several parts of it.

we're not just material reality

Firstly, it is possible to infinite power to create an immaterial cogitative substance. That there can be such a thing as a cogitative substance, that is, a substance endowed with consciousness and thought, is granted by all because every man's own experience convinces him that he himself is such a substance. Further, that if there be or can be any such thing as immaterial substances, then it is most reasonable to believe that substances as are endowed with consciousness and thought (properties the farthest distant from the known properties of matter, and the most unlike them that can possibly be imagined) are those immaterial substances, this also will, I think, be granted by all men. The only point, therefore, that remains to be proved is that immaterial substances are not impossible, or that a substance immaterial is not a contradictory notion.

Now whoever asserts that it is contradictory must affirm that whatever is not matter is nothing, and that to say anything exists which is not matter is saying that there exists something which is nothing. Which in other words is plainly this, that whatever we have not an idea of, is nothing and impossible to be. For there is no other way to reduce "immaterial substance" to a contradiction but by supposing "immaterial" to signify the same as having no existence. And there is no possible way to prove that but by saying we have no idea of it, and therefore it neither has nor can have any existence. By which same argument "material substance" will in like manner be a contradiction, for of that also (viz., of the substance to which solidity belongs) we have no idea. But supposing it were true (as it is indeed most false) that we had a clearer idea of the substance of matter than we have of immaterial substance, still, by the same argument wherewith an atheist will prove immaterial substance to be impossible, a man born blind may demonstrate irrefragably that light or color is an impossible and contradictory notion because it is not a sound or a smell. For the power of seeing light or color is to a man born blind altogether as incomprehensible and absolutely beyond the reach of all his ideas as either the operations and perceptions, or even the simple essence, of a pure immaterial substance or spirit can be to any of us. If, therefore, the blind man's want of ideas be not a sufficient proof of the impossibility of light or color, how comes our bare want of ideas to be a demonstration of the impossibility of the being of immaterial substances? A blind man, they will say, has testimony of the existence of light. Very true. So also have we of the existence of immaterial substances.

But there is this further advantage on our side in the comparison, that a blind man accepting the testimony of others finds not by any reasoning within himself the least likelihood or probability, no not in the lowest possible degree, that there can be any such thing as light or color. But we, besides testimony, have great and strong arguments both from experience and reason that there are such things as immaterial substances, though we have no knowledge of their simple essence, as indeed of the substance even of matter itself (its simple substance, considered as abstract from and as the foundation of that essential property of solidity) we have no idea. For to say that extension is the substance of matter is the same way of think-ing as to say that existence, or that duration, is the substance of matter. We have, I say, great and strong arguments both from experience and reason that there are such things as immaterial substances, though we have no idea of their simple essence. Even the very first and most universal principle of gravitation itself in all matter, since it is ever proportional not at all to the surfaces of bodies or of their particles, in any possible supposition, but exactly to the solid content of bodies, it is evident it cannot be caused by matter acting upon the surfaces of matter, which is all it [i.e., matter] can do, but must either immediately or mediately be caused by something which continually penetrates its solid substance. But in animals, which have a power of self-motion, and in the more perfect sorts of them, which have still higher faculties, the thing is yet more evident. For we see and feel, and observe daily in ourselves and others, such powers and operations and perceptions as undeniably evince themselves either to be the properties of immaterial substances; or else it will follow that matter is something of whose essential powers (as well as of its substance itself) we have altogether as little idea as we have of immaterial beings. And then, how are immaterial substances more impossible than material? But of this more hereafter.

From what has been said on this head, it will be easy to answer all the objections that have been brought by any atheists against the notion of human souls being immaterial substances and distinct from body. For, since it is possible there may be such things as immaterial substances, and since if any such substances can be, there is all the reason in the world to believe that conscious and thinking substance is such (these properties being the most remote from the known properties of matter that are possible to be conceived), the foundation of all the objections against the immateriality of the soul is entirely taken away. I shall not here tarry to consider the objections in particular which have been often and wholly answered by learned pens, but shall only mention one on which all the rest depend and to which they may all be reduced. And it is this: that seeing the only means we have of perception are the five senses, and these all plainly depend upon the organs of the body, therefore the soul without the body can have no perception, and consequently is nothing.[49] Now, besides that these very senses or perceptions, however they may be obstructed by bodily indisposition (and so do indeed depend upon the organs of the body as to their present exercise), yet in their nature are really entirely distinct powers and cannot possibly, as has been before shown, be absolutely founded in, or arise from, any of the known properties or qualities of

[49] "... si immortalis natura animae est,
et sentire potest secreta a corpore nostro,
quinque, ut opinor, eam faciendum est *sensibus* auctam;
nec ratione alia nosmet proponere nobis
possumus infernas animas Acherunte vagari.
Pictores itaque et scriptorum saecla priora
sic animas intro duxerunt sensibus auctas.
At neque seorsum oculi ..." etc.
"... Ne sensus ipsi seorsum consistere possunt
naribus atque manu, atque oculis, atque auribus, atque
lingua; nec per se possunt sentire, nec esse."

["... if the nature of the soul is immortal and can feel when separated from the body, I assume that it is endowed with the *five senses*; nor in any other way can we represent to ourselves the spirits below wandering in Acheron. Painters and writers of earlier times, therefore, have represented souls thus, endowed with senses. But apart from the body there can be no eyes ..." etc.]. T. Lucretius Caro, *De Rerum Natura*, book 3, vv. 624–31.

["The senses cannot stand on their own apart from the nostrils, the hands, the eyes, the ears, and the tongue, nor feel or exist on their own."]. The last three verses from Clarke's quotation are not in the standard editions of Lucretius' book. However, they were proposed by Dionysius Lambinus (Denys Lambin, 1516–72) as filling an alleged lacuna after v. 633. They are contained in a footnote in *Titi Lucretii Cari De Rerum Natura Libros Sex*, ed. Michael Fayvus (Paris, Federic Leonard, 1680), p. 237. Evidently Clarke accepted Lambinus' addition as justified, although modern critics have rejected it.

"ὅσων γάρ ἐστιν ἀρχῶν ἡ ἐνέργεια σωματική, δῆλον ὅτι ταύτας ἄνευ σώματος ἀ δύνατον ὑπάρχειν, οἷον βαδίζειν ἄνευ ποδῶν." ["Clearly, those principles whose activity is physical cannot exist without a physical body, as, for example, walking without feet."]. Aristotle, *De Generatione Animalium*, 736b19–21.

matter – besides this, I say, of him that thus argues I would only ask this one question. Are our five senses, by an absolute necessity in the nature of the thing, all and the only possible ways of perception? And is it impossible and contradictory that there should be any being in the universe endowed with ways of perception different from these that are the result of our present composition? Or are these things, on the contrary, purely arbitrary, and the same power that gave us these may have given others to other beings, and might, if he had pleased, have given to us others in this present state, and may yet have made us capable of different ones in another state? If they be purely arbitrary, then the want of these does by no means infer a total want of perception. But the same soul which in the present state has the powers of reflection, reason, and judgment, which are faculties entirely different from sense, may as easily in another state have different ways even of perception also. But if anyone will contend that these senses of ours are necessarily the only ways of perception, still the soul may be capable of having these very same ways of perception at any time restored to it. For as that which sees does not cease to exist when in the dark all objects are removed, so that which perceives does not necessarily cease to exist when by death all organs of perception are removed.

But what reason can any man allege why he should imagine these present senses of ours to be necessarily the only ways of perception? Is it not infinitely more reasonable to suppose that this is a mere prejudice arising from custom, and an attending to bare sense in opposition to reason?[50] For supposing men had been created only with four senses and had never known the use of sight, would they not then have had the very same reason to conclude there were but four possible ways of perception as they have now to fancy that there are but five? And would they not then have thought sight to have been an impossible, chimerical, and merely imaginary power, which is absolutely the same reason as they now presume

---

[50] "Has tamen imagines {*mortuorum*} *loqui* volebant, quod fieri nec sine lingua, nec sine palato, nec sine faucium, laterum, pulmonum vi et figura potest. Nihil enim *animo* {*speaking of such as attributed to spirits the same powers and senses only as they saw men endowed with in this present state*} videre poterant; ad oculos omnia referebant. Magni autem ingenii est revocare mentem a sensibus et cogitationem a consuetudine abducere." ["Nonetheless, they [the vulgar] wanted these phantoms {*of the dead*} to speak, which cannot occur without tongue or palate and without the form and activity of the throat, the chest and the lungs. In fact, they {*speaking of such as attributed to spirits the same powers and senses only as they saw men endowed with in this present state*} could not see anything with their souls and brought everything to the bar of eyesight. Indeed, a powerful intellect is required to turn the mind away from the senses and thought from habit."]. M. T. Cicero, *Tusculanae Disputationes*, Book I, Chapter 16.

the faculties of immaterial beings to be so, that is, with no reason at all? One would think men should be ashamed, therefore, to be so vain as, from their own mere negative ignorance, without any appearance or pretence of any positive argument, to dispute against the possibility of the being of things which (excepting only that they cannot frame to themselves an image or notion of them) there is a concurrence of all the reasons in the world to persuade them that such things really are. And then, as to the difficulty of conceiving the nature and manner of the union between soul and body, we know altogether as much of that as we do of the nature of the union or cohesion of the infinitely divisible parts of body, which yet no man doubts of. And therefore, our ignorance can be no more an argument against the truth of the one than it is a bar to our belief of the other.

Secondly, it is possible to infinite power to endow a creature with the power of beginning motion. This is constantly denied by all atheists because the consequence of it is a liberty of will, of which I shall have occasion to speak presently. But that the proposition is true, I thus prove. If the power of beginning motion be in itself a possible thing, and also possible to be communicated, then a creature may be endowed with that power. Now that the power of beginning motion is in itself a possible thing, I have already proved by showing that there must necessarily be somewhere a power of beginning motion because otherwise motion must have been from eternity, without any external cause of its being, and yet it is a thing that has no necessity of existence in its own nature. So that if there be not somewhere a principle or power of beginning motion, motion must exist without any cause or reason at all of its existence either within itself or from without which, as I have before shown, is an express contradiction. Wherefore a principle or power of beginning motion, there must of necessity be somewhere or other, and consequently it is not in itself an impossible thing.

I add: as a power of beginning motion is not itself an impossible thing because it must of necessity be in the supreme cause, so neither is it impossible to be communicated to created beings. The reason is plain, because no powers are impossible to be communicated but only those which imply self-existence and absolute independence. That a subordinate being should be self-existent or absolutely independent is indeed a contradiction. But it is no contradiction to suppose it endowed with any other power whatsoever separate from these. I know the maintainers of fate are very confident that a power of beginning motion is nothing less than being really independent, or being able to act independently from any superior cause.

But this is only a childish trifling with words. For a power of acting independently in this sense, communicated at the pleasure of the supreme cause and continued only during the same good pleasure, is no more a real and absolute independency than the power of existing (which I suppose the defenders of fate are not so fond to make a continual creation, as they are to make the power of self-motion a continual external impulse), or than the power of being conscious, or any other power whatsoever can be said to imply independence. In reality, it is altogether as hard to conceive how consciousness or the power of perception should be communicated to a created being, as how the power of self-motion should be so, unless perception be nothing else but a mere passive reception of impulse, which I suppose is as clear that it is not, as that a triangle is not a sound or that a globe is not a color. Yet no man doubts but that he himself and all others have truly a power of perception. And therefore in like manner, however hard it may be to conceive as to the manner of it, yet, since as has been now proved it can never be shown to be impossible and expressly contradictory that a power of self-motion should be communicated, I suppose no considering man can doubt but that he actually has also a power of self-motion. For the arguments drawn from continual experience and observation to prove that we have such a power are so strong, that nothing less than a strict demonstration that the thing is absolutely impossible and that it implies an express contradiction can make us in the least doubt that we have it not. We have all the same experience, the same marks and evidence exactly of our having really a power of self-motion, as the most rigid fatalist could possibly contrive to require if he was to make the supposition of a man's being endowed with that power. There is no one thing that such a man can imagine ought to follow from the supposition of self-motion, which every man does not now as much feel and actually experience in himself as it can possibly be imagined any man would do, supposing the thing were true.

Wherefore to affirm, notwithstanding all this, that the spirits by which a man moves the members of his body and ranges the thoughts of his mind are themselves moved wholly by air or subtler matter inspired into the body, and that again by other external matter, and so on (as the wheels of a clock are moved by the weights and those weights by gravitation and so on) without a man's having the least power by any principle within himself to think any one thought, or impel his own spirits in order to move any member of his body – all this is so contrary to experience and the reason of things, that unless the idea of self-motion were itself as evidently and clearly a contradiction as that two and two should make five, a man ought to be ashamed to talk at that rate.[b] Nay, a man of any considerable degree of modesty would even in that case be almost tempted rather to doubt the truth of his faculties than take upon him to assert one such intolerable absurdity merely for the avoiding of another. There are some, indeed, who denying man the power of beginning motion would yet seem in some manner to account for their actions by allowing them a power of determining motion.[c] But this also is a mere ludicrous trifling with words. For if that power of determining motion be no other in a man than that which is in a stone to reflect a ball one certain way, this is just nothing at all. But if he has a power of determining the motion of his spirits any way as he himself pleases, this is in all respects the very same as the power of beginning motion.

Thirdly, it is possible to infinite power to endow a creature with freedom or liberty of will. It might suffice that this is at once proved by the same argument and in the same method as I just now proved self-motion or a power of beginning motion to be possible, viz., because liberty must of necessity be in the supreme cause (as is at large proved in the ninth general head of this discourse), and therefore cannot be impossible and contradictory in the nature of the thing itself; and because it implies no contradiction to suppose it communicated (as being no harder to conceive than the aforementioned power of beginning motion); and because the arguments drawn from experience and observation are stronger on the one side of the question, than those arising merely from the difficulty of our apprehending the thing can be on the other. But forasmuch as this is a question of the greatest concern of all in matters both of religion and human life, and both Spinoza and Mr. Hobbes and their followers have with great noise and confidence denied it, I shall therefore, not contenting myself with this, endeavor to show moreover in particular the weakness of the principal arguments by which these men have pretended to demonstrate that there cannot possibly be any such power in men as a liberty of will. As to the propriety of the terms, whether the will be properly the seat

---

[b] Animal spirits were thought to be some sort of subtle fluid flowing through the nerves and instrumental in moving one's body and reacting to bodily impressions. See, for example, Descartes' account in *The Passions of the Soul*, part 1, sections 7–16.

[c] Here Clarke was contrasting initiating or causing new motion with merely modifying an existing motion; for example, by changing its direction.

of liberty or not, is not now to the purpose to enquire, the question being not *where* the seat of liberty is, but *whether* there be at all in man any such power as a liberty of choice and of determining his own actions or, on the contrary, his actions be all as necessary as the motions of a clock. The arguments by which Spinoza and Mr. Hobbes have attempted to maintain the latter side of the question are all plainly reducible to these two.

Firstly, that since every effect must needs be produced by some cause, therefore, as every motion in a body must have been caused by the impulse of some other body, and the motion of that by the impulse of a third, so every volition or determination of the will of man must needs be produced by some external cause. Therefore, as every motion in a body must have been caused by the impulse of some other body, and the motion of that by the impulse of a third, so every volition or determination of the will of man must needs be produced by some external cause, and that in like manner by the effect of some third. And consequently, there cannot possibly be any such thing in nature as liberty or freedom of will.

Secondly, that thinking and all its modes, as willing and the like, are qualities or affections of matter. And, consequently, since it is manifest that matter has not in itself a power of beginning motion or giving itself any manner of determination whatsoever, therefore it is evident likewise that it is impossible there should be any such thing as freedom of will.

Now to these arguments I oppose, and shall endeavor briefly to demonstrate, the three following propositions.

Firstly, that every effect cannot possibly be the product of external causes, but there must of necessity be somewhere a beginning of operation or a power of acting without being antecedently acted upon, and that this power may be, and is, in man.

Secondly, that thinking and willing neither are nor can be qualities and affections of matter, and consequently are not concluded under the laws thereof.

Thirdly, that even supposing the soul not to be a distinct substance from body, but that thinking and willing could be, and were indeed, only qualities or affections of matter, yet even this would not at all affect the present question, nor prove freedom of will to be impossible.

Firstly, every effect cannot possibly be the product of external causes, but there must of necessity be somewhere a beginning of operation, or a power of acting without being antecedently acted upon, and this power may be, and is, in man. The several parts of this proposition have been already proved in the second and ninth general heads of this discourse, and in that part of this tenth head which is concerning the possibility of the power of self-motion being communicated to created beings. I shall not, therefore, here repeat the proofs, but only apply them to Spinoza's and Mr. Hobbes's arguments, so far as is necessary to show the weakness of what they have said upon this head in opposition to the possibility of liberty or freedom of will. Now the manner of their arguing upon this head is this: that every effect must needs be owing to some cause, and that cause must produce the effect necessarily, because if it be a sufficient cause, the effect cannot but follow, and if it be not a sufficient cause, it will not be at all a cause of that thing (thus, for instance, whatever body is moved must be moved by some other body, which itself, likewise, must be moved by some third, and so on without end); that the will, in like manner, of any voluntary agent must of necessity be determined by some external cause and not by any power of determining itself inherent in itself, and that external cause must be determined necessarily by some other cause external to it, and so on without end.[51]

From all which it evidently appears that all that these men urge against the possibility of freedom extends equally to all other beings (not excepting the supreme) as well as to man; and Spinoza in express words confesses

---

[51] "... Quicumque unquam effectus productus sit, productus est a causa necessaria. Nam quod productum est ... causam habuit integram, hoc est, omnia ea quibus suppositis effectum non sequi intelligi non possit, ea vero causa necessaria est." ["... Whatsoever effect is produced at any time, is produced by a necessary cause. In fact what is produced ... had a complete cause, that is, all that which being supposed, it is unintelligible how the effect would not follow, for that cause is a necessary one."]. T. Hobbes, *De corpore*, Part II, Chapter 9, Section 5.

"Corpus motum, vel quiescens ad motum, vel quietem determinari debuit ab alio corpore, quod etiam ad motum, vel quietem determinatum fuit ab alio, et illud iterum ab alio, et sic in infinitum." ["A body in motion or at rest must have been determined to motion or rest by another body, which itself was determined to motion or rest by another body, and that body by another, and so on *ad infinitum*."]. *E*, Part II, Proposition 13, Lemma 3.

"... unaquaeque volitio non potest existere, neque ad operandum determinari, nisi ab alia causa determinetur, et haec rursus ab alia, et sic porro in infinitum." ["... no volition can exist or be determined to act but by being determined by another cause, and this cause again by another, and so on *ad infinitum*."]. *E*, Part I, Proposition 32, Proof.

"I conceive nothing taketh beginning from itself, but from the action of some immediate agent without itself. And that therefore, when first a man had an appetite or will to something to which immediately before he had no appetite or will, the cause of his will is not the will itself but something else not in his own disposing." Hobbes' debate with Bishop Bramhall, in *The English Works of Thomas Hobbes*, ed. W. Molesworth (London, John Bohn, 1849; reprint Darmstadt, Scientia Verlag, 1966), vol. 5, pp. 372–3.

"In mente nulla est absoluta sive libera voluntas, sed mens ad hoc vel illud volendum determinatur a causa quae etiam ab alia determinata est, et haec iterum ab alia, et sic in infinitum." ["In the mind there is no absolute or free will. The mind is determined to will this or that by a cause which is also determined by another cause, which is itself determined by another, and so on *ad infinitum*."]. *E*, Part II, Proposition 48.

it.[52] Wherefore, consequently, whatever noise they make of the strength and demonstrative force of their arguments, all that they say amounts at last to no more but this one most absurd conclusion: that there neither is anywhere, nor can possibly be, any principle of motion or beginning of operation at all, but everything is caused necessarily by an eternal chain of dependent causes and effects, without any independent original. All their arguments, therefore, on this head are already answered in the second and ninth general heads of this discourse, where I proved that there must of necessity be an original, independent, and free principle of motion or action, and that to suppose an endless succession of dependent causes and effects, without any original or first and self-actuating principle, is supposing a series of dependent things to be from eternity produced by nothing, which is the very same absurdity and contradiction as to suppose things produced by nothing at any definite time (the ability of nothing to produce anything being plainly the same in time or in eternity). And I have, moreover, proved *ex abundanti* [abundantly] in the foregoing part of this tenth head that the power of beginning motion is not only possible and certain in itself, but also possible to be communicated to finite beings, and that it actually is in man.

Secondly, thinking and willing neither are, nor can be, qualities or affections of matter, and consequently are not concluded under the laws thereof. That it is possible there may be immaterial substances, the notion not implying a contradiction in itself, has already been shown under the present general proposition. Further, that thinking and willing are powers entirely different from solidity, figure, and motion, and if they be different that then they cannot possibly arise from them or be compounded of them, has likewise been already proved under the eighth general head of this discourse. It follows, therefore, that thinking and willing may possibly be, nay, that they certainly and necessarily are, faculties or powers of immaterial substances, seeing they cannot possibly be qualities or affections of matter (unless we will confound, as some have done, the ideas of things, and mean by "matter" not what that word in all other cases signifies, a solid substance capable of division, figure and motion, and of whatever properties can arise from the modifications of these, but substance in general, capable of unknown powers or properties entirely different from these and from whatever can possibly result from these). In which confused sense of the word, could matter be supposed never so capable of thinking and willing;

---

[52] "Hinc sequitur *Deum* non operari ex libertate voluntatis." ["Hence it follows that *God* does not act from freedom of the will."]. *E*, Part I, Proposition 32, Corollary 1.

yet in that sense, as I shall show presently, it would signify nothing at all to the purpose or advantage of our adversaries.

In the meantime, how great an absurdity it is to suppose thinking and willing to be qualities or affections of matter, in the proper and usual sense of the word, may sufficiently appear without any foreign argument from the senselessness of Mr. Hobbes's own explication of the nature and original of sensation and consciousness. The immediate cause of sensation, says he, is this: the object, or something flowing from it, presses the outermost part of the organ, and that pressure is communicated to the innermost parts of the organ where, by the resistance or reaction of the organ causing a pressure outwards contrary to the pressure of the object inwards, there is made up a phantasm or image, which phantasm, says he, is the sensation itself.[53] Again, the cause of sensation, says he, is an object pressing the organ, which pressure is by means of the nerves conveyed to the brain and so to the heart where, by the resistance or counterpressure of the heart outwards, is made an image or phantasm, which is sensation.[54] Now

---

[53] "... ex quo intelligitur sensionis immediatam causam esse in eo, quod sensionis organum primum et tangit at premit. Si enim organi pars extima prematur, illa cedente premetur quoque pars, quae versus interiora illi proxima est, et ita propagabitur pressio sive motus ille per partes omnes usque ad intimam ... Quoniam {*autem*} ... motui, ab objecto per media ad organi partem intimam propagato, fit aliqua totius organi resistentia sive reactio, per motum ipsius organi internum naturalem, fit propterea conatui ab obiecto conatus ab organo contrarius; ut cum conatus ille ad intima ultimus actus sit eorum qui fiunt in actu sensionis, tum demum ex ea reactione aliquandiu durante ipsum existat *phantasma*; quod propter conatum versus externa, semper videtur ... tanquam aliquid situm extra organum." ["... from which it is clear that the immediate cause of sensation is in that which touches and presses the first organ of sense. In fact, when the outermost part of the organ is pressed, as it yields the part next within is pressed as well, and in this way that pressure or motion is transmitted through all the parts of the organ to the innermost ... Hence, as there is in the whole organ, because of its internal natural motion, a resistance or reaction to the motion which is transmitted through mediums from the object to the inner part of the organ, there is also in the organ an endeavor opposite to that of the object. Hence, when that endeavor inwards is the last action among those occurring in the act of sensation, then from the reaction, no matter how short, arises a *phantasm* which, since the endeavor is outwards, always seems ... something located outside the organ."]. T. Hobbes, *De Corpore*, Part IV, Chapter 25, Section 2.

"... Phantasma est sentiendi actus." ["... The phantasm is the act of sense."]. T. Hobbes, *De Corpore*, Part IV, Chapter 25, Section. 3.

[54] "Causa sensionis est externum corpus sive obiectum quod premit organum proprium ... et premendo (mediantibus nervis ... et membranis) continuum efficit motum introrsum ad cerebrum et inde ad cor; unde nascitur cordis resistentia et contra pressio seu ἀντιτυπία, sive conatus cordis liberantis se a pressione per motum tendentem extrorsam; qui motus propterea apparit tanquam aliquid externum: atque apparitio haec, sive phantasma, est id quod vocamus *sensionem*." ["The cause of sense is the external body or object which presses the organ ... and pressing (through the mediation of nerves ... and membranes) produces a continuous motion inwards to the brain and then to the heart; and hence there arises a resistance or counterpressure or ἀντιτυπία, or an endeavor of the heart to free itself from pressure through an outwards motion which therefore appears as something external. And this apparition or phantasm is what we call *sense*."]. T. Hobbes, *Leviathan*, Chapter 1.

what is there in all this, that does in any the least measure tend to explain or make intelligible the real and inward nature of sense or consciousness? The object, by communicating a pressure through the organ to the sensory, does indeed raise a *phantasm* or image, that is, make a certain *impression* on the brain. But wherein consists the power of perceiving this impression and of being sensible of it? Or what similitude has this impression to the sense itself, that is, to the thought excited in the mind? Why, exactly the very same that a square has to blueness, or a triangle to sound, or a needle to the sense of pain, or the reflecting of a tennis ball to the reason and understanding of a man. So that Mr. Hobbes's definition of sensation, that it is itself (the inmost and formal nature of it) nothing but the phantasm or image made in the brain by the pressure communicated from the object is, in other words, defining blueness to be the image of a square, or sound the picture of a triangle, or pain the similitude of a sharp pointed needle. I do not here misrepresent him in the least. For he himself expressly confesses that all sensible qualities such as color, sound, and the like, are in the objects themselves nothing but motion; and because motion can produce nothing but motion (as likewise it is evident that figure and all its possible compositions can produce nothing but figure), therefore in us also the perceptions of these sensible qualities are nothing but different motions.[55] If then the phantasm, that is, the image of the object made in the brain by figure and motion, be, as he says, the sensation itself, is not sensation bare figure and motion? And are not all the aforementioned absurdities unavoidable consequences of his opinion?

Mr. Hobbes, as I have elsewhere observed, seems indeed not to have been altogether unaware of this insuperable difficulty, but he industriously endeavors to conceal it from his readers, to impose upon them by the ambiguity of the word "phantasm." Yet for a reserve, in case he should be too hard pressed, he gives us a hint that possibly sensation may be something more, viz., a power of perception or consciousness naturally and essentially inherent in all matter; only that it wants the organs and memory

[55] "... quae qualitates omnes nominari solent sensibiles, et sunt in ipso obiecto nihil aliud praeter materiae motum, quo obiectum in organa sensuum diversimode operatur. Neque in *nobis* aliud sunt quam diversi motus. Motus enim nihil generat praeter motum." ["... all which qualities are usually called 'sensible,' and are in the object nothing else but the motion of matter by which the object operates on the organs of sense differently. Nor are they in *us* anything but different motions, for motion does not produce but motion."]. T. Hobbes, *Leviathan*, Chapter 1.

See *Four Defences of a Letter to Mr Dodwell* [that is, the correspondence with Anthony Collins at *W* III, 721–913].

of animals to express its sensation; and [he hints] that, as a man, if he were supposed to have no other sense but seeing, and that so ordered as that his eyes were always immovably fixed upon one and the same object, and that also unchangeable and without the least variety – such a man could not properly be said to see, but only to be under an unintelligible kind of amazement; so all unorganized bodies may possibly have sensation or perception, but because for want of organs there is no variety in it, neither any memory or means of expressing that sensation, therefore to us it seems as if they had no such thing at all.[56] This opinion, I say, Mr. Hobbes mentions as possible. But he does it with such hesitancy, diffidence, and sparingness, as shows plainly that he meant it only as a last subterfuge to recur to when he should be pressed with the aforementioned absurdities, unavoidably consequent upon the supposition of sensation being only figure and motion. And indeed well might he be sparing and, as it were, ashamed of this subterfuge. For it is a thing altogether as absurd as even the other opinion itself of thought being near motion. For what can be

---

[56] "Scio fuisse philosophos quosdam, eosdemque *viros doctos*, qui *corpora omnia sensu preadita* esse sustinuerunt; *nec video*, si natura sensionis in reactione sola collocaretur, *quomodo refutari possint*. Sed etsi ex reactione etiam corporum aliorum phantasma aliquod nasceretur, illud tamen remoto obiecto statim cessaret; nam nisi ad retinendum motum impressum, etiam remoto obiecto, apta habeant organa, ut habent animalia, ita tantum sentient, ut nunquam sensisse se recordentur ... Sensioni ergo ... quae vulgo ita appellatur, necessario adhaeret memoria aliqua" etc. ["I know that there have been philosophers, and those *learned men*, who have maintained that *all bodies are endowed with sense. Nor do I see how they can be refuted*, if the nature of sense be placed in reaction only. And though by the reaction of other bodies a phantasm might arise, it would nevertheless cease as soon as the object were removed. For unless those bodies had organs, as animals have, fit for the retaining of motion made in them, their sense would be such as that they would never remember they sensed ... Hence, some memory necessarily pertains to sense as it is commonly understood." Italics by Clarke.]. T. Hobbes, *De Corpore*, Part IV, Chapter 25, Section 5.

See also numbers 2 and 11 of the appendix to a collection of papers which passed between Mr Leibniz and Dr. Clarke [supplementary text IX].

"... Itaque et sensioni adhaeret propriae dictae, ut ei aliqua insita sit perpetua phantasmatum varietas, ita ut aliud ab alio discerni possit. Si supponemus enim esse hominem, oculis quidem claris caeterisque videndi organis recte se habentibus compositum, nullo autem alio sensu praeditum, eumque ad eandem rem eodem semper colore et specie sine ulla vel minima varietate apparentem obversum esse, mihi certe, quicquid dicant alii, non ... *videre* videretur ... Attonitum esse et fortasse aspectare eum, sed stupentem dicerem, videre non dicerem; adeo *sentire semper idem, et non sentire*, ad idem recidunt." ["Wherefore sense, properly so called, necessarily has some memory adhering to it, so that an inner variety of phantasms is perpetually present and one phantasm can be distinguished from another. For if we suppose a man to be made with clear eyes and all the rest of his organs of sight well disposed, but endowed with no other sense, and that he looks only at one thing which is always the same color and figure without the least appearance of variety, he would seem to me, whatsoever others may say, not to *see* ... I might perhaps say that he would be astonished and look at it, but not that he would see it; indeed, *sensing always the same thing and not sensing* amount to the same."]. T. Hobbes, *De Corpore*, Part IV, Chapter 25, Section 5.

[handwritten marginalia: If consciousness arises from matter, and matter is divisible all the way down, so all matter has consciousness.]

more ridiculous than to imagine that matter is as essentially conscious as it is extended? Will it not follow from this supposition that every piece of matter, being made up of entirely separable parts (that is, of parts which are as really distinct beings, notwithstanding their contiguity, as if they had been at never so great a distance one from another) is made up also of innumerable consciousnesses and infinite confusion? But it is a shame to trouble the reader with so much as the mention of any of the numberless absurdities following from that monstrous supposition.

Others, therefore, who would make thinking to be an affection of matter, and yet are ashamed to use either of the aforementioned ways, contend that God by his almighty and supreme power endows certain systems of matter with a faculty of thinking, according to his own good pleasure.[d] But this also amounts to nothing. For besides the absurdity of supposing God to make an innumerable company of distinct beings, such as the particles of every system of matter necessarily are, to be at the same time one individual conscious being – besides this, I say, either our idea of matter is a true and distinct idea, or it is not. If it be a true and distinct idea, that is, if our idea (not of the substance of matter, for of simple substance we have no idea, but if our idea of the properties which essentially distinguish and denominate the substance) be a right idea, viz., that matter is nothing but a solid substance capable only of division, figure, and motion, with all the possible effects of their several compositions (as to us it appears to be, upon the best examination we are able to make of it and the greatest part of our adversaries themselves readily allow), then it is absolutely impossible for thinking to belong to matter because thinking, as has been before shown, cannot possibly arise from any modification or composition of any or all of these qualities. But if any man will say that our idea of matter is wrong and that by "matter" he will not here mean, as in all other cases, a solid substance capable only of division, figure, and motion with all the possible effects of their several compositions, but that he means substance in general capable of thinking and of numberless unknown properties besides, then he trifles only in putting an ambiguous signification upon the word "matter," where he ought to use the word "substance." And in that sense, to suppose thinking or any other active property possible to be in matter,

---

[d] While matter by itself could not think, God, who can do anything which is logically and metaphysically possible, "superadds" the power of thought to matter. This hypothesis became the focus of much discussion after Locke toyed with it in *An Essay concerning Human Understanding*, book 4, chapter 3, section 6. Clarke vigorously opposed it in his debate with Collins on whether matter can think (*W* III, 721–913). For Clarke's main argument, see supplementary text VIII.

and signifying only substance in general of whose powers and capacities we have no certain idea, would make nothing at all to the present purpose in our adversaries' advantage, and is at least not a clear and more intelligible way of talking than to attribute those same properties to an immaterial substance, and keep the idea of matter and its properties clear and distinct.

For I affirm, thirdly, that even supposing in these men's confused way that the soul was really not a distinct substance from body, but that thinking and willing could be and were indeed only qualities or affections of matter, yet even *this* would not at all affect the present question about liberty, nor prove freedom of will to be an impossible thing. For since it has been already demonstrated that thinking and willing cannot possibly be effects or compositions of figure and motion, whosoever will make thinking and willing to be qualities or affections of matter must suppose matter capable of certain properties entirely different from figure and motion. And if it be capable of properties entirely different from figure and motion, then it can never be proved, from the effects of figure and motion being all necessary, that the effects of other and totally distinct properties must likewise be necessary.

Mr. Hobbes, therefore, and his followers are guilty of a most shameful fallacy in that very argument wherein they place their main and chief strength. For, supposing matter to be capable of thinking and willing, they contend that the soul is mere matter, and knowing that the effects of figure and motion must needs be all necessary, they conclude that the operations of the mind must all *therefore* be necessary. That is, when they would prove the soul to be mere matter, then they suppose matter capable not only of figure and motion but also of other unknown properties; and when they would prove the will and all other operations of the soul to be necessary, then they divest matter again of all its unknown properties, and make it mere solidity endowed only with figure and motion again. Wherefore, distinguishing their ambiguous and confused use of the word "matter," they are unavoidably reduced to one of these two concessions. If by "matter" they mean a solid substance endowed only with figure and motion and all the possible effects of the variations and compositions of these qualities, then the soul cannot be mere matter because, as Mr. Hobbes himself confesses, figure and motion can never produce anything but figure and motion, and consequently (as has been before demonstrated) they can never produce so much as any secondary quality, sound, color and the like, much less thinking and reasoning.[57] From whence it follows that the soul being unavoidably a substance immaterial, they have no argument left to prove that it cannot have a power of beginning motion, which is a plain instance of liberty. But if, on the other hand, they will by "matter" mean substance in general, capable of unknown properties totally different from figure and motion, then they must no longer argue against the possibility of liberty from the effects of figure and motion being all unavoidably necessary, because liberty will not consist in the effects of figure and motion, but in those other unknown properties of matter which these men can no more explain or argue about than about immaterial substances.

The truth, therefore, is they must needs suppose thinking to be merely an effect or composition of figure and motion, if they will give any strength to their arguments against liberty. And then the question will be not whether God can make matter think or not (for in that question they only trifle with a word, abusing the word "matter" to signify substance in general), but the question will be whether figure and motion, in any composition or division, can possibly be perception and thought, which (as has been before said) is just such a question as if a man should ask whether it be possible that a triangle should be a sound or a globe a color. The sum is this: if the soul be an immaterial substance (as it must needs be if we have any true idea of the nature and properties of matter), then Mr. Hobbes's arguments against the possibility of liberty, [being] drawn all from the properties of matter, are vain and nothing to the purpose. But if our adversaries will be so absurd as to contend that the soul is nothing but mere matter, then either by "matter" they must understand substance in general, substance endowed with unknown powers, with active as well as passive properties (which is confounding and taking away our idea of matter, and at the same time destroying all their own arguments against liberty which they have founded wholly on the known properties of matter), or else they must speak out, as they really mean, that thinking and willing are nothing but effects and compositions of figure and motion, which I have already shown to be a contradiction in terms.

There are some other arguments against the possibility of liberty which men by attempting to answer have made to appear considerable, when in reality they are altogether beside the question. As for instance, those drawn

---

[57] "Motus nihil generat praeter motum." ["Motion produces nothing but motion."]. T. Hobbes, *Leviathan*, Chapter I.

from the necessity of the will's being determined by the last judgment of the understanding, and from the certainty of the divine prescience.

As to the former, viz., the necessity of the will's being determined by the last judgment of the understanding, this is only a necessity upon supposition, that is to say, a necessity that a man should will a thing, when it is supposed that he does will it; just as if one should affirm that everything which is, is therefore necessary to be, because when it is it cannot but be. It is exactly the same kind of argument as that by which the true church is proved to be infallible, because truth cannot err, and they who are in the right cannot possibly, while they are so, be in the wrong. Thus, whatever a man at any time freely wills or does, it is evident (even upon supposition of the most perfect liberty) that he cannot at that time but will or do it, because it is impossible anything should be willed and not willed, whether it be freely or necessarily, or that it should be done and not done at the same time. The necessity of the will's being determined by the last judgment of the understanding is, I say, only a necessity upon supposition, a necessity that a man should will a thing, when it is supposed that he does will it. For the last judgment of the understanding is nothing else but a man's final determining, after more or less consideration, either to choose or not to choose a thing; that is, it is the very same with the act of volition. Or else, if the act of volition be distinguished from the last judgment of the understanding, then the act of volition, or rather the beginning of action consequent upon the last judgment of the understanding, is not determined or caused by that last judgment as by the physical efficient, but only as the moral motive. For the true, proper, immediate, physical efficient cause of action is the power of self-motion in men, which exerts itself freely in consequence of the last judgment of the understanding. But the last judgment of the understanding is not itself a physical efficient, but merely a moral motive upon which the physical efficient or motive power begins to act.

The necessity, therefore, by which the power of acting follows the judgment of the understanding is only a moral necessity, that is, no necessity at all in the sense wherein the opposers of liberty understand necessity. For moral necessity is evidently consistent with the most perfect natural liberty. For instance, a man entirely free from all pain of body and disorder of mind judges it unreasonable for him to hurt or destroy himself; and being under no temptation or external violence, he cannot possibly act contrary to this judgment, not because he wants a natural or physical power so to do, but because it is absurd and mischievous, and morally impossible, for him to choose to do it. Which also is the very reason why the most perfect rational creatures superior to men cannot do evil; not because they want a natural power to perform the material action, but because it is morally impossible that, with a perfect knowledge of what is best and without any temptation to evil, their will should determine itself to choose to act foolishly and unreasonably. Here, therefore, seems at last really to lie the fundamental error both of those who argue against the liberty of the will and of those who but too confusedly defend it. They do not make a clear distinction between moral motives and causes physically efficient, which two things have no similitude at all. Lastly, if the maintainers of fate shall allege that, after all, they think a man free from all pain of body and disorder of mind is under not only a moral but also a natural impossibility of hurting or destroying himself, because neither his judgment nor his will, without some impulse external to both, can any more possibly be determined to any action than one body can begin to move without being impelled by another, I answer this is forsaking the argument drawn from the necessity of the will's following the understanding, and recurs to the former argument of the absolute impossibility of there being anywhere a first principle of motion at all, which has been abundantly answered already.

Some ingenious and able writers have spoken with much confusion upon this head by mistaking, as it seems to me, the subject of the question and wherein the nature of liberty consists.

For it being evident that a free agent cannot choose whether he shall have a will or no will, that is, whether he shall be what he is or not, but (the two contradictories of acting or not acting being always necessarily before him) he must of necessity and essentially to his being a free agent perpetually will one of these two things, either to act or to forbear [from] acting, this has raised in the minds even of some considerate persons great doubts concerning the possibility of liberty.

But this difficulty, if it be any difficulty, arises merely from not apprehending rightly what liberty is. For the essence of liberty consists, not in the agent's choosing whether he shall have a will or no will, that is, whether he shall be at all an agent or no, whether he shall be what he is or no, but it consists in his being an agent, that is, in his having a continual power of choosing whether he shall act or whether he shall forbear [from] acting. Which power of agency or free choice (for these are precisely

74

identical terms, and a necessary agent is an express contradiction) is not at all prevented by chains or prisons. For a man who chooses or endeavors to move out of his place is therein as much a free agent as he that actually moves out of his place. Nor is this free agency at all diminished by the impossibility of his choosing two contradictories at once or by the necessity that one of two contradictories must always be done. A man that sits, whether he be or be not a free agent, cannot possibly both sit and rise up at the same time; nor can he possibly choose both to act or not to act at the same time – not for want of freedom, but because the exercise of that very freedom, his freely choosing the one, does in itself necessarily make the contrary to be at that time impossible. Nor does freedom of will in any manner suppose a power in the agent of choosing whether he shall will at all, or not. For a free agent may be, and indeed essentially every free agent *must* be, necessarily free; that is, has it not in his power not to be free.

God is, by necessity of nature, a free agent, and he can no more possibly cease to be so than he can cease to exist. He must of necessity every moment, either choose to act or choose to forbear [from] acting because two contradictories cannot possibly be true at once. But which of these two he shall choose, in this he is at perfect liberty, and to suppose him not to be so is contradictorily supposing him not to be the first cause, but to be acted by some superior power so as to be himself no agent at all.

Man also is by necessity (not in the nature of things, but through God's appointment) a free agent. And it is no otherwise in his power to cease to be such, than by depriving himself of life.

The necessity, therefore, of continually choosing one of the two, either to act or forbear [from] acting (which necessity nothing but a free agent can possibly be capable of, for necessary agents, as they are called, can neither choose to act nor to forbear [from] acting, they being indeed no agents at all) – the necessity, I say, of continually choosing one of the two, either to act or to forbear [from] acting, is not inconsistent with, or an argument against, liberty, but is itself the very essence of liberty.

The other argument which I said has also frequently been urged against the possibility of liberty is the certainty of the divine prescience. But this also is entirely besides the question. For if there be no other arguments by which it can be proved antecedently that all actions are necessary, it is certain it can never be made to appear to follow from prescience alone that they must be so. That is, if upon other accounts there be no impossibility but that the actions of men may be free, the bare certainty of the divine foreknowledge can never be proved to destroy that freedom, or make any alteration in the nature of men's actions. And, consequently, the certainty of prescience, separated from other arguments, is altogether besides the question concerning liberty. As to the other arguments usually intermingled with this question, they have all, I think, been answered already. And now, that the bare certainty of the divine foreknowledge (if upon other accounts there be no impossibility for the actions of men to be free) can never be proved to destroy that freedom, is very evident. For bare foreknowledge has no influence at all in any respect, nor affects in any measure the manner of the existence of anything. All that the greatest opponents of liberty have ever urged or can urge upon this head, amounts only to this, that foreknowledge implies certainty, and certainty implies necessity. But neither is it true that certainty implies necessity, neither does foreknowledge imply any other certainty than such a certainty only as would be equally in things though there was no foreknowledge.

For first, the certainty of foreknowledge does not cause the certainty of things but is itself founded on the reality of their existence. Whatever now is, it is certain that it is, and it was yesterday and from eternity as certainly true that the thing would be today as it is now certain that it is. And this certainty of event is equally the same whether it be supposed that the thing could be foreknown or not. For whatever at any time is, it was certainly true from eternity, as to the event, that that thing would be; and this certain truth of every future event would not at all have been the less though there had been no such thing as foreknowledge. Bare prescience, therefore, has no influence at all upon anything, nor contributes in the least towards the making it necessary.

We may illustrate this in some measure by the comparison of our own knowledge. We know certainly that some things are, and when we know that they are, they cannot but be; yet it is evident our knowledge does not at all affect the things to make them more necessary or more certain. Now foreknowledge in God is the very same as knowledge. All things are to him as if they were equally present to all the purposes of knowledge and power. He knows perfectly everything that is, and he knows whatever shall be in the same manner as he knows what is. As, therefore, knowledge has no influence on things that are, so neither has foreknowledge on things that shall be. It is true the manner how God can foresee future things without a chain of necessary causes is impossible for us to explain distinctly, though some sort of general notion we may conceive of it. For, as a man who has no influence over another person's actions can yet often perceive beforehand what that other will do, and a wiser and more experienced man will still with greater probability foresee what another, whose disposition he is perfectly acquainted with, will in certain circumstances do, and an angel, with still much less degree of error may have a further prospect into men's future actions, so it is very reasonable to apprehend that God, without influencing men's wills by his power, yet by his foresight cannot but have as much more certain a knowledge of future free events, than either men or angels can possibly have, as the perfection of his nature is greater than that of theirs.

The distinct manner how he foresees these things is indeed impossible for us to explain. But so also are numberless other things which yet no man doubts the truth of. And if there were any strength in this argument, it would prove not against liberty but against prescience itself. For if these two things were really inconsistent and one of them must be destroyed, the introducing an absolute and universal fatality, which evidently destroys all religion and morality, would tend more of the two to the dishonor of God than the denying him a foreknowledge, which upon this supposition would be impossible and imply a contradiction to conceive him to have, and the denying of which would in such case be no more a diminution of his omniscience than the denying him the power of working contradictions is taking away his omnipotence. But the case is not thus. For though we cannot indeed clearly and distinctly explain the manner of God's foreseeing the actions of free agents, yet thus much we know, that the bare foreknowledge of any action that would upon all other accounts be free cannot alter or diminish that freedom, it being evident that foreknowledge adds no other certainty to anything than what it would equally have though there was no foreknowledge. Unless, therefore, we be antecedently certain that nothing can possibly be free and that liberty is in itself absolutely an inconsistent and contradictory notion (as I have above shown that it is not), bare foreknowledge, which makes no alteration at all in anything, will not be any way inconsistent with liberty, how great difficulty soever there may be in comprehending the manner of such foreknowledge. For if liberty be in itself possible, the bare foresight of a free action before it be done is nothing different, to any purpose in the present question, from a simple knowledge of it when it is done, both these kinds of knowledge implying plainly a certainty only of the event (which would be the same though there was no such knowledge), and not at all any necessity of the thing.

For, secondly, as foreknowledge implies not any other certainty than such as would be equally in things though there was no foreknowledge, so neither does this certainty of event in any sort imply necessity. For let a fatalist suppose what he does not yet grant, that there was in man, as we assert, a power of beginning motion, that is, of acting freely; and let him suppose further, if he please, that those actions could not possibly be foreknown. Will there not yet, notwithstanding this supposition, be in the nature of things the same certainty of event in every one of the man's actions as if they were never so fatal and necessary? For instance, suppose the man by an internal principle of motion and an absolute freedom of will, without any external cause or impulse at all, does some particular action today; and suppose it was not possible that this action should have been foreseen yesterday. Was there not nevertheless the same certainty of event as if it had been foreseen? That is, would it not, notwithstanding the supposed freedom, have been as certain a truth yesterday and from eternity that this action was an event to be performed today (though supposed never so impossible to have been foreknown) as it is now a certain and infallible truth that it is performed? Mere certainty of event, therefore, does not in any measure imply necessity; and, consequently, foreknowledge, however difficult to be explained as to the manner of it, yet (since it is manifest it implies no other certainty but only that certainty of event which the things would equally have without being foreknown) it is evident that it also implies no necessity.

And now having, as I hope, sufficiently proved both the possibility and the real existence of liberty, I shall, from what has been said on this head, draw only this one inference, that hereby we are enabled to answer that ancient and great question, πόθεν τὸ κακόν, what is the cause and original of evil. For liberty implying a natural power of doing evil as well as good; and the imperfect nature of finite beings making it possible for them to abuse this their liberty to an actual commission of evil; and it being necessary to the order and beauty of the whole and for displaying the infinite wisdom of the creator that there should be different and various degrees of creatures whereof consequently some must be less perfect than others, hence there necessarily arises a possibility of evil, notwithstanding that the creator is infinitely good. In short, thus: all that we call evil is either an evil of imperfection, as the want of certain faculties and excellencies which other creatures have, or natural evil, as pain, death, and the like, or moral evil, as all kinds of vice. The first of these is not properly an evil. For every power, faculty or perfection which any creature enjoys being the free gift of God, which he was no more obliged to bestow than he was to confer being or existence itself, it is plain [that] the want of any certain faculty or perfection in any kind of creatures, which never belonged to their nature, is no more an evil to them than their never having been created or brought into being at all could properly have been called an evil. The second kind of evil, which we call natural evil, is either a necessary consequence of the former, as death to a creature on whose nature immortality was never conferred (and then it is no more properly an evil than the former); or else it is counterpoised in the whole with as great or greater good, as the afflictions and sufferings of good men (and then also it is not properly an evil); or else, lastly, it is a punishment (and then it is a necessary consequent of the third and last sort of evil, viz., moral evil). And this arises wholly from the abuse of liberty which God gave to his creatures for other purposes, and which it was reasonable and fit to give them for the perfection and order of the whole creation. Only they, contrary to God's intention and command, have abused what was necessary for the perfection of the whole to the corruption and depravation of themselves. And thus all sorts of evils have entered into the world, without any diminution to the infinite goodness of the creator and governor thereof.

Moral evil

XI

The supreme cause and author of all things must of necessity be infinitely wise. This proposition is evidently consequent upon those that have already been proved; and these being established, this, as admitting no further dispute, needs not to be largely insisted upon. For nothing is more evident than that an infinite, omnipresent, intelligent being, must know perfectly all things that are; and that he who alone is self-existent and eternal, the sole cause and author of all things, from whom alone all the powers of all things are derived and on whom they continually depend, must also know perfectly all the consequences of those powers, that is, all possibilities of things to come and what in every respect is best and wisest to be done; and that, having infinite power, he can never be controlled or prevented from doing what he so knows to be fittest. From all [of] which it manifestly follows that every effect of the supreme cause must be the product of infinite wisdom. More particularly, the supreme being, because he is infinite, must be everywhere present. And because he is an infinite mind or intelligence, therefore wherever he is, his knowledge is, which is inseparable from his being and must therefore be infinite likewise. And wherever his knowledge is, it must necessarily have a full and perfect prospect of all things, and nothing can be concealed from its inspection. He includes and surrounds everything with his boundless presence and penetrates every part of their substance with his all-seeing eye, so that the inmost nature and essence of all things are perfectly naked and open to his view, and even the deepest thoughts of intelligent beings themselves [are] manifest in his sight.

Further, all things being not only present to him but also entirely depending upon him, and having received both their being itself and all their powers and faculties from him, it is manifest that as he knows all things that are, so he must likewise know all possibilities of things, that is all effects that can be. For being himself alone self-existent, and having alone given to all things all the power and faculties they are endowed with, it is evident he must of necessity know perfectly what all and each of those powers and faculties, which are derived wholly from himself, can possibly produce. And seeing at one boundless view all the possible compositions and divisions, variations and changes, circumstances and dependencies of things, all their possible relations one to another, and their dispositions or fitnesses to certain and respective ends, he must without possibility of error know exactly what is best and most proper in everyone of the infinite possible cases or methods of disposing things, and understand perfectly how to order and direct the respective means to bring about what he so knows to be, in its kind or in the whole, the best and fittest in the end. This is what we mean by infinite wisdom. And having before shown (which indeed is also evident of itself) that the supreme cause is moreover all-powerful, so that he can no more be prevented by force or opposition than he can be hindered by error or mistake from effecting always what is absolutely fittest and wisest to be done, it follows undeniably that he is actually and effectually in the highest and most complete sense infinitely wise, and that the world and all things therein must be, and are, effects of infinite wisdom. This is demonstration *a priori*.

The proof *a posteriori* of the infinite excellency of his work is no less strong and undeniable. But I shall not enlarge upon this argument because it has often already been accurately and strongly urged, to the everlasting shame and confusion of atheists, by the ablest and most learned writers both of ancient and modern times.[58] I shall here observe only this one thing, that the older the world grows and the deeper men inquire into things, and the more accurate observations they make, and the more and greater discoveries they find out, the stronger this argument continually grows, which is a certain evidence of its being founded in truth.[59] If Galen so many ages since, could find in the construction and constitution of the parts of a human body, such undeniable marks of contrivance and design as forced him then to acknowledge and admire the wisdom of its author, what would he have said if he had known the late discoveries in anatomy and physics, the circulation of the blood, the exact structure of the heart and brain, the uses of numberless glands and valves for the secretion and motion of the juices in the body, besides several veins and other vessels and receptacles not at all known or so much as imagined to have any existence in his days, but which now are discovered to serve the wisest and most exquisite ends imaginable? If the arguments against the belief of the being of an all-wise creator and governor of the world, which Epicurus and his follower Lucretius drew from the faults which they imagined they could find in the frame and constitution of the earth, were so poor and inconsiderable that even in that infancy of natural philosophy the generality of men contemned and despised them as of no force, how would they have been ashamed if they had lived in these days, when those very things which they thought to be faults and blunders in the constitution of nature are discovered to be very useful and of exceeding benefit to the preservation and well-being of the whole?

And to mention no more, if Tully, from the partial and very imperfect knowledge in astronomy which his times afforded, could be so confident of the heavenly bodies being disposed and moved by a wise and understanding mind as to declare that in his opinion whoever asserted the contrary was himself void of all understanding, what would he have said if he had known the modern discoveries in astronomy?[60] The immense

---

[58] See Galen, *De Usu Partium Corporis Humani*; Tully [Cicero], *De Natura Deorum*; Boyle, *A Disquisition about the Final Causes of Natural Things* [1688]; Mr Ray, *Of the Wisdom of God manifested in the Works of the Creation* [1691]; Mr Derham's *Physico-Theology, or a Demonstration of the Being and Attributes of God from his Works of Creation* [the 1711–12 Boyle Lectures] etc.

[59] "Opinionum . . . commenta delet dies, naturae judicia confirmat." [". . . time obliterates the inventions of imagination, but confirms the judgments of nature."]. M. T. Cicero, *De Natura Deorum*, Book II, Chapter 2.

[60] "Coelestem ergo admirabilem ordinem incredibilemque constantiam, ex qua conservatio et salus omnium omnis oritur, qui vacare mente putat is ipse mentis expers habendus est." ["Anyone who thinks that the admirable order and the incredible regularity of the heavens, from which alone the preservation and the safety of everything arises, is not rational, himself cannot be taken to be rational."]. M. T. Cicero, *De Natura Deorum*, Book II, Chapter 21.

greatness of the world (I mean of that part of it which falls under our observation), which is now known to be as much greater than what in his time they imagined it to be, as the world itself, according to their system, was greater than Archimedes' sphere? The exquisite regularity of all the planets' motions without epicycles, stations, retrogradations, or any other deviation or confusion whatsoever? The inexpressible niceties of the adjustments of the primary velocities and original directions of the annual motions of the planets, with their distance from the central body and their force of gravitation towards it? The wonderful proportion of the diurnal motion of the Earth and other planets about their own centre for the distinction of light and darkness, without that monstrously disproportionate whirling of the whole heavens which the ancient astronomers were forced to suppose? The exact accommodating of the densities of the planets to their distances from the sun, and consequently to the proportion of heat which each of them is to bear respectively, so that neither those which are nearest to the sun are destroyed by the heat nor those which are farthest off by the cold, but each enjoys a temperature suited to its proper uses, as the Earth to ours?[61] The admirable order, number, and usefulness of the several moons, as I may very properly call them, never dreamt of by antiquity, but now by the help of telescopes clearly and distinctly seen to move about their respective planets, and whose motions are so exactly known that their very eclipses are as certainly calculated and foretold as those of our own moon? The strange adjustment of our moon's motion about its own centre once in a month, with its motion about the Earth in the same period of time, to such a degree of exactness that by that means the same face is always obverted to the Earth without any sensible variation? The wonderful motions of the comets, which are now known to be as exact, regular, and periodical as the motions of other planets? Lastly, the preservation of the several systems and of the several planets and comets in the same system from falling upon each other, which in infinite past time

---

[61] "Planetarum ... densitates ... fere sunt ... ut radices diametrorum apparentium applicatae ad diametros veras, hoc est, reciproce ut distantiae planetarum a Sole, ductae in radices diametrorum apparentium. Collocavit igitur Deus planetas in diversis distantiis a Sole, ut *quilibet, pro gradu densitatis, calore Solis maiore vel minore fruantur.*" ["The densities of the planets ... are about ... as the roots of the apparent diameters applied to the true diameters, that is, inversely as the distances of the planets from the Sun multiplied by the roots of the apparent diameters. Hence, God placed the planets at different distances from the Sun so that *they might enjoy greater or smaller heat of the Sun according to their degrees of density.*" Clarke's italics.]. *NP*, Book 3, Proposition 8, Corollary 4, pp. 582–3. [Clarke is quoting from the first (1687) edition; in subsequent editions, the passage was considerably altered.]

(had there been no intelligent governor of the whole) could not but have been the effect of the smallest possible resistance made by the finest ether and even by the rays of light themselves to the motions (supposing it possible there ever could have been any motion) of those bodies? What, I say, would Tully, that great master of reason, have thought and said, if these and other newly discovered instances of the inexpressible accuracy and wisdom of the works of God had been found out and known in his time? Certainly atheism, which then was altogether unable to withstand the arguments drawn from this topic, must now, upon the additional strength of these later observations which are every one an unanswerable proof of the incomprehensible wisdom of the creator, be utterly ashamed to show its head. We now see with how great reason the author of the book of *Ecclesiasticus*, after he had described the beauty of the Sun and stars and all the then visible works of God in heaven and Earth, concluded, ch. xliii, v. 32 (as we after all the discoveries of later ages may no doubt still truly say) "there are yet hid greater things than these, and we have seen but a few of his works."

XII

Lastly, the supreme cause and author of all things must of necessity be a being of infinite goodness, justice, and truth, and all other moral perfections such as become the supreme governor and judge of the world. That there are different relations of things one towards another is as certain as that there are different things in the world. And that from these different relations of different things there necessarily arises an agreement or disagreement of some things to others, or a fitness or unfitness of the application of different things or different relations one to another, is likewise as certain as that there is any difference in the nature of things, or that different things do exist. Further, that there is a fitness or suitableness of certain circumstances to certain persons and an unsuitableness of others founded in the nature of things and in the qualifications of persons, antecedent to will and to all arbitrary or positive appointment whatsoever, must unavoidably be acknowledged by everyone who will not affirm that it is equally fit and suitable in the nature and reason of things that an innocent being should be extremely and eternally miserable as that it should be free from such misery. There is, therefore, such a thing as fitness and unfitness, eternally, necessarily, and unchangeably in the nature and reason of things.

Now, what these relations of things absolutely and necessarily are in themselves, that also they appear to be to the understanding of all intelligent beings, except those only who understand things to be what they are not, that is, whose understandings are either very imperfect or very much depraved. And by this understanding or knowledge of the nature and necessary relations of things, the actions likewise of all intelligent beings are constantly directed (which by the way is the true ground and foundation of all morality), unless their will be corrupted by particular interest or affection, or swayed by some unreasonable and prevailing lust. The supreme cause, therefore, and author of all things, since (as has already been proved) he must of necessity have infinite knowledge and the perfection of wisdom (so that it is absolutely impossible he should err, or be in any respect ignorant of the true relations and fitness or unfitness of things, or be by any means deceived or imposed upon herein), and since he is likewise self-existent, absolutely independent and all-powerful (so that having no want of anything it is impossible his will should be influenced by any wrong affection, and having no dependence, it is impossible his power should be limited by any superior strength), it is evident he must of necessity (meaning not a necessity of fate, but such a moral necessity as I before said was consistent with the most perfect liberty) do always what he knows to be fittest to be done. That is, he must act always according to the strictest rules of infinite goodness, justice, and truth, and all other moral perfections.

In particular, the supreme cause must in the first place be infinitely *good*, that is, he must have an unalterable disposition to do and to communicate good or happiness because, being himself necessarily happy in the eternal enjoyment of his own infinite perfections, he cannot possibly have any other motives to make any creatures at all but only that he may communicate to them his own perfection, according to their different capacities arising from that variety of nature which it was fit for infinite wisdom to produce, and according to their different improvements arising from that liberty which is essentially necessary to the constitution of intelligent and active beings. That he must be infinitely good appears likewise further from hence, that being necessarily all-sufficient, he must consequently be infinitely removed from all malice and envy and from all other possible causes or temptations of doing evil, which, it is evident, can only be effects of want and weakness, of imperfection or depravation.

Again, the supreme cause and author of all things must in like manner be infinitely *just* because (the rule of equity being nothing else but the very nature of things and their necessary relations one to another; and the execution of justice being nothing else but a suiting the circumstances of things to the qualifications of persons according to the original fitness and agreeableness, which I have before shown to be necessarily in nature antecedent to will and to all positive appointment) it is manifest that he who knows perfectly this rule of equity, and necessarily judges of things as they are, who has complete power to execute justice according to that knowledge and no possible temptation to deviate in the least therefrom, who can neither be imposed upon by any deceit, nor swayed by any bias, nor awed by any power, must of necessity do always that which is right without iniquity and without partiality, without prejudice and without respect of persons.

Lastly, that the supreme cause and author of all things must be *true* and *faithful* in all his declarations and all his promises is most evident. For the only possible reason of falsifying is either rashness or forgetfulness, inconstancy or impotency, fear of evil or hope of gain; from all [of] which an infinitely wise, all-sufficient, and good being must of necessity be infinitely removed.[62] And, consequently, as it is impossible for him to be deceived himself, so neither is it possible for him in any wise to deceive others. In a word, all evil and all imperfections whatsoever arise plainly either from shortness of understanding, defect of power, or faultiness of will, and this last evidently from some impotency, corruption, or depravation, being nothing else but a direct choosing to act contrary to the known reason and nature of things. From all [of] which, it being manifest that the supreme cause and author of all things cannot but be infinitely removed, it follows undeniably that he must of necessity be a being of infinite goodness, justice, and truth, and all other moral perfections.

To this argumentation *a priori* there can be opposed but one objection that I know of, drawn on the contrary *a posteriori* from experience and observation of the unequal distributions of providence in the world. But (besides the just vindication of the wisdom and goodness of providence in its dispensations, even with respect to this present world only, which Plutarch and other heathen writers have judiciously made) the objection

---

[62] Οὐκ ἄρα ἔστιν οὗ ἕνεκα ἂν θεὸς ψεύδοιτο ... Κομιδῇ ἄρα ὁ θεὸς ἁπλοῦν καὶ ἀληθὲς ἔν τε ἔργῳ καὶ λόγῳ, καὶ οὔτε αὐτὸς μεθίσταται οὔ τε ἄλλους ἐξαπατᾷ, οὔτε κατὰ φαντασίας οὔτε κατὰ λόγους οὔτε κατὰ σημείων πομπάς, οὔθ' ὕπαρ οὔτ' ὄναρ." ["There is no reason for God to lie ... God, then, is altogether simple and true in word and deed. He himself does not change or deceive others by images, or words, or by sending signs in visions or dreams."]. Plato, *Republic*, 382e4–11.

85

itself is entirely wide of the question. For concerning the justice and goodness of God, as of any governor whatsoever, no judgment is to be made from a partial view of a few small portions of his dispensations, but from an entire consideration of the whole; and, consequently, not only the short duration of this present state, but moreover all that is past and that is still to come must be taken into the account, and then everything will clearly appear just and right.

From this account of the moral attributes of God, it follows:

Firstly, that though all the actions of God are entirely free, and consequently the exercise of his moral attributes cannot be said to be necessary in the same sense of necessity as his existence and eternity are necessary, yet these moral attributes are really and truly necessary by such a necessity as though it be not at all inconsistent with liberty, yet is equally certain, infallible, and to be depended upon, as even the existence itself or the eternity of God. For though nothing is more certain (as has been already proved in the ninth proposition of this discourse) than that God acts not necessarily but voluntarily with particular intention and design, knowing that he does good and intending to do so freely and out of choice, and, when he has no other constraint upon him but this his goodness, inclines his will to communicate himself and to do good, so that the divine nature is under no necessity but such as is consistent with the most perfect liberty and freest choice (which is the ground of all our prayers and thanksgivings, the reason why we pray to him to be good to us and gracious, and thank him for being just and merciful, whereas no man prays to him to be omnipresent, or thanks him for being omnipotent or for knowing all things) – though nothing, I say, is more certain than that God acts not necessarily but voluntarily, yet it is nevertheless as truly and absolutely impossible for God not to do, or to do anything contrary to, what his moral attributes require him to do as if he was really not a free but a necessary agent. And the reason hereof is plain: because infinite knowledge, power, and goodness in conjunction may, notwithstanding the most perfect freedom and choice, act with altogether as much certainty and unalterable steadiness as even the necessity of fate can be supposed to do. Nay, these perfections cannot possibly but so act because free choice in a being of infinite knowledge, power, and goodness, can no more choose to act contrary to these perfections than knowledge can be ignorance, power be weakness, or goodness malice, so that free choice in such a being may be as certain and steady a principle of action as the necessity of fate.

We may, therefore, as certainly and infallibly rely upon the moral as upon the natural attributes of God, it being as absolutely impossible for him to act contrary to the one as to divest himself of the other, and as much a contradiction to suppose him choosing to do anything inconsistent with his justice, goodness, and truth, as to suppose him divested of infinity, power, or existence. The one is contrary to the immediate and absolute necessity of his nature, the other to the unalterable rectitude of his will. The one is itself an immediate contradiction in the terms; the other is an express contradiction to the necessary perfections of the divine nature. To suppose the one, is saying absolutely that something is, at the same time that it is not; to suppose the other, is to say that infinite knowledge can act ignorantly, infinite power weakly, or that infinite wisdom and goodness can do things not good or wise to be done. All [of] which are equally great and equally manifest absurdities. This, I conceive, is a very intelligible account of the moral attributes of God, satisfactory to the mind and without perplexity and confusion of ideas. I might have said it at once, as the truth most certainly is, that justice, goodness, and all the other moral attributes of God are as essential to the divine nature as the natural attributes of eternity, infinity, and the like. But because all atheistical persons, after they are fully convinced that there must needs be in the universe some one eternal, necessary, infinite and all-powerful being, will still with unreasonable obstinacy contend that they can by no means see any necessary connection of goodness, justice, or any other moral attributes with these natural perfections, therefore I chose to endeavor to demonstrate the moral attributes by a particular deduction in the manner I have now done.

Secondly, from hence it follows that though God is a most perfectly free agent, yet he cannot but do always what is best and wisest in the whole. The reason is evident, because perfect wisdom and goodness are steady and certain principles of action as necessity itself. And an infinitely wise and good being endowed with the most perfect liberty can no more choose to act in contradiction to wisdom and goodness, than a necessary agent can act contrary to the necessity by which it is acted, it being as great an absurdity and impossibility in choice for infinite wisdom to choose to act unwisely, or infinite goodness to choose what is not good, as it would be in nature for absolute necessity to fail of producing its necessary effect. There was indeed no necessity in nature that God should at first create such beings as he has created, or indeed any beings at all, because he is in himself infinitely happy and all-sufficient. There was also no necessity in nature that he should preserve and continue things in being after they were created, because he would be as self-sufficient without their continuance as he was before their creation. But it was fit, and wise, and good, that infinite wisdom should manifest, and infinite goodness communicate itself. And therefore, it was necessary (in the sense of necessity I am now speaking of) that things should be made at such time, and continued so long, and endowed with various perfections in such degrees, as infinite wisdom and goodness saw it wisest and best that they should. And when and whilst things are in being, the same moral perfection makes it necessary that they should be disposed and governed according to the most exact and most unchangeable laws of eternal justice, goodness, and truth because while things and their several relations are, they cannot but be what they are, and an infinitely wise being cannot but know them to be what they are, and judge always rightly concerning the several fitnesses or unfitnesses of them. And an infinitely good being cannot but choose to act always according to this knowledge of the respective fitness of things, it being as truly impossible for such a free agent, who is absolutely incapable of being deceived or depraved, to choose, by acting contrary to these laws, to destroy its own perfections, as for necessary existence to be able to destroy its own being.

Thirdly, from hence it follows that, though God is both perfectly free and also infinitely powerful, yet he cannot possibly do anything that is evil. The reason of this also is evident because, as it is manifest, infinite power cannot extend to natural contradictions, which imply a destruction of that very power by which they must be supposed to be effected, so neither can it extend to moral contradictions which imply a destruction of some other attributes as necessarily belonging to the divine nature as power. I have already shown that justice, goodness, and truth, are necessarily in God, even as necessarily as power, and understanding, and knowledge of the nature of things. It is, therefore, as impossible and contradictory to suppose his will should choose to do anything contrary to justice, goodness, or truth, as that his power should be able to do anything inconsistent with power. It is no diminution of power not to be able to do things which are no object of power; and it is, in like manner, no diminution either of power or liberty to have such a perfect and unalterable rectitude of will, as never possibly to choose to do anything inconsistent with that rectitude.

Fourthly, from hence it follows that liberty, properly speaking, is not in itself an imperfection but a perfection. For it is in the highest and most complete degree in God himself, every act wherein he exercises any moral attribute as goodness, justice, or truth, proceeding from the most perfect liberty and freest choice (without which goodness would not be goodness, nor justice and truth any excellencies), these things, in the very idea and formal notion of them, utterly excluding all necessity. It has indeed been sometimes taught that liberty is a great imperfection because it is the occasion of all sin and misery. But, if we will speak properly, it is not liberty that exposes us to misery, but only the abuse of liberty. It is true liberty makes men capable of sin, and consequently liable to misery, neither of which they could possibly be without liberty. But he that will say everything is an imperfection, by the abuse whereof a creature may be more unhappy than if God had never given it that power at all, must say that a stone is a more excellent and perfect creature than man because it is not capable of making itself miserable as man is. And by the same argument, reason and knowledge, and every other perfection, nay, even existence itself, will be proved to be an imperfection because it is that without which a creature could not be miserable. The truth, therefore, is [that] the abuse of liberty, that is, the corruption and depravation of that without which no creatures could be happy, is alone the cause of their misery; but as for liberty itself, it is a great perfection, and the more perfect any creature is, the more perfect is its liberty. And the most perfect liberty of all is such liberty as can never by any ignorance, deceit, or corruption be biased or diverted from choosing what is the proper object of free choice, the greatest good.

Fifthly, from hence it follows that though probably no rational creature can be in a strict philosophical sense impeccable, yet we may easily conceive how God can place such creatures, as he judges worthy of so excellent a gift, in such a state of knowledge and near communion with himself (where goodness and holiness shall appear so amiable and where they shall be exempt from all means of temptation and corruption) that it shall never be possible for them, notwithstanding the natural liberty of their will, to be seduced from their unchangeable happiness in the everlasting choice and enjoyment of their greatest good. Which is the state of good angels and of the saints in heaven.

Lastly, from what has been said upon this head, it follows that the true ground and foundation of all eternal moral obligations is this, that the same reasons (viz., the aforementioned necessary and eternal different relations which different things bear one to another, and the consequent fitness or unfitness of the application of different things, or different relations one to another, unavoidably arising from that difference of the things themselves) – these very same reasons, I say, which always and necessarily *do* determine the will of God, as has been before shown, *ought* also constantly to determine the will of all subordinate intelligent beings. And when they do not, then such beings, setting up their own unreasonable self-will in opposition to the nature and reason of things, endeavor, as much as in them lies, to make things be what they are not and cannot be, which is the highest presumption and greatest insolence imaginable. It is acting contrary to their own reason and knowledge; it is an attempting to destroy that order by which the universe subsists, and it is also, by consequence, offering the highest affront imaginable to the creator of all things, who himself governs all his actions by these rules and cannot but require the same of all his reasonable creatures. They who found all moral obligations only upon laws made for the good of societies, hold an opinion which (besides that it is fully confuted by what has been already said concerning the eternal and necessary difference of things) is, moreover, so directly and manifestly contradictory and inconsistent with itself, that it seems strange it should not have been more commonly taken notice of. For if there be no difference between good and evil antecedent to all laws, there can be no reason given why any laws should be made at all when all things are naturally indifferent. To say that laws are necessary to be made for the good of mankind, is confessing that certain things tend to the good of mankind, that is, to the preserving and perfecting of their nature, which wise men therefore think necessary to be established by laws. And if the reason why certain things are established by wise and good laws is because those things tend to the good of mankind, it is manifest they were good antecedent to their being confirmed by laws. Otherwise, if they were not good antecedent to all laws, it is evident there could be no reason why such laws should be made rather than the contrary, which is the greatest absurdity in the world.

And now from what has been said upon this argument, I hope it is in the whole sufficiently clear that the being and attributes of God are, to attentive and considering minds, abundantly capable of just proof and demonstration, and that the adversaries of God and religion have not reason on their side (to which they would pretend to be strict adherers), but mere vain confidence and great blindness and prejudice, when they desire it should be thought that in the fabric of the world God has left himself wholly without witness, and that all the arguments of nature are on the side of atheism and irreligion. Some men, I know, there are, who, having never turned their thoughts to matters of this nature, think that these things are all absolutely above our comprehension, and that we talk about we know not what when we dispute about these questions. But, since the most considerable atheists that ever appeared in the world, and the pleaders for universal fatality, have all thought fit to argue in this way in their attempts to remove the first foundations of religion, it is reasonable and necessary that they should be opposed in their own way, it being most certain that no argumentation of what kind soever can possibly be made use of on the side of error, but may also be used with much greater advantage on the behalf of truth.

From what has been said upon this argument, we may see how it comes to pass that though nothing is so certain and undeniable as the necessary existence of God and the consequent deduction of all his attributes, yet men who have never attended to the evidence of reason and to the notices that God has given us of himself may easily be in great measure ignorant of both. That the three angles of a triangle are equal to two right ones, is so certain and evident that whoever affirms the contrary affirms what may very easily be reduced to an express contradiction; yet whoever turns not his mind to consider it at all may easily be ignorant of this and numberless other the like mathematical and most infallible truths.

Yet the notices that God has been pleased to give us of himself are so many and so obvious in the constitution, order, beauty, and harmony of the several parts of the world, in the frame and structure of our own bodies and the wonderful powers and faculties of our souls, in the unavoidable apprehensions of our own minds and the common consent of all other men, in everything within us and everything without us, that no man of the meanest capacity and greatest disadvantages whatsoever, with the slightest and most superficial observation of the works of God and the lowest and most obvious attendance to the reason of things, can be ignorant of him, but he must be utterly without excuse. Possibly, he may not indeed be able to understand or be affected by nice and metaphysical demonstrations of the being and attributes of God. But then, for the same reason, he is obliged also not to suffer himself to be shaken and unsettled by the subtle sophistries of skeptical and atheistical men, which he cannot perhaps answer because he cannot understand. But he is bound to adhere to those things which he knows and those reasonings he is capable to judge of, which are abundantly sufficient to determine and to guide the practice of sober and considering men.

But this is not all. God has moreover finally, by a clear and express revelation of himself brought down from heaven by his own son, our blessed Lord and Redeemer, and suited to every capacity and understanding, put to silence the ignorance of foolish and the vanity of skeptical and profane men. And by declaring to us himself his own nature and attributes, he has effectually prevented all mistakes which the weakness of our reason, the negligence of our application, the corruption of our nature, or the false philosophy of wicked and profane men might have led us into. And so [he] has infallibly furnished us with sufficient knowledge to enable us to perform our duty in this life, and to obtain our happiness in that which is to come. But this exceeds the bounds of my present subject and deserves to be handled in a particular discourse.

Other writings

I.

Several Letters to the Reverend Dr. Clarke from a Gentleman in Gloucestershire relating to the "Discourse concerning the Being and Attributes of God"

[*Editor's Note*: The "Gentleman in Gloucestershire" was none other than Joseph Butler (1692–1752), who went on to become one of the most important British moral philosophers and natural theologians of the eighteenth century. The exchange dealt mainly with divine omnipresence and divine necessity. The first topic was to become one of the most important in the controversy between Leibniz and Clarke. This selection should be read in conjunction with supplementary text II. The text is from W II, 737–50.]

Butler's First Letter [W II, 737–9]

Reverend Sir,

   I suppose you will wonder at the present trouble from one who is a perfect stranger to you, though you are not so to him, but I hope the occasion will excuse my boldness. I have made it, sir, my business ever since I thought myself capable of such sort of reasoning, to prove to myself the being and attributes of God. And being sensible that it is a matter of the last consequence, I endeavored after a *demonstrative* proof not only more fully to satisfy my own mind, but also in order to defend the great truths of natural religion and those of the Christian revelation which follow from them against all opposers. But I must own with concern that hitherto I have been unsuccessful, and though I have got very probable arguments, yet I can go but a very little way with *demonstration* in the proof of those things. When first your book on those subjects (which by all whom I have discoursed with is so justly esteemed) was recommended to me, I was in great hopes of having all my enquiries answered. But since in some places, either through my not understanding your meaning, or what else I know not, even that has failed me, I almost despair of ever arriving to such a satisfaction as I aim at, unless by the method I now use. You cannot but know, sir, that of two different expressions of the same thing, though equally clear to some persons, yet to others one of them is sometimes very obscure, though the other be perfectly intelligible. Perhaps this may be my case here, and could I see those of your arguments of which I

95

doubt differently proposed, possibly I might yield a ready assent to them. This, sir, I cannot but think a sufficient excuse for the present trouble, it being such a one as I hope may prevail for an answer with one who seems to aim at nothing more than that good work of instructing others.

In your *Demonstration of the Being and Attributes of God*, Prop. VI [pp. 33–5], you propose to prove the infinity or omnipresence of the self-existent being. The former part of the proof seems highly probable; but the latter part, which seems to aim at demonstration, is not to me convincing. The latter part of the paragraph is, if I mistake not, an entire argument of itself, which runs thus: "To suppose a finite being to be self-existent, is to say that it is a contradiction for that being not to exist, the absence of which may yet be conceived without a contradiction. Which is the greatest absurdity in the world." The sense of these words ("the absence of which") seems plainly to be determined by the following sentence to mean its absence from any particular place. Which sentence is to prove it to be an absurdity, and is this: "For if a being can, without a contradiction be absent from one place, it may, without a contradiction, be absent from another place, and from all places." Now supposing this to be a consequence, all that it proves is that if a being can without a contradiction be absent from one place at *one time*, it may without a contradiction be absent from another place, and so from all places, at *different times* (for I cannot see that if a being can be absent from *one place* at *one time*, therefore it may without a contradiction be absent from *all places* at the *same time*, i.e., may cease to exist.) Now, if it proves no more than this, I cannot see that it reduces the supposition to any absurdity. Suppose I could *demonstrate* that any particular man should live a thousand years; this man might, without a contradiction, be absent from one, and from all places at different times; but it would not from thence follow that he might be absent from all places at the same time, i.e., that he might cease to exist. No; this would be a contradiction, because I am supposed to have demonstrated that he should live a thousand years. It would be exactly the same if, instead of a thousand years, I should say "forever", and the proof seems the same whether it be applied to a self-existent or a dependent being.

What else I have to offer is in relation to your proof that the self-existent being must of necessity be but one. Which proof is as follows, in Prop. VII [pp. 35–6]: "To suppose two or more different natures existing of themselves, necessarily and independent from each other, implies this plain contradiction, that each of them being independent from the other, they may either of them be supposed to exist alone, so that it will be no contradiction to imagine the other not to exist and consequently neither of them will be necessarily existing." The supposition indeed implies that since each of these beings is independent from the other, they may either of them exist alone, i.e., without any relation to or dependence on the other. But where is the third idea, to connect this proposition and the following one, viz., so that it will be no contradiction to imagine the other not to exist? Were this a consequence of the former proposition, I allow it would be [a] demonstration, by the first corollary of Prop. III [p. 13]. But since these two propositions, "they may either of them be supposed to exist alone" and "so that it will be no contradiction to imagine the other not to exist," are very widely different, and since likewise it is no immediate consequence that because either may be supposed to exist independent from the other, therefore the other may be supposed not to exist at all, how is what was proposed proved? That the propositions are different, I think is plain; and whether there be an immediate connection, everybody that reads your book must judge for themselves. I must say, for my own part, the absurdity does not appear at first sight any more than the absurdity of saying that the angles below the base in an isosceles triangle are unequal; which, though it is absolutely false, yet I suppose no one will lay down the contrary for an axiom because, though it is true, yet there is need of a proof to make it appear so.

Perhaps it may be answered that I have not rightly explained the words "to exist alone", and that they do not mean only "to exist independent from the other" but that "existing alone" means that nothing exists with it. Whether this or the other was meant I cannot determine, but which ever it was, what I have said will hold. For if this last be the sense of those words "They either of them may be supposed to exist alone," it indeed implies that it will be no contradiction to suppose the other not to exist; but then I ask: how come these two propositions to be connected, that to suppose two different natures existing of themselves necessarily and independent from each other implies that each of them may be supposed to exist alone in this sense? Which is exactly the same as I said before, only applied to different sentences. So that if "existing alone" be understood as I first took it, I allow it is implied in the supposition, but cannot see that the consequence is, that it will be no contradiction to suppose the other not to exist. But if the words "existing alone" are meant in the latter sense, I grant that if either of them may be supposed thus to exist alone, it will be no contradiction to suppose the other not to exist. But then I cannot see that to suppose two different natures existing, of themselves, necessarily and independent from each other, implies that either of them may be supposed to exist alone in *this* sense of the words, but only that either of them may be supposed to exist without having any relation to the other, and that there will be no need of the existence of the one in order to [have] the existence of the other. But though upon this account, were there no other principle of its existence, it might cease to exist, yet on the account of the necessity of its own nature, which is quite distinct from the other, it is an absolute absurdity to suppose it not to exist.

Thus, sir, I have proposed my doubts with the reasons of them. In which if I have wrested your words to another sense than you defined them, or in any respect argued unfairly, I assure you it was without design. So I hope you will impute it to mistake. And if it will be not too great a trouble, let me once more beg the favor of a line from you, by which you will lay me under a particular obligation to be what with the rest of the world I now am,

Reverend Sir,
Your most obliged servant, etc.

Nov. the 4th, 1713

Clarke's answer to Butler's First Letter [*W* II, 739–40]

Sir,

Did men who publish controversial papers accustom themselves to write with that candor and ingenuity with which you propose your difficulties, I am persuaded almost all disputes might be very amicably terminated, either by men's coming at last to agree in opinion, or at least finding reason to suffer each other friendly to differ.

Your two objections are very ingenious, and urged with great strength and acuteness. Yet I am not without hopes of being able to give you satisfaction in both of them. To your first, therefore, I answer: Whatever may, without a contradiction, be absent from any one place at any one time may also, without a contradiction, be absent from all places at all times. For, whatever is *absolutely necessary* at all is absolutely necessary in *every part of space* and in *every point of duration*. Whatever can at any time be conceived possible to be absent from any one part of space may for the same reason (viz., the implying no contradiction in the nature of things) be conceived possible to be absent from every other part of space at the same time either by ceasing to be, or by supposing it never to have begun to be. Your instance about demonstrating a man to live 1000 years is what, I think, led you into the mistake, and is a good instance to lead you out of it again. You may suppose a man shall live 1000 years, or God may reveal and promise he shall live 1000 years; and upon that supposition it shall not be possible for the man to be absent from all places in any part of that time. Very true. But why shall it not be possible? Only because it is contrary to the supposition, or to the promise of God, but not contrary to the absolute nature of things, which would be the case if the man existed necessarily, as every part of space does. In supposing you could *demonstrate* a man should live 1000 years or one year, you make an impossible and contradictory supposition. For though you may know certainly (by Revelation suppose) that he will live so long, yet this is only the certainty of a thing true in fact, not in itself necessary; and demonstration is applicable to nothing but what is necessary in itself, necessary in all places and at all times equally.

To your second difficulty, I answer: What exists necessarily, not only must so exist alone as to be independent of any thing else but, being self-sufficient, may also so exist alone as that everything else may possibly (or without any contradiction in the nature of things) be supposed not to exist at all. And, consequently, since that which may possibly be supposed not to exist at all is not necessarily existent, *no other thing* can be necessarily existent. Whatever is necessarily existing, there is need of its existence in order to the supposal of the existence of any other thing, so that nothing can possibly be supposed to exist without presupposing and including antecedently the existence of that which is necessary. For instance, the supposal of the existence of anything whatever includes necessarily a presupposition of the existence of space and time, and if any thing could exist without space or time, it would follow that space and time were not necessarily existing. Therefore, the supposing anything possibly to exist alone, so as not necessarily to include the presupposal of some other thing, proves demonstrably that that other thing is not necessarily existing, because whatever has necessity of existence cannot possibly, in any conception whatsoever, be supposed away. There cannot possibly be any notion of the existence of anything, there cannot possibly be any notion of existence at all, but what shall necessarily pre-include the notion of that which has necessary existence. And, consequently, the two propositions which you judged independent are really necessarily connected. These sorts of things are indeed very difficult to express, and not easy to be conceived but by very attentive minds; but to such as can and will attend, nothing, I think, is more demonstrably convincing.

If anything still sticks with you in this or any other part of my books, I shall be very willing to be informed of it; who am,

Sir,

Your assured friend, and servant, S.C.

Nov. 10, 1713

P.S. Many readers, I observe, have misunderstood my Second General Proposition, as if the words "some one unchangeable and independent being," meant "one only ... being." Whereas the true meaning, and all that the argument there requires, is "some one at least." That there can be *but* one, is the thing proved afterwards, in the Seventh Proposition.

Butler's Second Letter [*W* II, 741–2]

Reverend Sir,

I have often thought that the chief occasion of men's differing so much in their opinions were either their not understanding each other, or else that, instead of ingenuously searching after truth, they have made it their business to find out arguments for the proof of what they have once asserted. However, it is certain there may be other reasons for persons not agreeing in their opinions; and where it is so, I cannot but think with you that they will find reason to suffer each other to differ friendly, every man having a way of thinking, in some respects, peculiarly his own.

I am sorry I must tell you your answers to my objections are not satisfactory. The reasons why I think them not so are as follow.

You say: "Whatever is *absolutely necessary* at all, is absolutely necessary in *every part of space* and in *every point of duration*." Were this evident, it would certainly prove what you bring it for, viz., "that whatever may, without a contradiction, be absent from one place at one time, may also [...] be absent from all places at all times." But I do not conceive that the idea of ubiquity is contained in the idea of self-existence, or directly follows from it any otherwise than as, "whatever exists must exist somewhere." You add: "Whatever can at any time be conceived possible to be absent from any one part of space, may for the same reason (viz., the implying no contradiction in the nature of things) be conceived possible to be absent from every other part of space at the same time." Now I cannot see that I can make these two suppositions for the same reason or upon the same account. The reason why I conceive this being may be absent from one place, is because it does not contradict the former proof (drawn from the nature of things), in which I proved only that it must necessarily exist. But the other supposition, viz., that I can conceive it possible to be absent from every part of space at one and the same time, directly contradicts the proof that it must exist *somewhere,* and so is an express contradiction; unless it be said that as when we have proved the three angles of a triangle equal to two right ones, that relation of the equality of its angles to two right ones will be wherever a triangle exists, so when we have proved the necessary existence of a being, this being must exist everywhere. But there is a great difference between these two things, the one being the proof of a certain relation upon supposition of such a being's existence with such particular properties; and, consequently, wherever this being and these properties exist, this relation must exist too. But from the proof of the necessary existence of a being, it is no evident consequence that it exists every where. My using the word "demonstration," instead of "proof" which leaves no room for doubt, was through negligence, for I never heard of strict demonstration of matter of fact.

In your answer to my second difficulty, you say: "Whatsoever is necessarily existing, there is need of its existence, in order to the supposal of the existence of any other thing." All the consequences you draw from this proposition, I see proved demonstrably, and consequently that the two propositions I thought independent are closely connected. But how, or upon what account, is there need of the existence of what is necessarily existing in order to the existence of any other thing? Is it as there is need of space and duration in order to the existence of any thing, or is it needful only as the cause of the existence of all other things? If the former be said, as your instance seems to intimate, I answer: space and duration are very abstruse in their natures and, I think, cannot properly be called things, but are considered rather as affections which belong, and in the order of our thoughts are antecedently necessary, to the existence of all things. And I can no more conceive how a necessarily existing being can, on the same account or in the same manner as space and duration are, be needful in order to the existence of any other being, than I can conceive extension attributed to a thought (that idea no more belonging to a thing existing than extension belongs to thought). But if the latter be said, that there is need of the existence of whatever is a necessary being, in order to the existence of any other thing only as this necessary being must be the cause of the existence of all other things, I think this is plainly begging the question, for it supposes that no other being exists but what is casual, and so not necessary. And on what other account, or in what other manner than one of these two, there can be need of the existence of a necessary being in order to the existence of anything else, I cannot conceive.

Thus, sir, you see I entirely agree with you in all the consequences you have drawn from your suppositions, but cannot see the truth of the suppositions themselves.

I have aimed at nothing in my style but only to be intelligible, being sensible that it is very difficult (as you observe) to express oneself on these sorts of subjects, especially for one who is altogether unaccustomed to write upon them.

I have nothing at present more to add, but my sincerest thanks for your trouble in answering my letter, and for your professed readiness to be acquainted with any other difficulty that I may meet with in any of your writings. I am willing to interpret this, as somewhat like a promise of an answer to what I have now written, if there be anything in it which deserves one.

I am, Reverend Sir,
Your most obliged humble servant.

Nov. 23, 1713

Clarke's Answer to Butler's Second Letter [W II, 743]

Sir,

It seems to me that the reason why you do not apprehend ubiquity to be necessarily connected with self-existence is because, in the order of your ideas, you first conceive a being (a finite being, suppose), and then conceive self-existence to be a property of that being, as the angles are properties of a triangle, when a triangle exists. Whereas, on the contrary, necessity of existence, not being a property consequent upon the supposition of the thing's existing, but antecedently the cause or ground of that existence, it is evident this necessity, being not limited to any antecedent subject, as angles are to a triangle, but being itself original, absolute, and (in order of nature) antecedent to all existence, cannot but be everywhere for the same reason that it is anywhere.[63] By applying this reasoning to the instance of space, you will find that by consequence it belongs truly to that substance whereof space is a property or mode of existence, as duration also is. What you say about a necessary being existing somewhere supposes it to be finite; and being finite supposes some cause which determined that such a certain quantity of that being should exist, neither more nor less; and that cause must either be a voluntary cause, or else such a necessary cause the quantity of whose power must be determined and limited by some other cause. But in original absolute necessity, antecedent (in order of nature) to the existence of any thing, nothing of all this can have place, but the necessity is necessarily everywhere alike.

Concerning the second difficulty, I answer: That which exists necessarily is needful to the existence of any other thing; not considered now as a cause (for that indeed is begging the question) but as a *sine qua non*, in the sense as space is necessary to every thing, and nothing can possibly be conceived to exist without thereby presupposing space, which therefore I apprehend to be a property or mode of the self-existent substance. And [I apprehend] that [space], by being evidently necessary itself, proves that the substance of which it is a mode must also be necessary, necessary both in itself and needful to the existence of anything else whatsoever. Extension indeed does not belong to thought because thought is not a being; but there is need of extension to the existence of every being, to a being which has or has not thought, or any other quality whatsoever.

I am, Sir,

Your real friend and servant,

London, Nov. 28, 1713

Butler's Third Letter [*W* II, 744]

Reverend Sir,

I don't very well understand your meaning, when you say that you think, "in the order of my ideas I first conceive a being (finite, suppose) to exist, and then conceive self-existence to be a property of that being." If you mean that I first suppose a finite being to exist I know not why, affirming necessity of existence to be only a consequent of its existence, and that when I have supposed it finite I very safely conclude it is not infinite, I am utterly at a loss upon what expressions in my letter this

---

[63] See the conclusion of the answer to the Seventh Letter [Supplementary text III].

conjecture can be founded. But if you mean that I first of all prove a being to exist from eternity and then, from the reasons of things, prove that such a being must be eternally necessary, I freely own it. Neither do I conceive it to be irregular or absurd, for there is a great difference between the order in which things exist and the order in which I prove to myself that they exist. Neither do I think my saying a necessary being exists somewhere supposes it to be finite; it only supposes that this being exists in space, without determining whether here, or there, or everywhere.

To my second objection, you say: "That which exists necessarily is needful to the existence of any other thing [. . .] as a *sine qua non*, in the sense space is necessary to every thing"; which is proved (you say) by this consideration, that space is a property of the self-existent substance, and being both necessary in itself and needful to the existence of everything else, consequently the substance of which it is a property must be so too. Space, I own, is *in one sense* a property of the self-existent substance; but *in the same sense*, it is also a property of all other substances. The only difference is in respect to the quantity. And since every part of space, as well as the whole, is necessary, every substance, consequently, must be self-existent because it has this self-existent property. Which since you will not admit for true, if it directly follows from your arguments, they cannot be conclusive.

What you say under the first head proves, I think, to a very great probability, though not to me with the evidence of demonstration; but your arguments under the second, I am not able to see the force of.

I am so far from being pleased that I can form objections to your arguments that, besides the satisfaction it would have given me in my own mind, I should have thought it an honour to have entered into your reasonings and seen the force of them. I cannot desire to trespass any more upon your better employed time; so shall only add my hearty thanks for your trouble on my account, and that I am with the greatest respect,

Reverend Sir,
Your most obliged humble servant,

Dec. the 5th, 1713

Clarke's Answer to Butler's Third Letter [*W* II, 745–6]

Sir,

Though when I turn my thoughts every way I fully persuade myself there is no defect in the argument itself, yet in my manner of expression I am satisfied there must be some want of clearness when there remains any difficulty to a person of your abilities and sagacity. I did not mean that your saying a necessary being exists somewhere does *necessarily* suppose it to be finite, but that the manner of expression is *apt* to excite in the mind an idea of a finite being at the same time that you are thinking of a necessary being, without accurately attending to the nature of that necessity by which it exists.

Necessity absolute and antecedent in the order of nature to the existence of any subject has nothing to limit it; but if it operates at all (as it must needs do), it must operate (if I may so speak) everywhere and at all times alike. Determination of a particular quantity, or particular time or place of existence of any thing, cannot arise but from somewhat external to the thing itself. For example: why there should exist just such a small determinate quantity of matter, neither more nor less, interspersed in the immense vacuities of space, no reason can be given. Nor can there be anything in nature which could have determined a thing so indifferent in itself as is the measure of that quantity but only the will of an intelligent and free agent. To suppose matter or any other substance necessarily existing in a finite determinate quantity (in an inch-cube, for instance, or in any certain number of cube-inches, and no more) is exactly the same absurdity as supposing it to exist necessarily, and yet for a finite duration only, which every one sees to be a plain contradiction. The argument is likewise the same in the question about the origin of motion. Motion cannot be necessarily existing because, it being evident that all determinations of motion are equally possible in themselves, the original determination of the motion of any particular body this way rather than the contrary way could not be necessary in itself, but was either caused by the will of an intelligent and free agent, or else was an effect produced and determined without any cause at all, which is an express contradiction: as I have shown in my *Demonstration of the Being and Attributes of God* [p. 19].

To the second head of argument, I answer: space is a property or mode of the self-existent substance, but not of any other substances. All other substances are *in* space and are *penetrated* by it; but the self-existent substance is *not in space nor penetrated* by it, but is itself (if I may so speak) the *substratum* of space, the ground of the existence of space and duration itself. Which (space and duration) being evidently necessary and yet themselves not substances but properties or modes, show evidently that the substance without which these modes could not subsist is itself much more (if that were possible) necessary. And as space and duration are needful (i.e., *sine qua non*) to the existence of everything else, so consequently is the substance to which these modes belong in that peculiar manner which I before mentioned.

I am, Sir,

Your affectionate friend and servant

Dec. 10, 1713

Butler's Fourth Letter [*W* II, 746–7]

Reverend Sir,

Whatever is the occasion of my not seeing the force of your reasonings, I cannot impute it to (what *you* do) the want of clearness in your expression. I am too well acquainted with myself to think my not understanding an argument a sufficient reason to conclude that it is either improperly expressed or not conclusive, unless I can clearly show the defect of it. It is with the greatest satisfaction I must tell you that the more I reflect on your first argument, the more I am convinced of the truth of it; and it now seems to me altogether unreasonable to suppose absolute necessity can have any relation to one part of space more than to another; and if so, an absolutely necessary being must exist everywhere.

I wish I was as well satisfied in respect to the other. You say: all substances, except the self-existent one, are in space, and are penetrated by it. All substancess doubtless, whether body or spirit, exist in space; but when I say that a spirit exists in space, were I put upon telling my meaning, I know not how I could do it any other way than by saying such a particular quantity of space terminates the capacity of acting in finite spirits at one and the same time, so that they cannot act beyond that determined quantity.[e] Not but that I think there is *somewhat* in the manner of existence of spirits in respect of space that more directly answers to the manner of the existence of body; but what that is, or of the manner of their existence, I cannot possibly form an idea. And it seems (if possible) much more difficult to determine what relation the self-existent being has to space. To say he exists in space, after the same

---

[e] Here Butler was thinking of operational, as contrasted to substantial, presence; see the section on God in the introduction.

manner that other substances do, somewhat like which I too rashly asserted in my last, perhaps would be placing the Creator too much on a level with the creature; or, however, it is not plainly and evidently true. And to say the self-existent substance is the *substratum* of space, in the common sense of the word, is scarce intelligible, or at least is not evident. Now though there may be an hundred relations distinct from either of these, yet how we should come by ideas of them, I cannot conceive. We may indeed have ideas to the words and not altogether depart from the common sense of them when we say the self-existent substance is the *substratum* of space or the ground of its existence; but I see no reason to think it true because space seems to me to be as absolutely self-existent as it is possible any thing can be. So that, make what other supposition you please, yet we cannot help supposing immense space because there must be either an infinity of being or (if you will allow the expression) an infinite vacuity of being. Perhaps it may be objected to this that though space is really necessary, yet the reason of its being necessary is its being a property of the self-existent substance; and that it being so evidently necessary, and its dependence on the self-existent substance not so evident, we are ready to conclude it absolutely self-existing as well as necessary; and that this is the reason why the idea of space forces itself on our minds, antecedent to, and exclusive of (as to the ground of its existence), all other things. Now this, though it is really an objection, yet it is no direct answer to what I have said because it supposes the only thing to be proved, viz., that the reason why space is necessary is its being a property of a self-existent substance. And supposing it not to be evident that space is absolutely self-existent, yet, while it is doubtful, we cannot argue as though the contrary were certain and we were sure that space was only a property of the self-existent substance. But now, if space be not absolutely independent, I do not see what we can conclude is so, for it is manifestly necessary itself as well as antecedently needful to the existence of all other things, not excepting, as I think, even the self-existent substance.

All your consequences I see follow demonstrably from your supposition, and were *that* evident, I believe it would serve to prove several other things as well as what you bring it for. Upon which account, I should be extremely pleased to see it proved by anyone. For, as I design the search after truth as the business of my life, I shall not be ashamed to learn from any person, though at the same time I cannot but be sensible that instruction from some men is like the gift of a prince: it reflects an honor on the person on whom it lays an obligation.

> I am,
> Reverend Sir,
> Your obliged servant.

Dec. the 16th, 1713

Clarke's Answer to Butler's Fourth Letter [*W* II, 747–8]

Sir,

My being out of town most part of the month of January and some other accidental avocations hindered me from answering your letter sooner. The sum of the difficulties it contains is, I think, this: that it is difficult to determine what relation the self-existent substance has to space; that to say it is the *substratum* of space in the common sense of the word is scarce intelligible, or at least is not evident; that space seems to be as absolutely self-existent as it is possible any thing can be; and that its being a property of the self-existent substance is supposing the thing that was to be proved. This is entering into the very bottom of the matter, and I will endeavor to give you as brief and clear an answer as I can.

That the self-existent substance is the *substratum* of space, or space a *property* of the self-existent substance, are not perhaps very proper expressions; nor is it easy to find such. But what I mean is this. The idea of space, as also of time or duration, is an *abstract* or *partial* idea, an idea of a certain quality or relation which we evidently see to be necessarily existing and yet which, not being itself a substance, at the same time necessarily presupposes a substance without which it could not exist. Which substance, consequently, must be itself much more, if possible, necessarily existing. I know not how to explain this so well as by the following similitude. A blind man, when he tries to frame to himself the idea of body, his idea is nothing but that of hardness. A man that had eyes, but no power of motion or sense of feeling at all, when he tried to frame to himself the idea of body, his idea would be nothing but that of color. Now as in these cases hardness is not body and color is not body, but yet to the understanding of these persons those properties necessarily infer the being of a substance, of which substance itself the persons have no idea, so space to us is not itself substance, but it necessarily infers the being of a substance which affects none of our present senses; and being itself necessary, it follows that the substance which it infers is much more necessary.

I am, Sir,

Your affectionate friend and servant.

Jan. 29, 1714

Butler's Fifth Letter [*W* II, 748–9]

Reverend Sir,

You have very comprehensively expressed in six or seven lines all the difficulties of my letter, which I should have endeavored to have made shorter had I not been afraid an improper expression might possibly occasion a mistake of my meaning. I am very glad the debate is come into so narrow a compass; for I think now it entirely turns upon this, whether our ideas of space and duration are *partial*, so as to presuppose the existence of some other thing. Your similitude of the blind man is very apt to explain your meaning, which I think I fully understand, but does not seem to come entirely up to the matter. For what is the reason that the blind man concludes there must be somewhat external to give him that idea of hardness? It is because he supposes it impossible for him to be thus affected unless there were some cause of it; which cause, should it be removed, the effect would immediately cease too and he would no more have the idea of hardness but by remembrance. Now, to apply this to the instance of space and duration, since a man from his having these ideas very justly concludes that there must be somewhat external which is the cause of them; consequently, should this cause (whatever it is) be taken away, his ideas would be so too. Therefore if what is supposed to be the cause be removed, and yet the idea remains, that supposed cause cannot be the real one. Now, granting the self-existent substance to be the *substratum* of these ideas, could we make the supposition of its ceasing to be, yet space and duration would still remain *unaltered*, which seems to show that the self-existent substance is not the *substratum* of space and duration. Nor would it be an answer to the difficulty, to say that every property of the self-existent substance is as necessary as the substance itself, since that will only hold while the substance itself exists, for there is implied in the idea of a property an impossibility of subsisting without its *substratum*. I grant the supposition is absurd; but how otherwise can we know whether any thing be a property of such a substance but by examining whether it would cease to be, if its supposed substance should do so? Notwithstanding what I have now said, I cannot say that I believe your argument not conclusive, for I must own my ignorance that I am really at a loss about the nature of space and duration. But did it plainly appear that they were *properties* of a substance, we should have an easy way with the atheists, for it would at once prove demonstrably an eternal, necessary, self-existent being; that there is but one such; and that he is needful in order to the existence of all other things. Which makes me think that though it may be true, yet it is not obvious to every capacity, otherwise it would have been generally used as a fundamental argument to prove the being of God.

I must add one thing more, that your argument for the omnipresence of God seemed always to me very probable. But being very desirous to have it appear demonstrably conclusive, I was sometimes forced to say what was not altogether my opinion. Not that I did this for the sake of disputing, for besides the particular disagreeableness of this to my own temper, I should surely have chosen another person to have trifled with, but I did it to set off the objection to advantage, that it might be more fully answered. I heartily wish you as fair treatment from your opponents in print as I have always had from you, though I must own I cannot see in those that I have read that unprejudiced search after truth which I would have hoped for. I am,

Reverend Sir,
Your most humble servant.

Feb. 3, 1714

Clarke's Answer to Butler's Fifth Letter [*W* II, 750]

Sir,

In a multitude of business I mislaid your last letter, and could not answer it until it came again to my hands by chance. We seem to have pushed the matter in question between us as far as it will go, and upon the whole I cannot but take notice I have very seldom met with persons so reasonable and unprejudiced as yourself in such debates as these.

I think all I need say in answer to the reasoning in your letter is that your granting the absurdity of the supposition you were endeavoring to make is consequently granting the necessary truth of my argument. If space and duration necessarily remain even after they are supposed to be taken away and be not, as it is plain they are not, themselves substances, then the substance on whose existence they depend will necessarily remain likewise even after it is supposed to be taken away, which shows that supposition to be impossible and contradictory.[64]

As to your observation at the end of your letter (that the argument I have insisted on, if it were obvious to every capacity, should have more frequently been used as a fundamental argument for a proof of the being of God), the true cause why it has been seldom urged is, I think, this: that the universal prevalency of Descartes' absurd notions (teaching that matter is necessarily infinite and necessarily eternal, and ascribing all things to mere mechanical laws of motion, exclusive of final causes and of all will and intelligence and divine providence from the government of the world) has incredibly blinded the eyes of common reason, and prevented men from discerning him in whom they live and move and have their being.[65] The like has happened in some other instances. How universally have men for many ages believed that eternity is no duration at all and infinity no amplitude? Something of the like kind has happened in the matter of transubstantiation and, I think, in the Scholastic notion of the Trinity, etc.

I am, Sir,

Your affectionate friend and servant.

April 8, 1714

[64] "Ut partium temporis ordo est immutabilis, sic etiam ordo partium spatii. Moveantur haec de locis suis, et movebuntur (ut ita dicam) de seipsis." ["As the order of the parts of time is immutable, so is the order of the parts of space. Suppose the parts of space to be moved out of their places, and they will be moved (if I may say so) out of themselves."]. *NP*, Book I, Scholium to Definition 8, p. 48.

"{Deus} non est aeternitas vel infinitas, sed aeternus et infinitus; non est duratio vel spatium, sed durat et adest. Durat semper, et adest ubique; et existendo semper et ubique, durationem et spatium, aeternitatem et infinitatem, constituit. Cum unaquaeque spatii particula sit *semper*, et unumquodque durationis indivisibile momentum *ubique*, certe rerum omnium Fabricator ac Dominus non erit *nunquam nusquam* ... Omnipraesens est, non per virtutem solam, sed etiam per substantiam: nam virtus sine substantia subsistere non potest. In ipso continentur et moventur universa, etc." ["{God} is not eternity or infinity, but is eternal and infinite; he is not duration or space, but he endures and is present. He endures forever and is present everywhere; and by existing always and everywhere, he constitutes duration and space, eternity and infinity. Since each and every particle of space is *always*, and each and every indivisible moment of duration is *everywhere*, certainly the Maker and Lord of all things will not be *never* and *nowhere* ... He is omnipresent not only by operation but also by substance; for operation cannot subsist without substance. In him all things are contained and moved, etc."]. *NP* III, Scholium Generale, 761–2.

[65] "... puto implicare contradictionem ut mundus {meaning the material world} sit finitus", i.e., "... I think it implies a contradiction for the world to be finite." R. Descartes, Letter to More of 15 April 1649, in *Oeuvres de Descartes*. eds. C. Adam and P. Tannery (Paris, 1897–1913, reprint Paris, J. Vrin, 1964–76), vol. 5, p. 345.

II

The Answer to a Sixth Letter Being part of a letter written to another gentleman, who had proposed several of the same objections with the foregoing

[*Editor's Note*: We do not know the name of Clarke's correspondent. Clarke's letter dealt extensively with the issue of divine immensity and its compatibility with the fact that God is an immaterial thinking substance. It should be read in conjunction with supplementary text I. The text is from *W* II, 751–4.]

Sir,

You will give me leave, without any preface or apology, to propose directly the best answer I can to the objections you have offered.

There are but *two* ways by which the being and all or any of the attributes of God can possibly be proved. The one, *a priori*; the other, *a posteriori*.[f]

The proof *a posteriori* is level to all men's capacities because there is an endless gradation of wise and useful phenomena of nature, from the most obvious to the most abstruse, which afford at least a moral and reasonable proof of the being of God to the several capacities of all unprejudiced men who have any probity of mind.[66] And this is what, I suppose, God expects, as a moral governor, that moral agents should be determined by.

The proof *a priori* is, I fully believe, strictly *demonstrative* but, like

---

[f] Here, as elsewhere, Clarke and his correspondents use "a priori" and "a posteriori" in their Scholastic sense, in which "a priori" refers to a type of argument moving from principles, reasons, or causes to their consequences or effects. By contrast, "a posteriori" refers to a type of argument moving from consequences or effects to their principles or causes. Thus, an argument inferring God's existence from the divine nature, e.g., the ontological argument, is *a priori*, while one inferring God's existence from the effects of which God is the author, e.g., the argument from design, or Descartes' argument in the third Meditation from our idea of God, is *a posteriori*. Clarke considered his argument, or at least the part moving from the very nature of necessity to the existence of God, *a priori*.

[66] "The invisible things of Him from the creation of the world are clearly seen, being understood by the things that are made, even his eternal power and Godhead." Rom. I, 20.

numberless mathematical demonstrations, capable of being understood only by a few attentive minds because it is of use only against learned and metaphysical difficulties. And therefore it must never be expected that this should be made obvious to the generality of men any more than astronomy or mathematics can be.

This being premised in general, I proceed to particulars.

Concerning the notion of self-existence, I explain myself thus. Of every thing that is, there is a reason which now does, or once and always did, determine the existence rather than the non-existence of that thing. Of that which derives not its being from any other thing, this reason or ground of existence, whether we can attain to any idea of it or no, must be *in* the thing itself. For though the bare proof by ratiocination, that there cannot but exist such a being, does not indeed give us any distinct notion of self-existence but only shows the certainty of the thing, yet when once a thing is known by reasoning *a posteriori* to be certain, it unavoidably follows that there is in nature a reason *a priori*, whether we can discover it or no, of the existence of that which we know cannot but exist. Since, therefore, in that which derives not its being from any other thing, the ground or reason why it exists rather than not exists must be in the thing itself, and it is a plain contradiction to suppose its own will by way of *efficient* cause to be the reason of its existence, it remains that *absolute necessity* (the same necessity that is the cause of the unalterable proportion between 2 and 4) be by way of *formal* cause the ground of that existence. And this necessity is indeed *antecedent*, though not in time yet in the order of nature, to the existence of the being itself; whereas on the contrary its own will is, in the order of nature, subsequent to the supposition of the existence of the being and therefore cannot be the formal cause of that existence.

Nothing can be more absurd than to suppose that any thing or any circumstance of any thing is, and yet that there be absolutely no reason why it is rather than not. It is easy to conceive that we may indeed be utterly ignorant of the reasons, or grounds, or causes of many things. But that any thing is, and that there is a *real* reason in nature why it is rather than is not, these two are as necessarily and essentially connected as any two correlates whatever, as height and depth, etc.

The scholastic way of proving the existence of the self-existent being from the absolute perfection of his nature is ὕστερον πρότερον. For all or any perfections presuppose existence, which is *petitio principii*. But bare necessity of existence does not presuppose, but infers existence. That which exists by absolute necessity of nature will always, whether you will or no, be supposed or included in any possible idea of things, even where you never so expressly endeavor to exclude it, just as the proportion between 2 and 4 remains included in the very terms, wherein any man would endeavor expressly to deny it.

To exist at all and to exist everywhere are one and the very same thing where the cause or ground of the existence is not either confined to, or operates only in, some particular place. For 2 and 4 to have at all a certain proportion to each other, and to have that same proportion everywhere, is the very same thing. And the like is true of every thing that is necessary in itself. To suppose, as you suggest, that the self-existent may be limited by its own nature is presupposing a nature or limiting quality; whereas in this case, here nothing must be presupposed, no nature, no quality whatsoever but what arises (and consequently everywhere alike) from a necessity absolutely in itself and antecedent, in the order of our ideas, to any nature, place, quality, time, or thing whatsoever.

When I say that necessity, absolutely such in itself, has no relation to time or place, my meaning is that it has no relation to, or dependence upon, any particular time or place, or any thing in any particular time or place, but that it is the same in all time and in all place. What you mean by time and place being finite, I understand not. The Schoolmen's notion of time's depending on the motions or existence of the material world is as senseless as the supposing it to depend on the turning or not-turning of an hourglass. The same also is true of place.

Infinite space is infinite extension, and eternity is infinite duration. They are the two first and most obvious and simple ideas that every man has in his mind. Time and place are the *sine qua non* of all other things and of all other ideas. To suppose either of them finite is an express contradiction in the idea itself. No man does, or can, possibly imagine either of them to be finite but only if either by non-attention or by choice he attends perhaps to part of his idea and forbears attending to the remainder. All the difficulty that has ever arisen about this matter is nothing but dust thrown by men's using words (or rather sounds only) in their philosophy, instead of ideas. And the arguments drawn from the jargon of the schoolmen will equally prove every axiom in Euclid to be uncertain and unintelligible.

They who remove the idea of infinity (or of a being whose attribute infinity is) by supposing space to be nothing but a relation between two bodies are guilty of the absurdity of supposing that which is nothing to have *real* qualities. For the space which is between two bodies is always unalterably just what it was and has the very same dimensions, quantity, and figure whether these, or any other bodies be there, or anywhere else, or not at all, just as time or duration is the same whether you turn your hour-glass, or no; or whether the sun moves or stands still; or whether there was or was not any sun, or any material world at all.[67]

The Schoolmen's distinctions about spirits existing in *ubi* and not in *loco* are mere empty sounds, without any manner of signification.[g]

To set bounds to space is to suppose it bounded by something which itself takes up space, and that is a contradiction, or else that it is bounded by nothing, and then the idea of that nothing will still be space, which is another contradiction. Beings which exist in time, and in space (as every finite thing must needs do) presuppose time and space. But that being whose existence makes duration and space must be infinite and eternal because duration and space can have no bounds. Not that duration and space are the formal cause of that existence, but that necessary attributes do necessarily and inseparably infer, or show to us a necessary substance, of which substance itself we have no image because it is the object of none of our senses. But we perceive its existence by its effects, and the necessity of that existence by the necessity of certain attributes and by other arguments of reason and inference. To suppose space removed, destroyed, or taken away amounts to the absurd supposition of removing a thing away from itself. That is, if in your imagination you annihilate the whole of infinite space, the whole infinite space will still remain; and if you annihilate any part of it, that part will still necessarily remain, as appears by the unmoved situation of the rest. And to suppose it divided or divisible amounts to the same contradiction.

The objection of immensity being inconsistent with *spirituality* and *simplicity* arises merely from the jargon of the Schoolmen who, in order to help out transubstantiation, have used themselves to speak of this and of many other things in phrases which had no meaning or ideas belonging to them. By denying the *real* immensity and the *real* eternal duration of God, they in true consequence, though it is reasonable to suppose they saw not

---

g In Scholastic jargon, a substance is somewhere *in loco* if it is there locally, as a body would be; by contrast, it is somewhere in *ubi* if it is there operationally, by acting there.

67 "Eadem est duratio seu perseverantia existentiae rerum; sive motus sint celeres, sive tardi, sive nulli." ["the duration or continuation of the existence of things is the same whether motions be fast, slow, or non-existent."]. *NP*, Scholium to Definition 8, p. 48.

that consequence, denied his being. The immensity of space, it being throughout *absolutely uniform* and *essentially indivisible*, is no more inconsistent with simplicity than the *uniform successive flowing of the parts of duration*, as you most rightly observe, are inconsistent with simplicity. There is no difficulty at all in this point, but a mere prejudice and false notion of simplicity.

As to spirituality, the individual consciousness of the one immense Being is as truly one as the present moment of time is individually one in all places at once. And the one can no more properly be said to be an ell or a mile of consciousness, which is the sum of your objection, than the other can be said to be an ell or a mile of time. This suggestion seems to deserve particular consideration.

To the objection that the supposing God to be really and substantially omnipresent is supposing him to be the soul of the world, I answer: this is a great mistake. For the word "soul" signifies a part of a whole whereof body is the other part; and they, being united, mutually affect each other as parts of the same whole. But God is present to every part of the universe not as a soul but as a governor, so as to act upon everything, in what manner he pleases, himself being acted upon by nothing.

What you suggest about space having no parts, because it is infinite, is a mere quibble indeed and has nothing in it. The meaning of "parts," in questions of this nature, is "separable, compounded, un-united parts," such as are the parts of matter which, for that reason, is always a *compound*, not a simple substance. No matter is *one* substance, but a *heap* of substances. And that I take to be the reason why matter is a subject incapable of thought. Not because it is extended, but because its parts are distinct substances, un-united and independent of each other. Which, I believe, is not the case of other substances. The kinds of substance may perhaps be more and more different from each other than we, at present, for want of more senses are aware of. Matter and spirit is no other division than matter and not-matter, just as if one should divide the species of animals into horses and not-horses.

As to the question why absolute necessity will not admit of the existence of two distinct independent beings, as well as of different attributes and properties in one independent being, I answer: absolute necessity, in which there is nowhere any variation, cannot be the ground of existence of a number of finite beings, however agreeing and harmonious, because that (viz., number or finiteness) is itself a manifest deformity or inequality. But it may be the ground or existence of one uniform infinite being. The different attributes of one uniform being are not a variety of parts or an un-uniformness, if I may so speak, of the necessity by which it exists, but they are all and each of them attributes of the whole, attributes of the one simple infinite being, just as the powers of hearing and seeing are not inequalities or deformities in the soul of man but each of them, powers of the whole soul.

As to the last argument you refer to, my meaning therein is this, that it is a contradiction to suppose two or more necessarily existing beings because each of them, by the supposition being independent and sufficient to itself though the other were supposed not to exist, they thereby each of them mutually destroy the supposed necessity of the other's existence and consequently neither of them indeed will be necessary or independent. For instance, if matter, or spirit, or any other substance could as possibly be conceived to exist without that in which they all exist as that in which they all exist can be conceived to exist without them, then there would be necessary-existence on neither part.

As to the question concerning the possible plurality of infinites, it is certainly true that the infinity of space neither excludes finite bodies nor finite spirits, nor infinite body, nor infinite spirit. But it excludes every thing of the *same* kind, whether finite or infinite, which is all that my argument requires. There can be but *one* infinite space and but *one* infinite time and but *one* infinite spirit (taking spirit to mean a particular positive distinct substance and not the mere negative non-matter, of which there may be innumerable kinds) and, if matter could be infinite, there could likewise be but one infinite body, and so on. For one infinite in all dimensions exhausts always the whole possibility of that kind, though it excludes not others.

The *ubi* of spirits being their perception only, and the omnipresence of God being his infinite knowledge only, are mere words without any sense at all. And by the like confusion anything may be said to be anything and we have in us no principles of knowledge at all, nor any use either of words or ideas.

> I am, Sir,
> Your assured friend
> and servant, etc.

III

The Answer to a Seventh Letter Concerning the Argument a priori

[*Editor's Note*: Clarke's critic was Daniel Waterland (1683–1740), a prominent English theologian who criticized Clarke's theological views on the nature of Christ, and divine immensity and eternity. Clarke's letter deals with the reasons for preferring an *a priori* argument for the existence and perfections of God rather than an *a posteriori* one. The text is at *W* II, 755–8.]

To the Reverend Dr. ***

Your objection against arguing at all *a priori* concerning the existence and perfections of the first cause is what many learned men have indeed stuck at. And it being evident that nothing can be prior to the first cause, they have therefore thought it sufficient to say that the first cause exists "absolutely without cause," and that therefore there can be no such thing as reasoning or arguing about it *a priori* at all. But if you attend carefully, you will find this way of speaking to be by no means satisfactory. For though it is indeed most evident that no thing, no being, can be prior to that being which is the first cause and original of all things, yet there must be in nature a ground or reason, a permanent ground or reason, of the existence of the first cause, otherwise its existence would be owing to and depend upon mere chance. And all that could be said upon this head would amount to this only, that it exists because it exists; that it therefore does and always did exist because it does and always did exist. Which the followers of Spinoza will, with equal strength of reason, affirm concerning every substance that exists at all.

If the idea of an eternal and infinite nothing were a possible idea and not contradictory in itself, the existence of the first cause would not be necessary, for necessity of being and possibility of not being are contradictory ideas.[68] And if the existence of the first cause was not necessary, it would be no contradiction to suppose it either not to have existed in time past or to cease to exist at any time to come. The existence therefore of the first cause, is necessary, necessary absolutely and in itself. And therefore that

---

[68] Nothing is that of which everything can be truly denied and nothing can truly be affirmed. So that the idea of nothing, if I may so speak, is absolutely the negation of all ideas. The idea, therefore, either of a finite or infinite nothing is a contradiction in terms.

necessity is, *a priori* and in the order of nature, the ground or reason of its existence. For that which exists necessarily, or in the idea of which existence and necessity are inseparably and necessarily connected, must either therefore be necessary because it exists, or else it must therefore exist because its existence is necessary. If it was, therefore, necessary because it existed, then for the same reason every thing that exists would exist necessarily, and either every thing, or nothing, would be the first cause. On the contrary, if the first cause does therefore exist because its existence is necessary, then necessity is the ground or reason or foundation of that existence, and the existence does not infer (that is, *a priori* or in the order of nature and consequence, antecede) the necessity of existing; but the necessity of existing does on the contrary infer (that is, *a priori* or in the order of nature, antecede) the supposition of the existence. Which is what I proposed to prove.

The argument *a posteriori* is indeed by far the most generally useful argument, most easy to be understood, and in some degree suited to all capacities, and therefore it ought always to be distinctly insisted upon. But forasmuch as atheistical writers have sometimes opposed the being and attributes of God by such metaphysical reasonings as can not otherwise be obviated than by arguing *a priori*, therefore this manner of arguing also is useful and necessary in its proper place.

The eternity of God cannot otherwise be proved than by considering *a priori* the nature of a necessary or self-existent cause. The temporary phenomena of nature prove indeed demonstrably *a posteriori* that there is, and has been from the beginning of those phenomena, a being of power and wisdom sufficient to produce and preserve those phenomena. But that this first cause has existed from eternity and shall exist to eternity cannot be proved from those temporary phenomena, but must be demonstrated from the intrinsic nature of necessary-existence. If the first cause exists "absolutely without any ground or reason of existence," it might as possibly in times past, without any reason, have not existed, and may as possibly in times to come, without any reason, cease to exist. Can it be proved *a posteriori* that the first cause of all things will exist tomorrow? Or can it be proved any otherwise than by showing that necessity is a certain ground of future as well as of present existence? And if so, then the ground or reason upon which the first cause now does, and hereafter always will and cannot but exist, is the very same ground or reason upon which it always did exist. And consequently it cannot with truth be affirmed that the first cause exists "absolutely without any ground or reason of existence." It is true indeed there is no antecedent reason why necessity is necessity. It is in itself essentially immediate, and it is absurd to suppose that it can be perceived otherwise than immediately and intuitively. Yet, I think, it is not an absurd question to ask why that which is now a necessary being must equally in all past time have been, and in all future time continue to be, a necessary being. And the answer to that question will express fully all that I mean, by affirming the necessity to be the ground or reason of the existence. When atheistical writers affirm that the material universe and every existing substance in particular was eternal "absolutely without any ground or reason of existence," can this assertion be confuted by him who shall himself affirm that God was eternal absolutely without any ground or reason of existence? Or can it be any other way confuted at all than by showing that something must be necessarily existent (else nothing would ever have existed), and that that which is necessarily existent cannot possibly be either finite, or moveable, or at any time capable of any alterations, limitations, variations, inequalities, or diversifications whatsoever, either in whole or in part, or in different parts either of space or time?

In like manner, the infinity or immensity or omnipresence of God can not otherwise be proved than by considering *a priori* the nature of a necessary or self-existent cause. The finite phenomena of nature prove indeed demonstrably *a posteriori* that there is a being which has extent of power and wisdom sufficient to produce and preserve all these phenomena. But that this author of nature is himself absolutely immense or infinite cannot be proved from these finite phenomena but must be demonstrated from the intrinsic nature of necessary existence. If the first cause exists "absolutely without any ground or reason of existence," it may as possibly be finite as infinite; it may as possibly be limited as be immense. It may as possibly in other places, without any reason, not exist as it does, without any reason, exist in those places where the phenomena of nature prove that it does exist. Can it be proved *a posteriori* that that governing wisdom and power, which the phenomena of nature in this material world demonstrate to be present here, must therefore be immense, infinite, or omnipresent, and must be present likewise in those boundless spaces where we know of no phenomena or effects to prove its existence? Or can the immensity and omnipresence of the first cause be at all proved any other way than by showing that necessity of existence is capable of no limitation, but must for the same reason be the ground of immense or omnipresent existence, as it is the ground or foundation of any existence at all?

Again, the unity of God (which, I think, has always been allowed to be a principle of natural religion; otherwise St. Paul could not justly have blamed the heathen as inexcusable in that they did not like to retain God in their knowledge, and that when they knew God they glorified him not as God) – the unity of God, I say, can not otherwise be demonstrated than by considering *a priori* the nature of a necessary or self-existent cause. The phenomena of nature which come within the reach of our observation prove indeed demonstrably that there is a supreme author and director of that nature or of those phenomena whereof we have any knowledge. But that this supreme author and governor of this nature or of these phenomena is likewise the supreme author and governor of universal nature cannot be proved by us from our partial and imperfect knowledge of a few phenomena in that small part of the universe which comes within the reach of our senses, but must be demonstrated from the intrinsic nature of necessary existence. If the first cause exists "absolutely without any ground or reason of existence," it is altogether as possible, and as probable and as reasonable to suppose, that there may, without any reason, exist numberless finite independent co-existent first causes (either of like nature and substance to each other or of different nature and substance from each other) in different parts of the immense universe as that there should, without any reason, exist one only, infinite, immense, omnipresent, first cause, author, and governor of the whole.

That there is and cannot be but one, and one only, such first cause, author, and governor of the universe is, I conceive, capable of strict demonstration, including that part of the argument which is deduced *a priori*. The subject of the question is no trifle. If any sober-minded man is persuaded he can find any flaw in that demonstration, or cares not to examine it lest any of its consequences should prove inconsistent with some other notions he may perhaps through prejudice have imbibed, I should be very thankful to him to show how the unity of God (the first principle of natural religion) can *at all* be proved by reason *a posteriori* only.

Some such considerations as these (I suppose) they were, or others of the like nature, which moved Mr Limborch to write thus to Mr Locke: "Argumentum desiderat {*vir magnificus*}, quo probetur ens, cujus existentia est necessaria, tantum posse esse *unum*; & quidem ut id argumentum a necessitate existentiae desumatur, & a priori (ut in scholis loquuntur,) non a posteriori concludat; hoc est, ex natura necessariae existentiae probetur, eam pluribus non posse esse communem." To which Mr. Locke replies: "Les theologiens, les philosophes, & Descartes lui-meme, supposent l'unite de Dieu, sans la prouver." After which, having suggested his own thoughts, he thus concludes: "C'est là, selon moi, une preuve a priori, que l'etre éternel independent n'est q'un."[69]

To argue, therefore, *a priori* concerning the existence and attributes of the first cause, is no absurdity. For though no thing, no being, can indeed be prior to the first cause, yet arguments may, and must, be drawn from the nature and consequences of that necessity, by which the first cause exists. Mathematically necessary truths are usually demonstrated *a priori*, and yet nothing is prior to truths eternally necessary. To confine, therefore, the use of the term to argumentations about such things only, as have other things prior to them in time, is only quibbling about the signification of words.

To the objection that an attribute cannot be the ground or reason of the existence of the substance itself, which is always on the contrary the support of the attributes, I answer that in strictness of speech necessity of existence is not an attribute in the sense that attributes are properly so styled, but it is (*sui generis*) the ground or foundation of existence both of the substance and of all the attributes. Thus, in other instances, immensity is not an attribute in the sense that wisdom, power, and the like are strictly so called, but it is (*sui generis*) a mode of existence both of the substance and of all the attributes. In like manner, eternity is not an attribute or property in the sense that other attributes, inhering in the substance and supported by it are, properly so called, but it is (*sui generis*) the duration of existence both of the substance and of all the attributes. Attributes or properties, strictly so called, cannot be predicated one of another. Wisdom cannot be properly said to be powerful or power to be

---

[69] ["He desires an argument by which it may be proved that a being whose existence is necessary can only be *one*, and indeed that that argument should be taken from the necessity of the existence and conclude *a priori* (as one says in the Schools) and not *a posteriori*; that is, that it should be proved from the nature of necessary existence that it cannot be common to several things."]. Philippus van Limbroch to John Locke, 4 April 1698. E. S. De Beer (ed.), *The Correspondence of John Locke* (Oxford, Clarendon Press, 1981), vol. VI, pp. 354–5. [Limbroch was referring to Mr Hudde, burgomaster of Amsterdam and a devoted Cartesian.]

 ["... Theologians, philosophers, Descartes himself, suppose the unity of God without proving it."]

 ["There, in my view, is an *a priori* proof that the eternal independent being is but one."]. John Locke to Philippus van Limbroch, April 21, 1698. E. S. De Beer (ed.), *The Correspondence of John Locke* (Oxford, Clarendon Press, 1981), vol. VI, pp. 405–6.]

wise. But immensity is a *mode* of existence both of the divine substance and of all the attributes. Eternity is the duration of existence both of the divine substance and of all the attributes. And necessity is the ground, or reason, or foundation of existence, both of the divine substance and of all the attributes.

I am, Sir,
Your very humble servant, etc.

IV

Letters to Dr. Clarke concerning Liberty and Necessity
from a Gentleman of the University of Cambridge,
with the Doctor's Answers to them

[*Editor's Note*: The "Gentleman of the University of Cambridge" was John Bulkeley (1694–1718). Their exchange revolved around the role of the last judgment of the understanding in volition, and it prompted Clarke to provide one of the clearest statements of his views on free will and the difference between moral and natural necessity. It should be read in conjunction with supplementary text V. The correspondence is at *W* IV, 713–18.]

Bulkeley's First Letter [*W* IV, 713]

Jan. 1, 1716–17

Reverend Sir,
        I have no other pretence to trouble you on this occasion but that right which all mankind may plead to the instructions of a great and good man. The small share of time I have spent in study has been employed in examining the fundamental principles of reason and philosophy. In this pursuit I must have been absolutely blind, if your *Discourse on the Being and Attributes of God* had escaped me, in which your account of liberty and necessity has silenced a great many difficulties which perplexed me very much. But I have one still remaining on my mind, which I could wish to get rid of, and therefore beg your assistance. I see plainly man is not over-ruled by any blind impulse; but that every volition is not necessary, this I cannot see. It is allowed that the will is no other but the last judgment of the understanding. It will likewise, I suppose, be granted that the last judgment of the understanding assenting to, or dissenting from, any speculative proposition is necessary. My enquiry then is, why the last judgment of the understanding assenting to, or dissenting from, any practical proposition (by which the man is determined to act) should not be equally necessary; and also, whether such a necessity be not, in all its consequences and effects, though not in its foundation, the very same which the fatalists maintain? To give an instance: a man judges it better to consult his present ease than to wait for the greatest happiness in reversion. Does he

not act by the same necessity by which another man judges the contrary to be more eligible? Or, to speak more properly, by the same necessity by which a mathematician judges that a triangle is one half of a square on the same base and between the same parallels? To pursue this matter a little farther: God is absolutely perfect; he judges, then, in every instance that to be best (i.e., wills that) which in nature and reality is best; he is, therefore, necessarily good and just. Every man is imperfect; he judges, then, in many instances that to be best (i.e., wills that) which in nature and reality is not best: every man, therefore, is by necessity imperfectly good and just, and that according to their several degrees of imperfection. How is any creature, then, accountable for the want of that perfection which God never gave it, neither was it in its power to give itself? Thus, Sir, I have opened my opinion as clearly and fully as I could, which will, I hope, save you some trouble. And now, when I look back, I cannot but suspect that I am got into a very odd train of thoughts; and yet, when I take a survey of my ideas on all sides, I am at a loss how or where the delusion could creep in. If you condescend to answer my letter, I shall receive it with the reverence and esteem due to so great a character, and forever think myself

Your most obliged
Humble servant, etc.

Clarke's Answer to Bulkeley's First Letter [*W* IV, 714]

Jan. 3, 1716–17

Sir,

You have put the argument against liberty more short and strong than I have usually seen it. The true answer to it, I think, is this. So far as any thing is passive, so far it is subject to necessity; so far as it is an agent, so far it is free: for action and freedom are, I think, perfectly identical ideas. To explain this in the instance you allege, truth and good are to the understanding what a luminous object is to the eye. The eye, when open, sees the object necessarily because it is passive in so doing. The understanding likewise, when open, perceives the truth of a speculative proposition, or the reasonableness of a practical proposition, necessarily because the understanding also is passive in so doing. Only, as a man by the action of shutting his eyes may avoid seeing, so by the action of withdrawing his attention he may avoid understanding. But allowing the last judgment of the understanding to be always necessary, as indeed I think it is, yet what follows from thence? *Judging* is one thing, and *acting* is another. They depend upon principles totally different from each other, and which have no more connection than activeness and passiveness. Neither God nor man can avoid seeing that to be true which they see is true, or judging that to be fit and reasonable which they see is fit and reasonable. But in all this there is no action, any more than God's being omnipresent (which depends not on his will) can be said to be a divine act. The physical power of acting (which both in God and man is the essence of liberty) continues exactly the same after the last judgment of the understanding as before. For example: it appears from several promises (suppose) that it is at this instant the last judgment of the divine understanding that it is not reasonable the world should be destroyed this day. Does it follow from thence that God's physical power of destroying it is not exactly the same this day as it will be at any time hereafter? And is it not evident that the necessity by which God is omnipresent or omniscient and the necessity by which he keeps his promise are things that have no similitude but in name, the one being *natural* and *literal*, the other merely *figurative* and *moral?* The sum is: there is no connection between *approbation* and *action*, between what is passive and what is active. The spring of action is not the understanding, for a being incapable of action might nevertheless be capable of perception. But the spring of action is *the self-motive power* which is (in all animals) spontaneity, and (in rational ones) what we call "liberty." All error in this matter has, I think, arisen from men's using the word "will" in a confused sense to express indistinctly partly what is passive and partly what is active.

I am, Sir, etc.

Bulkeley's Second Letter [*W* IV, 715]

Jan. 6, 1716–17

Reverend Sir,

      I shall detain you no longer than to acknowledge your great favor, and proceed to offer my reasons why I cannot apprehend how your argument satisfies the difficulty. But first it will be of use to settle my notion of necessity. Thus, therefore, when in any given circumstance it is a contradiction to suppose any being, mode, or action, to have been otherwise than it actually is, that being, mode, or action is in that instance necessary, absolutely and properly speaking. To apply this to the question before us, viz., whether human actions are strictly and properly necessary, the last judgment of the understanding is granted necessary in every instance of volition; every action therefore, or self-motion (be its cause or principle what it will) is, I think, also necessary. For it either necessarily follows a man's last judgment or volition, or it does not. If it does, it is then strictly and properly necessary; if it be said that it does not necessarily follow, is not that a contradiction in the very terms? Is it not to suppose the very same creature self-moving and not self-moving at the very same time? So that if the idea of freedom be the idea of self-motive power, it is so far from being opposed to necessity that it may be, and I think it is itself, necessary. Thus, then, necessity is consistent with perfect freedom, i.e., with self-motive power, and the divine being himself is in all his actions necessary in the natural and literal sense of the word. For it is as direct a contradiction in nature to suppose all-wisdom, if I may use that term, acting unjustly or cruelly, that is, unwisely, as to suppose omnipresence confined, since the *moral* attributes of God are as truly and properly *natural* as those which are distinguished by that name, and are therefore equally necessary. But this is a very high perfection in the creator; it cannot, therefore, be an imperfection in the creature. Nothing can be more clear. But then will it not unavoidably follow that no creature can be accountable for his actions? Every action of self-motion necessarily follows the last determination of the understanding; where, then, can the blame lie but at the understanding? What is sin but folly? And how can any man be accountable for it any more than for not being wiser than God made him? Nothing remains but to observe that I always use the word "necessity" in this argument to signify not an external necessity or blind impulse, but a necessity internal, which results from the very being and constitution of rational nature; which latter will, I think, as naturally infer the consequence I have deduced as the former; and to conclude myself

> Your most obliged
> Humble servant

Clarke's Answer to Bulkeley's Second Letter [*W* IV, 716]

> Jan. 8, 1716–17

Sir,

Your argument is urged with much ingenuity. But it plainly appears to me that there is an error which lies under the word "volition." Under that term you include both the final perception of the understanding, which is passive, and also the first operation or exertion of the active faculty or self-motive power. These two you suppose to be necessarily connected. I think there is no connection at all between them, and that in their not being connected lies the difference between action and passion, which difference is the essence of liberty. If the two things now mentioned were (as you suppose) connected by a true physical necessity, there would remain no difference between action and passion, but this only, that what we now call an agent would erroneously imagine itself to be an agent when in reality it was merely passive. Nay, indeed, there would be no such thing as an agent or action in the universe. Neither man, nor angel, nor even God himself, would act in any other sense than a balance determined on one side by an overplus of weight, supposing it endued with perception or understanding. Now the consequence of this is that there would be in the universe all patient and no agent, all effect and no cause, which is a manifest and most express contradiction.

Again: you plainly confound *moral* contradiction and *moral* necessity, with *natural* contradiction and *natural* necessity. It is indeed a contradiction in terms, *morally* speaking, that a wise man should do a foolish thing, or an honest man a dishonest thing; but it is no contradiction in physics. And in God himself, were his doing acts of goodness and mercy as physically necessary as his being omnipresent, it would be as absurd to thank him for doing good as for being omnipresent. Wherefore, were the moral perfections of God necessary in the same physical sense as the natural attributes are, which have no dependence on his will or power of acting, they would not be moral perfections at all.

I am, Sir,
Yours, etc.

Bulkeley's Third Letter [*W* IV, 716–17]

Jan 10, 1716–17

Reverend Sir,

You have now brought the debate into a very narrow compass. The only difficulty I find remaining is to disjoin in my mind the last judgment or perception of the understanding and the first exertion of the self-motive power. For let us suppose them disjoined and consider the consequence. Will it not follow that unintelligent substance may be capable of self-motion, and mere matter be as absolutely free as infinite wisdom itself? Nay, if in any instance action or self-motion does not follow the last perception or judgment of the understanding, the agent must in that instance be over-ruled by a blind impulse: there is no medium. To consider this matter more distinctly in the great author of all perfection, if his actions do not necessarily follow the final perception of his understanding, how can it be *proved* that he is infinitely just and good? It is no impossibility, on this hypothesis, but he may act in the worst conceivable manner, at the very same time when he judges and wills the best, for it is supposed that there is no connection between judgment and self-motion, between volition and action. I do not understand your distinction between physical and moral necessity because I, indeed, have no idea at all of the latter. If it means the same which I expressed by the term "necessity internal," it has, I think, as clear and distinct a foundation in nature as any physical necessity whatsoever. Which I desire you particularly to observe because I had reason to suspect from your last favor that my meaning was not sufficiently clear on that head.

> I am, Sir,
> Your most obliged
> Humble servant

Clarke's Answer to Bulkeley's Third Letter [*W* IV, 717–18]

> Jan. 12, 1716–17

Sir,

I think your remaining difficulty may be removed by the following similitude. The perception or last judgment of the understanding is as distinct from the actual exertion of the self-motive power as seeing the way is from walking in it. Nor will it follow, because the perception of the understanding is denied to be the immediate efficient necessary cause of the exertion of the self-motive power, that therefore unintelligent matter may be capable of self-motion, any more than it will follow, if a man's eyes be denied to be the immediate efficient necessary cause of his walking, that therefore the man may be capable of walking, though he has neither legs nor life. A man's understanding judges of what he is to do as his eyes discern the way; but a blind or winking man has power to walk without seeing, and every living agent has a physical power to act, whether he makes any use of his judgment and understanding or no. Unintelligent matter can be no agent because action supposes in the very notion of it life and con-sciousness. But that consciousness which makes action to be action is entirely a distinct thing from that perception or judgment by which a man determines before-hand concerning the reasonableness or fitness of what he is about to act. An agent over-ruled by a blind impulse is a contradic-tion in terms, for then he is not at all an agent but a mere patient. But an agent acting not according to the last judgment of his understanding (meaning always by "the last judgment of the understanding" the last passive perception and not the first active volition of the agent, which two things must by no means be confounded) – such an agent, I say, is like a man shutting his eyes and walking at a venture down a precipice.

God always discerns and approves what is just and good *necessarily*, and cannot do otherwise; but he always acts or does what is just and good *freely*, that is, having at the same time a full natural or physical power of acting differently. Otherwise justice, for example, in God would be nothing different from justice in a sword when it executes a just sentence, suppos-ing the sword to perceive what it is doing and yet cannot help doing it. The consequence whereof is that there could not possibly be in God *any* moral perfection at all. For every thing that is of a moral nature, implies in the very notion or essence of it the doing of something, which at the same time was in the agent's power not to have done. Moral necessity, therefore, is distinguished from physical necessity, just as all other figures of speech are from literal expressions, that is, it is in truth and philosophically speaking, *no necessity* at all. And yet every one easily sees that the justice and good-ness of an infinitely perfect free agent may as firmly and reasonably be relied on as the necessary effect of any necessary agent is known to be physically unavoidable.

I am, Sir, etc.

Bulkeley's Last Letter [*W* IV, 718]

Jan. 24, 1716–17

Sir,

I have now, to my great satisfaction, a clearer insight than I ever expected into so intricate a question as we have been upon. The consider-ation that the last judgment of the understanding can have no influence on self-motion because there is no resemblance between an action and a perception of the mind, and that, therefore, there must be some distinct principle of self-motion entirely independent on the perceptive faculty, weighs very much with me. And I think it is very probable, as you observe, that our want of clearly distinguishing between the perceptive and active faculty is the chief origin of all perplexity in this question. I shall trouble you no farther on this occasion, but leave the rest to time and repeated reflection. But it were perfect stupidity or, worse, ingratitude not to acknowledge your candor and even friendship to an entire stranger who appeared to be engaged in the pursuit of truth. I know not how to express my sentiments of it with truth and sincerity, unless in a manner which will certainly be disagreeable to you; but I should have no sense of anything that is serious and rational, if I knew not how to esteem it.

I am, Sir, etc.

V

From *Remarks Upon a Book, entitled "A Philosophical Enquiry Concerning Human Liberty"*

[*Editor's Note*: The author Clarke criticized was Anthony Collins (1676–1729), a free-thinker leaning toward materialism who was greatly influenced by Locke. Collins' book, which denied freedom of the will, was published in 1716, Clarke's review, which contains a very clear exposition of his theory of agent causation, a year later. This selection should be read in conjunction with supplementary text IV. For ease of reading, I have eliminated Clarke's copious page references to Collins' book. The text is from *W* IV, 721–5.]

In a book lately published, entitled *A Philosophical Enquiry Concerning Human Liberty*, the author [Anthony Collins] proposes six distinct arguments to prove that there neither is nor can be any liberty in human actions. The arguments he offers, have, I think, been already in great measure obviated in the papers which lately passed between me and the learned Mr. Leibniz. Yet, because some of them seem to be placed in such a light as may possibly deceive unwary persons whose thoughts have not been much conversant upon so nice a subject, I thought it not improper to set down particularly such brief remarks as might be sufficient to lay open to an intelligent reader the fallacy of the whole book.

... The question he undertakes to determine is thus stated by him: whether man be a free or necessary agent. And he is confident that men are necessary agents; that all allow mad men, and children, and beasts, to be necessary agents; that some actions are plainly actions that are necessary; that there can be no dispute but perception is a necessary action of man; and that causes act on necessary agents, to whom they are necessary causes of action. Now here I desire to know what idea the word "agent" or "action" carries along with it when joined with necessary. Vulgarly, indeed, in loose, figurative, and improper speech, we call clocks and watches, "necessary" agents. But in truth and strictness of speaking (which ought always to be carefully preserved in philosophical debates) a necessary agent or necessary action is a contradiction in terms. For whatever acts necessarily does not indeed act at all, but is only acted upon; is not at all an agent, but a mere patient; does not move, but is moved only.

Clocks and watches are in no sense agents; neither is their motion, in any sense, an action. Nor is it merely, "for want of sensation and intelligence, that clocks and watches are subject to an absolute, physical, and mechanical necessity." For the pulsation of the heart, though joined with sensation, is yet as necessary a motion as that of a clock; and the one is no more an action of the man, than the other is of the clock. Nor would a balance endowed with sensation and intelligence be any more an agent when it felt itself moved by the weights than it is now an agent without perception. A necessary agent, therefore, I say, whether with or without sensation, is no agent at all, but the terms are contradictory to each other. To be an agent signifies to have a *power of beginning motion*; and motion cannot begin necessarily, because necessity of motion supposes an efficiency superior to, and irresistible by, the thing moved; and consequently the beginning of the motion cannot be in that which is moved necessarily, but in the superior cause, or in the efficiency of some other cause still superior to that, until at length we arrive at some free agent. Which free agent may either (which is the case of men) have received the power of beginning motion from the will of a superior free agent; or (which is the case of God Almighty) he may be himself necessarily existent, necessarily all-knowing, necessarily all-powerful, because existence, knowledge, power, and the like are not actions. But he cannot be a necessary agent without an express contradiction in the very terms. All power of acting essentially implies at the same time a power of not acting, otherwise it is not acting but barely a being acted upon by that power (whatever it be) which causes the action.

 . . . These two things, [perception and action] . . . the author constantly confounds together as one individual by the ambiguous use of the words "willing" and "preferring" . . . [He argues] that because willing and preferring, so far as those words signify the last perception or approbation of the understanding, are passive and necessary, therefore willing and preferring, when the same words imply the first exertion of the self-moving power, which is essentially active, are necessary also. And [he argues that] because when "will" signifies the actual exertion of the self-moving power, a man then, indeed, must necessarily do that which he wills (because it is not possible that a man should not do a thing, when he is supposed to do it), therefore when the same word "will" signifies nothing more than the last approbation of the understanding, it shall still be true that a man must necessarily do (using the word "necessarily" in the physical and proper sense) what his understanding approves. Than which consequence, nothing can be more weak. For though the self-moving power (which if it is not free is a contradiction in terms) is an adequate cause of action, yet understanding, or judgment, or assent, or approbation or liking, or whatever name you please to call it by, can no more possibly be the efficient cause of action than rest can be the cause of motion. Nothing can possibly be the cause of an effect more considerable than itself. Nothing that is passive can possibly be the cause of anything that is active. An *occasion* indeed, it may be, and action may be consequent (though without any physical connection) upon perception or judgment; nay, it may easily (if you please) be supposed to be *always* consequent upon it, and yet that at the same time there be no manner of physical or necessary connection between them. For instance, God's performing his promise is always consequent upon his making it; yet there is no connection between them as between cause and effect, for not the promise of God but his active power is the alone physical or efficient cause of the performance.

Again, what has become of clear and distinct ideas, when we are told of "actions being determined by the causes preceding each action"; of man's being "Ever unavoidably determined in every point of time by the circumstances he is in, and the causes he is under, to do that one thing he does, and not possibly to do any other"; of "this first necessary action [viz. perception, which is no action at all], being the foundation and cause of all the other intelligent actions of man" and, of "pleasure and pain being *causes* to determine men's wills?" For what idea can any man frame how pleasure or pain, which are mere passive perceptions, or how reasons, motives, and arguments, which are mere abstract notions, can be the physical, necessary, and efficient cause of action? May not an abstract notion as well strike a ball as be the efficient cause of motion in a man's body? Occasions indeed there may be, and are, upon which that substance in man wherein the self-moving principle resides freely exerts its active power. But it is the self-moving principle and not at all the reason or motive which is the physical or efficient cause of action.

When we say, in vulgar speech, that motives or reasons determine a man, it is nothing but a mere figure or metaphor. It is the man that freely determines himself to act. Reasons, or perceptions of the understanding, can no more (properly and strictly speaking) determine an action, than an abstract notion can be a substance or agent, or can strike or move a piece of matter. Unless all that this gentleman advances about reasons and motives and perceptions of the understanding be mere cant, and his true meaning be that man is indeed no agent at all but is moved necessarily and mechanically by mere impulses of subtle matter. And then the question will still for ever return upon him about the original cause of motion; which must either finally be resolved into a first mover, in whom consequently there is liberty of action, or else into an infinite and eternal chain of effects without any cause at all, which is an express contradiction, except motion could be necessarily existent in its own nature; which that it is not, is evident because the idea of rest is no contradiction, and also because there being no motion without a particular determination one certain way, and no one determination being in nature more necessary than another, an essential and necessary tendency to motion in all determinations equally, could never have produced any motion at all.

Lastly, by what clear and distinct ideas can any man perceive that an indifference as to power (that is, an equal physical power either of acting or of forbearing to act) and an indifference as to inclination (that is, an equal approbation or liking of one thing or of the contrary) is one and the same thing? And yet these two are constantly confounded through the whole book, the author always supposing that if a man is not determined as necessarily and irresistably as a weight determines the motion of a balance, then he can in no degree be influenced by, nor can have any regard to, any motives or reasons of action whatsoever but must be totally indifferent to all actions alike... As if nothing could possibly be of any weight, or of any use with men, that did not necessitate them, and if a person be not determined irresistibly, then he must be totally indifferent to all actions alike and can have no regard to motives or reasons of action at all. Of which consequence no man can have a clear idea until it has first been proved that self-moving or active power is inconsistent with having any regard to reasons of acting.

In the next place, I observe, that the author endeavors to impose upon his reader a false definition of liberty. "I contend," says he, "for liberty, as it signifies a power in man, to do as he wills or pleases." And this he elsewhere styles a valuable liberty. Now in this definition, besides the forementioned ambiguity of the words "wills" or "pleases," it ought carefully to be remarked that the word "do" has no signification. For his meaning is not that the man acts or does any thing, but the liberty or power in man to do as he wills or pleases is, with him, exactly and only the same as the liberty or power in a balance would be, to move as it wills or pleases, supposing the balance endowed with such a sensation or intelligence, as enabled it to perceive which way the weights turned it, and to approve the motion, so as to fancy that it moved itself, when indeed it was only moved by the weights. That this is his real meaning appears plainly from hence, that he makes the difference between a man and a clock to consist only in sensation and intelligence, not in any power of acting. Whereas indeed the whole essence of liberty consists in the power of acting. *Action* and *liberty* are identical ideas: and the true definition of a free being is "one that is endowed with a power of acting as well as of being acted upon."

This mistake in the notion of physical liberty and necessity led him also into the like mistake in his notion of moral necessity. Moral necessity, in true and philosophical strictness, is not indeed any necessity at all, but it is merely a *figurative* manner of speaking which, like all other figurative expressions, has nothing at all of physical reality in it. When a man says, he cannot *possibly* be deceived in relying on the word of a person of known veracity, the meaning is not that the other person has no power to deceive him, or that (with regard to the physical action) it is not as easy for that person to depart from his promise as to keep it, but that the man has great reason to depend on such a person's character, that he shall not be deceived by him. But now this author makes moral necessity and physical necessity to be exactly and philosophically the same thing, only with this distinction, that physical necessity in an unintelligent subject is physical necessity, but that the same physical necessity in an intelligent subject is only moral necessity. When a stone falls, or a clock or watch moves, it moves by a physical necessity; but when a man falls, or when he is determined to do any action, which he is exactly under the same physical necessity of doing (only with this circumstance, that his understanding approves or is pleased with it) as he is of falling when he is thrown down a precipice, this (it seems) is moral necessity only. In which matter the author is guilty of a double absurdity. First, in supposing reasons or motives (unless those terms be mere cant) to make the same necessary impulse upon intelligent subjects as matter in motion does upon unintelligent subjects, which is supposing abstract notions to be substances. And secondly, in endeavoring to impose it upon his reader, as a thing taken for granted, that moral necessity and physical necessity do not differ intrinsically in their own nature but only with regard to the subject they are applied to, when on the contrary he well knows that by "moral necessity" consistent writers never mean anything more than to express in a figurative manner the certainty of such an event as may in reason be fully depended upon, though literally and in philosophical strictness of truth, there be *no necessity at all* of the event. Thus if God has promised that the world shall continue another year, it is a very natural and obvious manner of expression, to say that the world cannot possibly come to an end this year; and yet no reasonable person is by that manner of speaking led to imagine that God has not at this moment the very same physical power of destroying the world, as he will have at any time hereafter.

VI

From Clarke's *Sermons on Several Subjects.*

[*Editor's Note*: The sermons from which this selection is excerpted were first published in *W* I by Samuel's brother John in 1738. They expand and clarify many of Clarke's views about God's metaphysical and moral attributes.]

Sermon IV: *Of the Eternity of God* [*W* I, 22]

... It is worthy of observation, as to the manner of our conceiving the eternity of God, that the Scholastic writers have generally described it to be not a real perpetual duration but one point or instant comprehending eternity, and wherein all things are really coexistent at once. But un-intelligible ways of speaking have, I think, never done any service to religion. The true notion of the divine eternity does not consist in making past things to be still present and things future to be already come, which is an express contradiction. But it consists in this (and in this it infinitely transcends the manner of existence of all created beings, even of those which shall continue for ever): that whereas their finite minds can by no means comprehend all that is past or understand perfectly the things that are present, much less know or have in their power the things that are to come (but their thoughts and knowledge and power, must of necessity have degrees and periods, and be successive and transient as the things them-selves); the eternal, supreme cause, on the contrary, has such a perfect, independent, and unchangeable comprehension of all things that in every point or instant of his eternal duration all things past, present, and to come must be, not indeed themselves present at once (for that is a manifest con-tradiction), but they must be as entirely known and represented to him in one single thought or view, and all things present and future be as absolutely under his power and direction as if there were really no succes-sion at all, and as if all things had been (not that they really are) actually present at once.

Sermon VII: *Of the Immutability of God* [*W* I, 39–41]

... In order to explain the nature of this divine attribute of immutability and show distinctly wherein it consists, it is to be observed that both in reason and Scripture God is considered as unchangeable upon different accounts and in very different respects.

Firstly, in respect of his essence, God is absolutely unchangeable because his being is necessary and his essence self-existent; for whatever necessarily is, as it cannot but be, so it cannot but continue to be invariably what it is. That which depends upon nothing can be affected by nothing, can be acted upon by nothing, can be changed by nothing, can be influenced by no power, can be impaired by no time, can be varied by no accident.

Secondly, in respect of his perfections likewise, as well as his essence, God is absolutely unchangeable. Concerning those perfections which flow necessarily from his essence and depend not on his will, this is self-evident because whatever necessarily flows from any cause or principle, must likewise of necessity be as invariable as the cause or principle from which it necessarily proceeds. Of this kind are the power, the knowledge, the wisdom, and the other natural attributes of God which, having no dependence even upon his own will any more than his very being itself has, it is plain they can much less be subject to any alteration from any other cause or power whatsoever. Concerning those other perfections, the exercise whereof depends upon his will, such are his justice, veracity, goodness, mercy, and all other moral perfections, the absolute immutability of these is not indeed so obvious and self-evident because it depends on the unchangeableness not only of his essence, but of his will also. Nevertheless, upon careful consideration, the unchangeableness of these likewise will no less certainly appear, because in a being who always knows what is right to be done, and can never possibly be deceived, or awed, or tempted, or imposed upon, his general will or intention of doing always what is best and most fit and right will in reality, though not upon the same ground of natural necessity, yet, in event and upon the whole, be as certainly and truly unchangeable as his very essence itself.

... Thirdly, as God is unchangeable in his essence and in the general perfections of his nature, so is he also in the particular decrees and purposes of his will, and so likewise in his laws, in his promises, and in his threatenings. The reason is because, having all power and all knowledge, he can never resolve upon anything which shall be either not possible or not reasonable to be accomplished. All finite beings are frequently forced to change their designs because they often find it impossible to finish what they begin, or unreasonable to pursue their first intention; but in God these things have no place.

He is unchangeable in all his decrees and purposes because, having all things in his power and comprehending all things in his fore-knowledge, he can by no force be over-ruled; he can by no surprise or unexpected accident be prevented; he can by no unforeseen alteration in the reasons of things be himself changed in his purpose.

... Again, in his laws likewise, that is, in the uniform intention of all his commandments, God is perfectly unchangeable because they are always founded on the same immutable reasons, the eternal differences of good and evil, the original nature of things, and universal equity; and they always tend to the same regular end: the order and happiness of the whole creation. Of this, the law of nature was the primary institution; the law of Moses was the typical or figurative representation; and the Gospel of Christ, its completion or perfect restoration.

... Further; in his covenants or promises, such as are not declared to be conditional and annexed to certain particular qualifications, God is like-wise perfectly unchangeable. The reason is because covenants or promises of this kind are founded upon such grounds as cannot be altered, even upon the original, fixed, and permanent designs and intentions of all-wise providence.

Sermon XI: *Of the Omniscience of God* [*W* I, 69–70]

... But there is a further and still more wonderful object of the divine knowledge than even the hearts or thoughts of men, and that is future events. He that gave all things those powers and faculties which they enjoy, must be acknowledged to foresee what each of those powers and faculties will produce and, through an infinite series of causes, perceive at one view all things that ever shall be, as if they at present were. Even the most contingent futurities, the actions of free agents, cannot be conceived to be hidden from his foresight, who gave to his creatures those very powers of will and choice by which they are free agents ... The many predictions of future events which have been in the world were convincing evidences of the truth of this attribute to the heathen philosophers; and even the common reason of the vulgar taught them that it could not be imagined that the knowledge of the infinite and eternal God should be in any respect finite. There is in this matter one difficulty only which has in all ages employed the speculation of considering persons, namely the following question: how foreknowledge in God can be consistent with liberty of action in men. In order to remove which difficulty, it may not be improper to premise two things.

Firstly, that our finite understandings may very reasonably be allowed not to be able to comprehend all the ways of infinite knowledge. But this acknowledgement of the incomprehensibleness of the ways of God must always be understood with relation to such things only as do not imply any express contradiction. For whenever that is the case, it cannot be said concerning such things that they are incomprehensible or what we cannot understand but, on the contrary, that they are such things which we do clearly and distinctly understand that they cannot possibly be, the necessary falsity of all such things being as clear to our understandings as the self-evidence of the plainest truths. Also, it must be observed that this acknowledgment ought to be understood only of things expressly revealed, not of any human doctrines.

Secondly, it is further necessary to premise that in the matter before us the question is not whether men's actions be free, but whether or no, and how, that freedom of action which makes men to be men can be consistent with fore-knowledge of such actions. For if these two things were really inconsistent and could by no means be reconciled, it would follow not that men's actions were not free (for that would destroy *all* religion, and take away *all* the moral attributes of God at once), but on the other side it would follow that such free actions as men's are, and without which rational creatures could not be rational creatures, were not the objects of the divine fore-knowledge. And in such case it would be no more a diminution of God's omniscience not to know things impossible and contradictory to be known than it is a diminution of his omnipotence not to be able to do things impossible and contradictory to be done.

But this is not the case. For, these two things being premised, we may now to the difficulty itself, how fore-knowledge in God can be consistent with liberty of action in men, answer directly that they are therefore consistent, because fore-knowledge has no influence at all upon the things fore-known, and it has therefore no influence upon them, because things would be just as they are and not otherwise, though there was no fore-knowledge. Fore-knowledge does not cause things to be; but things that are to be hereafter, whether necessarily or freely, are the cause of it being fore-known that they shall so, whether necessarily or freely, be. The futurity of free actions is exactly the same and, in the nature of things themselves, of the like certainty in event, whether they can or could not be fore-known. And as our knowing a thing to be when we see it does not hinder an action from being free, notwithstanding that it is then certain and cannot but be when it is, so God's fore-seeing that any action will freely be done does not at all hinder its being free, though he knows it certainly, because his fore-seeing things to come does no more influence or alter the nature of things than our seeing them when they are.

The manner of God's knowing future free actions must not, indeed, be like his fore-knowledge of things necessary; I say, it must not be by fore-seeing a continued chain of causes, for that would indeed destroy their freedom, but it must be a power quite of another kind, a power whereof we can only have an obscure glimpse in some such manner as that which follows. What one man will freely do upon any particular occasion, another man, by observation and attention, may in some measure judge; and the wiser the person be who makes the observation, the more probable will his judgment be and the seldomer will he be deceived. An angel, in the like case, would make a judgment of the future event as much nearer to certainty than that of the wisest man, as the angelic nature and faculties are superior to the human. In God himself, whose powers are all in every respect infinitely transcending those of the highest creatures, this judgment of future free actions must needs be infallible; that is, as truly certain (though entirely of a different kind) as that fore-knowledge which he has of necessary events by seeing their necessary chain of causes.

Nor ought it to seem strange that this divine fore-knowledge of future free actions should be entirely of a different nature from his fore-knowledge of necessary events. For there is a not unlike distinction in some others also of the divine attributes. The omnipresence of God, is an attribute necessarily belonging to him by absolute necessity of *nature*, and altogether independent of his will; the goodness of God is, likewise, a necessary attribute, yet not in the same manner as his omnipresence, by a mere necessity of nature, but by the unalterable rectitude of his *will*, which is the true reason why we properly return to him thanks for being good but not for being omnipresent. Thus both are necessary, and yet by a necessity of a totally different sort or kind. In like manner, the fore-knowledge of God, both that of necessary and that of free events, is in the issue of things equally certain. Yet, in the one case this certainty is entirely of a different nature from that in the other, it arising, in the case of necessary events, from God's own fore-appointing a necessary chain of causes to produce those events; but, in the case of free events, it arises from and depends upon the mere futurity of the things themselves.

To illustrate this matter by an example, that Christ should die for the sins of men, God not only fore-knew but fore-appointed it also, and sent him into the world on purpose for that end. That Judas should betray our savior, God fore-knew but did not fore-appoint it; only he chose on purpose into the number of his disciples one such person, the wickedness of whose own heart, he saw would prompt him to accomplish that event.

Sermon XIV: *Of the Goodness of God* [*W* I, 88]

... God actually is, and cannot but be, good ... For, goodness being nothing else but a fixed disposition to do always what in the whole is best, and, so far as is consistent with right and justice, what is most beneficial to all, it is evident that the supreme being, having all knowledge so that his understanding can never err in judging what is best, and having no want of any thing to complete his own happiness so that his will can never be influenced by any wrong affection, or have any possible temptation laid before it to act otherwise than according to what he knows best – it is from hence, I say, very evident to reason that the supreme cause, being thus necessarily happy in the eternal enjoyment of his own infinite perfections and altogether incapable of being tempted with evil, could not possibly have any other motives to make any creatures at all but only that he might communicate to them his own perfections, goodness, and happiness, according to their different capacities arising from that variety of natures which it was fit for infinite wisdom to produce, and according to their different improvements and deserts arising from that liberty which is essentially necessary to the constitution of intelligent and active beings. God, therefore, is necessarily and essentially good ... This necessity arises wholly from the unalterable rectitude of his will, whereas his natural attributes, such as knowledge and power, arise immediately from absolute necessity of nature.

Sermon XVI: *Of the Justice of God* [*W* I, 100–1]

... That the supreme lord and governor of all things is and cannot but be just in all his actions may be made to appear in the following manner. There being necessarily in nature a difference of things, which is what we call natural good and evil, and a variety in the dispositions and qualifications of persons, which is what we call moral good and evil, from the due or undue adjustment of these natural qualities of things to the moral qualifications of persons arise unavoidably the notions of right and wrong. Now the will of every intelligent agent being always directed by some motive, it is plain the natural motive of action, where nothing irregular interposes, can be no other than this right or reason of things. Whenever, therefore, this right and reason are not made by the rule of action, it can only be, either because the agent is ignorant of what is right, or wants ability to pursue it, or else is knowingly and willingly diverted from it by the hope of some good, or fear of some evil. But now none of these causes of injustice can possibly have any place in God; his actions, therefore, must always necessarily be directed by right, and reason, and justice only. For, having all knowledge, it is impossible he can be deceived in judging what is right; having no want of any thing, his will cannot possibly be influenced by any wrong affection; and having no dependence, his power can never be limited by any superior strength. It is very evident, therefore, that he who knows thus perfectly the rule of equity, and necessarily judges of things as they really are; who has complete power to execute justice according to that knowledge, and no possible temptation to deviate in the least therefrom; who can neither be imposed upon by any deceit, nor moved by any bias, nor awed by any power; it is very evident, I say, that such a being will always do what is right without iniquity, and without partiality, without prejudice, and without respect of persons.

There is a shorter way, which has frequently been made use of, to prove that all the actions of God must needs be just: by alleging that whatever he does is therefore just, because he does it. Which argument is not proving but supposing the thing in question. For the reason why God's doing a thing proves it to be just is only upon this foundation that, knowing him to be a perfectly just being, we are sure, if the thing had not been in itself just, he would not have done it. And in this sense indeed the argument is very good and reasonable. But those who use it have generally turned it to a very different and very false meaning, as if because whatever God does is certainly just, therefore whatever unjust and unreasonable things they in their systems of divinity ascribe to him were made just and reasonable by their supposing God to be the author of them; or, because the essence of God is incomprehensible and all his attributes infinitely transcending the perfections of any finite beings, that therefore justice in him was not the same thing, nor to be judged of by the same notions, as justice among men; or that, God being all-powerful and having no superior to render an account to of what he does, therefore whatever is ascribed to him, though in itself it may seem unjust and would be unjust among men, yet by supreme power is made just and right. And upon this kind of reasoning is built the doctrine of absolute reprobation, and some other the like opinions. But now, in reality, what is this else but speaking deceitfully for God and destroying the truth of his divine attributes under the appearance of defending them? For if every thing that power can do is just, what, then, is justice but mere power only, and not anything really in the nature of things? And so, the worst and most cruel being in the world, with sufficient power annexed, would in these men's sense be as just as supreme goodness itself. The alleging in this manner the power of God to the destroying [of] our moral notion of justice is like alleging the same power, in the case of transubstantiation, to the destroying [of] the natural truth of things. The effect of both is the confounding [of] the whole nature of truth and falsehood, of right and wrong, and making every thing to be unintelligible and without meaning. One sense indeed there is, in which supreme power *may* be said to be the foundation of justice, and that is because such power sets the person who possesses it above all possibility of being tempted, or compelled by any fraud, or by any force, to do an unjust thing.

... In this sense, I say, power may be affirmed indeed to be the foundation of justice as setting the person who is possessed of it far above all temptation of doing wrong. But in any other sense, to make power the measure of justice, and to imagine that justice in God is not the same thing as justice among men, but something transcendent and we know not what, is in reality subverting the nature of things, taking away the intrinsic difference between good and evil, and overturning the ground of all religion. For though the essence of God, which it is not our business to understand, is really incomprehensible, as indeed are the essences of all other things, yet the notion of his moral attributes must be easy and familiar, and if we could not understand these, the whole doctrine of the Gospel would be insignificant to us. For all revelation from God supposes us to know beforehand what is meant by justice, goodness, and the like, so that no man can reasonably entertain any notion of God contradictory to these upon any pretense whatsoever. And it is very absurd for anyone to pretend that we cannot understand what justice in God is; for if we understand not this, it is all one to us whether God be just or not. Neither would it be possible for us to imitate his justice, for he who imitates endeavors to be like something that he knows, and must of necessity understand what it is he aims to be like. So that if we had no certain and settled notion of the justice and other moral attributes of God, religion, which consists in the imitation of him, would be altogether unintelligible to our minds and impossible to practice.

VII

From *A Discourse concerning the Unchangeable Obligations of Natural Religion and the Truth and Certainty of the Christian Revelation*

[*Editor's Note*: These eight sermons, delivered at St. Paul's Cathedral in 1705 constituted Clarke's second set of Boyle Lectures. The two selections deal with the passive nature of matter and clearly illustrate Clarke's radical views on this topic. The first excerpt is from *W* II, 601; the second from *W* II, 697–8.]

... Since matter is utterly incapable of obeying any laws, the very original laws of motion themselves cannot continue to take place but by something superior to matter continually exerting on it a certain force or power, according to such certain and determinate laws. And it is now evident beyond question that the bodies of all plants and animals, much the most considerable parts of the world, could not possibly have been formed by mere matter according to any general laws of motion. And not only so, but that most universal principle of gravitation itself, the spring of almost all the great and regular inanimate motions in the world, answering not at all to the surfaces of bodies (by which alone they can act upon one another) but entirely to their solid content, cannot possibly be the result of any motion originally impressed on matter, but must of necessity be caused (either *immediately* or *mediately*) by something which penetrates the very solid substance of all bodies and continually puts forth in them a force or power entirely different from that by which matter acts on matter. Which is, by the way, an evident demonstration not only of the world's being made originally by a supreme intelligent cause, but moreover that it depends every moment on some superior being for the preservation of its frame, and that all the great motions in it are caused by some immaterial power, not having *originally* impressed a certain quantity of motion upon matter but *perpetually* and *actually* exerting itself every moment in every part of the world. Which preserving and governing power, whether it be immediately the power and action of the same supreme cause that created the world ... or whether it be the action of some subordinate instruments appointed by him to direct and preside respectively over certain parts thereof, does either way equally give us a very noble idea of providence.

. . .

. . . What degrees of power God may reasonably be supposed to have communicated to created beings, to subordinate intelligences, to good or evil angels, is by no means possible for us to determine. Some things absolutely impossible for men to effect, it is evident, may easily be within the natural powers of angels; and some things beyond the power of inferior angels may as easily be supposed to be within the natural power of others that are superior to them, and so on. So that (unless we knew the limit of communicable and incommunicable power) we can hardly affirm with any certainty that any particular effect, how great or miraculous soever it may seem to us, is beyond the power of all created beings in the universe to have produced.

It is not, therefore, a right distinction to define a miracle (as some very learned and pious men have done) to be such an effect as could not have been produced by any less power than the divine omnipotence. There is no instance of any miracle in Scripture which to an ordinary spectator would necessarily imply the immediate operation of original, absolute, and underived power. And consequently, such a spectator could never be certain that the miraculous effect was beyond the power of all created beings in the universe to produce. There is one supposition indeed, upon which the opinion of all miracles being necessarily the immediate effects of the divine omnipotence may be defended; and that is, if God, together with the natural powers wherewith he has endowed all subordinate intelligent beings, has likewise given a law or restraint whereby they be hindered from ever interposing in this lower world to produce any of those effects which we call miraculous or supernatural. But then, how certain soever it is that all created beings are under some particular laws and restraints, yet it can never be proved that they are under such restraints universally, perpetually, and without exception; and without this, a spectator that sees a miracle can never be certain that it was not done by some created intelligence.

Reducing the natural power of created beings to as low a degree as any one can desire to suppose will help nothing in this matter. For supposing, which is very unreasonable to suppose, that the natural powers of the highest angels were no greater than the natural powers of men, yet, since thereby an angel would be enabled to do all that invisibly which a man can do visibly, he would even in this supposition be naturally able to do numberless things which we should esteem the greatest of miracles.

All things that are done in the world are done either immediately by God himself or by created intelligent beings, matter being evidently not at all capable of any laws or powers whatsoever any more than it is capable of intelligence, excepting only this one negative power, that every part of it will of itself always and necessarily continue in that state, whether of rest or motion, wherein it at present is. So that all those things which we commonly say are the effects of the natural powers of matter and laws of motion, of gravitation, attraction, or the like, are indeed (if we will speak strictly and properly) the effects of God's acting upon matter continually and every moment either immediately by himself, or mediately by some created intelligent beings (which observation, by the way, furnishes us . . . with an excellent natural demonstration of providence).

Consequently, there is no such thing as what men commonly call "the course of nature" or "the power of nature." The course of nature, truly and properly speaking, is nothing else but the will of God producing certain effects in a continued, regular, constant, and uniform manner; which course or manner of acting, being in every moment perfectly arbitrary, is as easy to be altered at any time as to be preserved. And if, as seems most probable, this continued acting upon matter be performed by the subserviency of created intelligences appointed to that purpose by the supreme creator, then it is as easy for any of them, and as much within their natural power, by the permission of God to alter the course of nature at any time or in any respect as to preserve or continue it.

It is not, therefore, a right distinction to define a miracle to be that which is against the course of nature, meaning by "the course of nature" the power of nature or the natural powers of created agents. For, in this sense, it is no more against the course of nature for an angel to keep a man from sinking in the water than for a man to hold a stone from falling in the air by overpowering the law of gravitation. And yet the one is a miracle, the other not so. In like manner, it is no more above the natural power of a created intelligence to stop the motion of the sun or of a planet than to continue to carry it on in its usual course. And yet the former is a miracle, the latter not so. But if by "the course of nature" be meant only, as it truly signifies, the constant and uniform manner of God's acting either immediately or mediately in preserving and continuing the order of the world, then, in that sense, indeed a miracle may be rightly defined to be an effect produced contrary to the usual course or order of nature by the unusual interposition of some intelligent being superior to men.

... And from this observation we may easily discover the vanity and unreasonableness of that obstinate prejudice, which modern deists have universally taken up, against the belief of miracles in general. They see that things generally go on in a constant and regular method; that the frame and order of the world is preserved by things being disposed and managed in a uniform manner; that certain causes produce certain effects in a continued succession, according to certain fixed laws or rules. And from hence they conclude, very weakly and unphilosophically, that there are in matter certain necessary laws or powers, the result of which is that which they call the course of nature, which they think is impossible to be changed or altered, and consequently that there can be no such thing as miracles.

Whereas, on the contrary, if they would consider things duly, they could not but see that dull and lifeless matter is utterly incapable of obeying any laws or of being endowed with any powers, and that therefore that order and disposition of things, which they vulgarly call "the course of nature," cannot possibly be anything else but the arbitrary will and pleasure of God exerting itself and acting upon matter continually (either immediately by itself, or mediately by some subordinate intelligent agents) according to certain rules of uniformity and proportion, fixed indeed and constant, but which yet are made such merely by arbitrary constitution, not by any sort of necessity in the things themselves ... And consequently, it cannot be denied but that it is altogether as easy to alter the course of nature as to preserve it; that is, that miracles, excepting only that they are more unusual, are in themselves and in the nature and reason of the thing as credible in all respects, and as easy to be believed, as any of those we call "natural effects."

VIII
From *Four Defences of a Letter to Mr. Dodwell*

[*Editor's Note*: The exchange between Clarke and Anthony Collins on whether matter can think originated with Clarke's letter to Henry Dodwell (1641–1711), who had adopted the mortalist thesis that at death only divine intervention can prevent the death of the soul. The first excerpt shows Clarke trying to reconcile his belief in the local extension of the soul with that of its immateriality; it also contains the best statement of Clarke's proof that matter cannot possibly be conscious. The second presents Clarke's views on the nature of gravitation and should be read in conjunction with supplementary text VII. The third reiterates Clarke's view on the successiveness of divine thinking and briefly addresses whether matter acts on the soul.]

From *A Second Defence of the Immateriality and Natural Immortality of the Soul* [*W* III, 794–9]

... To the difficulties arising from the supposition of immateriality not excluding extension, I answer:

1. That all these difficulties are wide of the main question. For if the foregoing proof, that matter is incapable of thinking, cannot be shown to be defective, it follows necessarily that the soul must be an immaterial indiscerpible substance.[h] But the difficulties that arise from any following hypothesis concerning other properties of that immaterial indiscerpible substance, as whether it be extended or unextended, whether it ever acts wholly separate or always in some material vehicle, finer or grosser, and the like – the difficulties, I say, that arise from any of these particular hypotheses affect only the particular hypothesis from which they arise, and not at all the foregoing general proof.

I take it to be demonstrated, that the soul is an immaterial indiscerpible substance. He that thinks the difficulties arising from the supposition of that immaterial indiscerpible substance being extended to be unsurmountable may try if he can find fewer difficulties in supposing it unextended; and he that thinks the difficulties that arise from supposing

---

[h] By "indiscerpible" Clarke means indivisible.

it unextended are not to be got over may try to solve the difficulties that arise from supposing it extended. But the main argument remains firm either way, and no difficulty arising from following hypotheses can be so great as to lessen the force of the following positive proof.

2. But conceiving immateriality not to exclude extension, and supposing the difficulties arising from that hypothesis to be such as could not be clearly answered, yet this would not weaken the foregoing proof, unless that argument could otherwise be shown to be in itself defective. For there are many demonstrations even in abstract mathematics themselves, which no man who understands them can in the least doubt of the certainty of, and which yet are attended with difficult consequences that cannot perfectly be cleared. The infinite divisibility of quantity is an instance of this kind, as also the eternity of God, than which nothing is more self-evident. And yet the difficulties consequent upon it are such as have reduced most of the Schoolmen to entertain that unintelligible notion of a *nunc stans* [permanent now]. And his immensity is attended with much the like difficulties.

3. But neither is this the true state of the case. For the difficulties arising from the supposition of immaterial indiscerpible extension are by no means like those before-mentioned. Space (which you [Anthony Collins] unphilosophically call "the mere absence of bodies," and yet confess it to be positively infinite) is without difficulty confessed by you to be an instance of such an extension: an extension whose parts (improperly so called) depend on each other for their existence not only because of its infinity but because of the contradiction which a separation of them manifestly would imply. And the only thing required in the present case is to conceive that God can create a finite substance which shall not, like the solid, rigid, determined extension of matter, consist of parts which are actually so many distinct beings independent of each other for their existence, but be a substance perfectly and essentially one, so that to suppose any division of it shall necessarily infer a destruction of the essence of that substance. This must indeed be confessed to be a considerable difficulty; but if the difficulties arising upon any other hypothesis be (as they certainly are) at least as great, nothing can thence be inferred to the weakening of the foregoing proof.

Your applying the argument, by which I proved that matter could not think, in the same words to prove that neither could immaterial substance be capable of thinking, is fallacious in the first sentence. For the supposition of the substance being by the power of God divided into two parts, which concerning matter is confessed to be always possible, may concerning immaterial substance (even though extension be not included) be denied to be possible, as being a supposition which destroys the very essence of the substance itself.

. . .

... By "consciousness" in the following propositions, the reader may understand indifferently either the reflex act, by which a man knows his thoughts to be his own thoughts which is the strict and properest sense of the word; or the direct act of thinking; or the power or capacity of thinking; or, which is of the same import, simple sensation; or the power of self-motion, or of beginning motion by the will – the argument holding equally in all or any of these senses, as has been before said.

I.   *Every system of matter consists of a multitude of distinct parts.*
This, I think, is granted by all.

II.   *Every real quality inheres in some subject.*
This also, I think, is granted by all. For whatever is called a quality, and yet inheres not in any subject, must either subsist of itself, and then it is a substance not a quality, or else it is nothing but a mere name.

III.   *No individual or single quality of one particle of matter can be the individual or single quality of another particle.*
The heat of one particle is not the heat of another. The gravity, the color, the figure, of one particle is not the same individual gravity, color, or figure of another particle. The consciousness or sensation of one particle (supposing it to be a quality of matter) is not the consciousness or sensation of another. If it was it would follow that the same thing could be two in the same sense and at the same time that it is but one.
... From hence may be drawn an evident confutation of that absurd notion which Mr. Hobbes suggests in his physics (*De Corpore*, chapter 25, section 5) that all matter is essentially endued with an obscure actual sense and perception, but that there is required a number and apt composition of parts to make up a clear and distinct sensation or consciousness. For from this notion it would follow that the resulting sensation or consciousness at last, being but one distinct sensation or consciousness (as is that of a man), the sensation or consciousness of every one of the constituent

particles would be the individual sensation or consciousness of all and each of the rest.

IV. *Every real simple quality that resides in any whole material system resides in all the parts of that system.*

The magnitude of every body is the sum of the magnitudes of its several parts. The motion of every body is the sum of the motions of its several parts. The weight of every body is the sum of the weights of its several parts. The heat of every body is the heat of its several parts.[70] The color of every body is the color of its several parts. And the same is universally true of every simple quality residing in any system. For residing in the whole and not residing in the parts, is residing in a thing and not residing in it, at the same time.

V. *Every real compound quality that resides in any whole material system is a number of simple qualities residing in all the parts of that system, some in one part, some in another.*

Thus in the instance of mixed colors. When the simples, blue, suppose, and yellow, make the whole appear green, in this case that portion of the system in which any one of the particular simple qualities resides is a whole system with respect to that quality, and the quality residing in it resides in the several particles of which that portion of the system is constituted, and so of the rest.

VI. *Every real quality, simple or compound, that results from any whole material system but does not reside in it, that is, neither in all its distinct parts nor in all the parts of some portion of it according to the explication of the two foregoing propositions, is the mode or quality of some other substance, and not of that.*

All sensible secondary qualities, heat, color, smell, taste, sound, and the like, are of this kind, being in reality not qualities of the bodies they are ascribed to, but modes of the mind that perceives them.

VII. *Every power, simple or compound, that results from any whole material system but does not reside in it (that is, in all its parts in the manner before explained), nor yet resides in any other substance as its subject, is no real quality at all; but must either be itself a real substance (which seems unintelligible), or else it is nothing but merely an abstract name or notion, as all universals are.*

---

[70] By "heat," here is meant that motion which causes in us the sensation of heat; by "color," that magnitude, and figure, which causes particular rays to be transmitted to us, etc.

Thus, the power resulting from the texture of a rose to excite in us the sensation of sweetness is nothing but an abstract name, signifying a particular motion and figure of certain parts emitted. The power of a clock to show the hour of the day is nothing but one new complex name to express at once the several motions of the parts, and particularly the determinate velocity of the last wheel to turn round once in twelve hours; upon the stopping which motion by the touch of a finger or any other impediment, without making any alteration at all in the number, figure, or disposition of the parts of the clock, the power wholly ceases; and upon removing the impediment, by which nothing is restored but mere motion, the power returns again, which is, therefore, no new real quality of the whole but only the mere motion of the parts. The power of a pin to prick is nothing distinct from its mere figure permitting it to enter the skin. The power of a weight in one scale of a balance to ascend or descend upon increasing or diminishing the counterpoise in the other scale is not a new real quality distinct from its absolute gravity (though it occasions a new effect), there being no alteration at all made in the weight itself. The power of the eye to see is not a real quality of the whole eye, but merely an abstract name signifying a transmitting and refracting of the rays of light in a certain manner through its several parts; which effect, by the interposition or removal of an opaque body, is destroyed or renewed without any alteration at all in the eye itself. A key, by having many new locks made to fit it, acquires a new power of producing effects which it could not before, and yet no new real quality is produced nor any alteration at all made in the key itself. And so universally of all powers of this kind. If these powers were anything else but mere abstract names, they would signify qualities subsisting without any subject at all, that is, such as must themselves be distinct substances, which is unintelligible.

VIII. *Consciousness is neither a mere abstract name (such as are the powers mentioned in Prop. VII), nor a power of exciting or occasioning different modes in a foreign substance (such as are all the sensible qualities of bodies, Prop. VI), but a real quality, truly and properly inherent in the subject itself, the thinking substance.*

If it was a mere abstract name, it would be nothing at all in the person that thinks, or in the thinking substance itself, but only a notion framed by the imagination of some other being. For all those powers which are only abstract names are not at all in the things whose powers they are called, but are only notions framed in imagination by the mind that observes, compares, and reasons about different objects without itself.

If it was a power of exciting or occasioning different modes in a foreign substance, then the power of thinking must be before in that foreign substance, and that foreign substance alone would in reality be conscious, and not *this* which excites the different modes in that foreign substance. For the power that is in one substance of exciting different modes in another substance presupposes necessarily in that other substance the foundation of those modes. Thus in the case of all the sensible qualities of bodies the power of thinking is beforehand in that being wherein those qualities excite or occasion different modes of thinking.

It remains, therefore, that it must of necessity be a real quality, truly and properly inhering in the subject itself, the thinking substance, there being no other species of powers or qualities left to which it can possibly be referred. And this, indeed, is of itself as evident by every man's experience as it can be rendered by any explication or proof whatsoever.

IX. *No real quality can result from the composition of different qualities so as to be a new quality in the same subject, [but] of a different kind or species from all and every one of the component qualities.*

If it could, it would be a creation of something out of nothing. From compound motions, can arise nothing but motion; from magnitudes, nothing but magnitude; from figure, nothing but figure; from compositions of magnitude, figure, and motion together, nothing but magnitude, figure, and motion; from mechanical powers, nothing but mechanical powers; from a composition of colors, nothing but color, which itself (as appears by microscopes) is still the simple colors of which it was compounded. From mixtures of chemical liquors, nothing but ferments, which are only mere motions of the particles in mixing, such motions as arise from the placing of iron and a lode-stone near each other. Gravity is not a quality of matter, arising from its texture or any other powers in it, but merely an endeavor to motion excited by some foreign force or power. Magnetism and electricity are not new qualities resulting from different and unknown powers but merely emissions of certain streams of matter which produce certain determinate motions. Compositions of colors can never contribute to produce a sound; nor compositions of magnitude and figure, to produce a motion; nor necessary and determined motions, to produce a free and indetermined power of self motion; nor any mechanical powers whatsoever, to produce a power not mechanical. And the same must of necessity hold universally true of all qualities and powers whatsoever, whether known or unknown, because otherwise, as has been before said, there would in the compound be something created out of nothing.

X.   *Consciousness, therefore, being a real quality (Prop. VIII.) and of a kind specifically different from all other qualities, whether known or unknown, which are themselves acknowledged to be void of consciousness, can never possibly result from any composition of such qualities.*

This is as evident from the foregoing propositions, as that a sound cannot be the result of a mixture of colors and smells; nor extension the result of a composition of parts unextended; nor solidity the result of parts not solid, whatever other different qualities, known or unknown, those constituent parts may be supposed to be endued with.

XI.   *No individual quality can be transferred from one subject to another.* This is granted by all.

XII.   *The spirits and particles of the brain, being loose and in perpetual flux, cannot therefore be the seat of that consciousness, by which a man not only remembers things done many years since, but also is conscious that he himself, the same individual conscious being, was the doer of them.*

This follows evidently from the foregoing.

XIII.   *The consciousness that a man has at one and the same time is one consciousness and not a multitude of consciousnesses as the solidity, motion, or color of any piece of matter is a multitude of distinct solidities, motions, or colors.*

This is granted by all who deny that the particles of the brain, which they suppose to constitute a conscious substance, are themselves each of them conscious.

XIV.   *Consciousness, therefore, cannot at all reside in the substance of the brain, or spirits, or in any other material system as its subject, but must be a quality of some immaterial substance.*

This follows necessarily from the foregoing propositions compared together. For since every possible power of matter, whether known or unknown, must needs be either, first, a real quality of the matter to which it is ascribed (and then it must inhere in the several distinct parts); or secondly, a power of exciting or occasioning certain modes in some other subject (and then it is truly the quality, not of the matter, but of that other subject); or thirdly, a mere abstract name or notion of what is, properly speaking, no real quality at all, and inheres in no real subject at all. And since consciousness is acknowledged to be none of these, it follows unavoidably that it must of necessity be a quality of some immaterial substance.

XV. *Difficulties that arise afterwards, concerning other qualities of that immaterial substance, as whether it be extended or unextended, do not at all affect the present argument.*

For thus even abstract mathematical demonstrations, as those concerning the infinite divisibility of quantity, the eternity of God, and his immensity, have almost insuperable difficulties on the other side, and yet no man who understands those matters thinks that those difficulties do at all weaken the force or diminish the certainty of the demonstrations.

From *A Third Defence of the Immateriality and Natural Immortality of the Soul* [*W* III, 848]

... You [Anthony Collins] say: Whether you take Mr. Clarke right or no, the incomparable Sir Isaac Newton (in the Preface to his *Principia*) is of opinion "that several phenomena of Nature may depend on certain forces or powers, whereby from causes yet undiscovered, the particles of bodies are mutually impelled against each other ... or recede and are driven from one another; which forces or powers being yet unknown, the philosophers hitherto have attempted nature in vain."[i] Now to insinuate to your reader by such a citation that this great man is of your opinion in the present question, when on the contrary, the very sentence you cite was spoken by him (as appears from the words immediately preceding those you have cited) not concerning gravitation but concerning other more particular phenomena of nature in express contradistinction to those of gravitation; and when in that whole book, from one end to the other, he is professedly confuting and showing the absolute impossibility of your notion of gravitation; and when he has elsewhere in express words declared that by the terms "forces" and "powers" he does not mean (as you did by "powers originally placed in matter by God") to signify the efficient cause of certain determinate motions of matter, but only to express the action itself

---

i *NP*, author's preface to the reader, 16.

by which the effect is regularly produced, without determining the immediate agent or cause of that action – after all this, I say, to insinuate to your reader by the citation of a piece of a single sentence that that great man is of your opinion, is (to use your own expressions once more) such a conduct as the world may justly demand a reason of from your self, for I cannot assign a good one for you.[71]

Lastly, as you declare it to be your opinion that gravitation is caused by material impulse, so you think it impossible that it should be owing to any immaterial cause; and you believe it to be as intelligible that matter might act without impulse by powers placed in it by God, as that an immaterial being should move matter without being able to impel it by contact.

This belief of yours is founded wholly upon the supposition that there is nothing in the world but tangible substance, which opinion you give no reason for, and therefore it is a mere prejudice. But further, I presume you will hardly deny but God himself is an immaterial being, and that he can move matter, though he does not impel it by contact. Other immaterial beings, therefore, though they do not impel matter by contact, yet it does not from thence follow that they cannot move it at all because from God's moving it, it is manifest that there are other ways of moving it besides that of impelling by contact. But powers or laws are not real beings; they are nothing but mere words or notions and can neither act in any sense, nor move matter either with contact or without it. I conceive an ordinary reader may be able to discern the difference between affirming that an immaterial substance, a real being, though not hard and solid, may move matter, and affirming that a law or power, a mere word or term of art, which is really no thing and has not truly any being or existence save only in imagination, can cause matter to move.

From *A Fourth Defence of the Immateriality and Natural Immortality of the Soul* [*W* III, 896–7]

Nor is it a less wonderful expression when you [Anthony Collins] affirm that thinking in God cannot be successive nor have any modes or distinct acts of thinking, but that it is one numerical individual act, fixed and permanent, and invariable and without succession, etc. That is to say, that God cannot vary his will, nor diversify his works, nor act successively, nor

---

[71] I. Newton, *Optice: sive de Reflexionibus, Refractionibus & Coloribus Lucis libri tres*, trans. S. Clarke. (London, 1706), Quaestio 23, p. 322.

govern the world, nor indeed have any power to will or do anything at all. I do not charge you with consequences, but I affirm they are too plain consequences of what you profess.

You observe that I allow matter to act upon the soul, which since it cannot do by contact, it must be by a power whereof we have no idea; and if there be in matter any such power whereof we have no idea, why may it not as well be capable of thinking?

I answer: the power by which matter acts upon the soul is not a real quality inhering in matter, as motion inheres in it and as thinking inheres in the thinking substance, but it is only a power or occasion of exciting certain modes or sensations in another substance; which power is one of those qualities I ranked under the second sort, and there is no analogy at all between a subject's being itself capable of sensation and its being the occasion of certain sensations being excited in another subject.[j]

[j] For Clarke's classification of qualities, see pp. 154–5.

IX

From *A Collection of Papers which passed between the late learned Mr. Leibniz and Dr. Clarke, in the Years 1715 and 1716 relating to the Principles of Natural Philosophy and Religion. With an Appendix*

[*Editor's Note*: These two selections are from the appendix to Clarke's edition of his exchange with Leibniz. I give Clarke's translation of Leibniz's texts and add their standard titles and references. With these texts, Clarke clearly tried to show that Leibniz's own words proved that he held that matter is a substance; that, consequently, it always acts; that it is imbued with a spiritual principle, and consequently that it has some sort of proto-perception. In short, Clarke viewed Leibniz as a dangerous crypto-hylozoist.]

2 [*W* IV, 701–4].

"We must know that spontaneity, strictly speaking, is common to us with all simple substances, and that this, in an intelligent and free substance, amounts to a dominion over its own actions. . . . Naturally, every simple substance has perception" etc. (*Theodicy*, p. 291) [section 291].

"But active force contains a certain act or efficacy, and is something of a middle nature between the faculty of acting and action itself. It involves a conatus or endeavor, and is of itself carried towards action; and stands in need of no help but only that the impediment be taken away. This may be illustrated by the examples of a heavy body stretching the string it is hung by, and of a bow bent. For though gravity and elasticity may, and ought to, be explained mechanically by the motion of the aether, yet the ultimate cause of motion in matter is a force, impressed at creation, which is in every part of matter but, according to the course of nature, is variously limited and restrained by bodies striking against each other. And this active faculty I affirm to be in all substance and that some action is always arising from it, so that not even corporeal substance, any more than spiritual, ever ceases acting. Which seems not to have been apprehended by those who have placed the essence of matter in extension alone or even in impenetrability, and fancied they could conceive a body absolutely at rest. It will appear also from what I have advanced, that one created substance does not receive from another the active force itself, but only the limits and determination of the endeavor or active faculty already pre-existing in it" (*Acta Eruditorum*, 1694, p. 112) [*De Prima Philosophiae Emendatione et de Notione Substantiae*, in *Die Philosophischen Schriften von G. W. Leibniz*, ed. C. I. Gerhardt (Berlin, 1875–90; reprint Hildesheim, G. Olms, 1961), vol. IV, pp. 468–70].

"To act, is the characteristic of substances." (*Acta Eruditorum*, 1695, p. 145) [*Specimen Dynamicum*, in *Die Mathematischen Schriften von G. W. Leibniz*, ed. C. I. Gerhardt (Berlin, 1875–90; reprint Hildesheim, G. Olms, 1963), vol. VI, pp. 234–46] .

"Which primitive active power is of itself in all corporeal substance; for, I think, a body absolutely at rest is inconsistent with the nature of things" (ibid., p. 146).

"Every part of matter is, by its form, continually acting" (ibid., p. 147).

"The active power which is in the form, and the inertia, or repugnance to motion, which is in the matter" (ibid., p. 151).

"Though I admit everywhere in bodies a principle superior to the {common} notion of matter, a principle active and, if I may so speak, vital" (ibid., p. 153).

"I have elsewhere explained, though it is a thing perhaps not yet well understood by all, that the very substance of things consists in the power of acting and being acted upon" (*Acta Eruditorum* 1698, p. 432) [*De Ipsa Natura*, in *Die Philosophischen Schriften von G. W. Leibniz*, ed. C. I. Gerhardt (Berlin, 1875–90; reprint Hildesheim, G. Olms, 1961), vol. IV, pp. 504–16].

"So that, not only every thing which acts is a single substance, but also every single substance does perpetually act, not excepting matter itself, in which there is never absolute rest" (ibid., p. 432).

"If we ascribe to our own minds an intrinsic power of producing imma-nent actions or, which is the same thing, of acting immanently, it is no way unreasonable (nay, it is very reasonable) to allow that there is the same power in other souls or forms, or, if that be a better expression, in the natures of substances. Unless a man will imagine that, in the whole extent of nature within the compass of our knowledge, our own minds are the only things endowed with active powers; or that all power of acting immanently and vitally, if I may so speak, is connected with understanding. Which kind of assertions, certainly, are neither founded on any reason, nor can be maintained, but in opposition to truth" (ibid., p. 433).

"Hence we may gather that there must needs be in corporeal substance an original efficacy or, as it were, prime recipient of active force; that is, there must be in it a primitive motive power, which, being added over and above the extension (or that which is merely geometrical) and over and above the bulk (or that which is merely material), acts indeed continually, but yet is variously modified by the conatuses and impetuses of bodies striking against each other. And this is that substantial principle which in living substances is styled "soul"; in others "the substantial form" (ibid., p. 434).

"The materia prima is indeed merely passive, but it is not a complete substance. To make it complete substance, there must be, moreover, a soul or a form analogous to soul, or an original efficacy, that is, a certain endeavor or primitive power of acting, which is an innate law impressed by the decree of God. Which opinion, I think, is not different from that of an eminent and ingenious gentleman who has lately maintained that body consists of matter and spirit, meaning by the word "spirit" not, as usually, an intelligent thing, but a soul or form analogous to a soul; and not a simple modification, but a substantial permanent constituent, which used to becalled a "monad," in which is, as it were, perception and desire" (ibid., p. 435).

"On the contrary, I am rather of opinion that it is neither agreeable to the order, nor beauty, nor reason of things, that there should be a vital principle or power of acting immanently only in a very small part of matter, when it would be an argument of greater perfection for it to be in all matter. And nothing hinders but that there may everywhere be souls, or at least something analogous to souls, though souls endowed with dominion and understanding, such as are human souls, cannot be everywhere" (ibid., p. 436).

"What does not act, what wants active power, what is void of discernibility, what wants the whole ground and foundation of subsistence, can no way be a substance" (ibid., p. 439).

11 [*W* IV, 708–9]

"In my doctrine of a pre-established harmony, I show that every single substance is naturally endowed with perception; and that its individuality consists in that perpetual law which causes its appointed succession of perceptions, arising naturally in order one from the other, so as to represent its own body and, by the same means, the whole universe according to the point of view proper to that single substance, without it needing to receive any physical influence from the body. And the body, likewise on its part, acts correspondingly to the volitions of the soul by its own proper laws; and consequently, does not obey the soul any otherwise than as those laws are correspondent" (*Theodicy*, p. 291) [section 291].

"It must also be confessed that every soul represents to itself the universe according to its point of view and by a relation peculiar to it; but there is always a perfect harmony between them" (ibid., p. 552) [section 357].

"The operations of spiritual machines, that is, of souls, is not mechanical. But it contains eminently whatever is excellent in mechanism, the motions which appear actually in bodies being concentrated by representation in the soul, as in an ideal world which represents the laws of the actual world and the series of their being put in execution, differing in this from the perfect ideal world which is in God, that most of the perceptions in human souls are but confused. For we must know that every single substance includes the universe in its indistinct perceptions; and that the succession of these perceptions is regulated by the particular nature of the substance, but yet in a manner which always represents whole universal nature.[k] And every present perception, as every motion which such perception represents, tends towards a new motion. But it is impossible the soul should be able to understand distinctly its own whole nature and to apprehend how this numberless number of little perceptions, heaped up or, rather, concentrated together, are produced. In order to [do] this, it would be requisite that the soul understood perfectly the whole universe which is included within it; that is, it must be a God" (ibid., p. 603) [section 403].

---

[k] Clarke mistranslated this and the two previous occurrences of the French "substance simple" as "single substance."

Index

Cambridge Texts in the History of Philosophy

Titles published in the series thus far

Antoine Arnauld and Pierre Nicole *Logic or the Art of Thinking* (edited by Jill Vance Buroker)

Boyle *A Free Enquiry into the Vulgarly Received Notion of Nature* (edited by Edward B. Davis and Michael Hunter)

Clarke *A Demonstration of the Being and Attributes of God and Other Writings* (edited by Ezio Vailati)

Conway *The Principles of the Most Ancient and Modern Philosophy* (edited by Allison P. Coudert and Taylor Corse)

Cudworth *A Treatise Concerning Eternal and Immutable Morality* with *A Treatise of Freewill* (edited by Sarah Hutton)

Descartes *Meditations on First Philosophy*, with selections from the *Objections and Replies* (edited with an introduction by John Cottingham)

Kant *Critique of Practical Reason* (edited by Mary Gregor with an introduction by Andrews Reath)

Kant *Groundwork of the Metaphysics of Morals* (edited by Mary Gregor with an introduction by Christine M. Korsgaard)

Kant *The Metaphysics of Morals* (edited by Mary Gregor with an introduction by Roger Sullivan)

Kant *Prolegomena to any Future Metaphysics* (edited by Gary Hatfield)

La Mettrie *Machine Man and Other Writings* (edited by Ann Thomson)

Leibniz *New Essays on Human Understanding* (edited by Peter Remnant and Jonathan Bennett)

Malebranche *Dialogues on Metaphysics and on Religion* (edited by Nicholas Jolley and David Scott)

Malebranche *The Search after Truth* (edited by Thomas M. Lennon and Paul J. Olscamp)

Mendelssohn *Philosophical Writings* (edited by Daniel O. Dahlstrom)

Nietzsche *Daybreak* (edited by Maudemarie Clark and Brian Leiter, translated by R. J. Hollingdale)

Nietzsche *Human, all too Human* (translated by R. J. Hollingdale with an introduction by Richard Schacht)

Nietzsche *Untimely Meditations* (edited by Daniel Breazeale, translated by R. J. Hollingdale)

Schleiermacher *On Religion: Speeches to its Cultured Despisers* (edited by Richard Crouter)

Printed in the United States
19881LVS00007B/145-165